RULES

CONTEMPORARY STUDIES IN DESCRIPTIVE LINGUISTICS

VOL. 34

Edited by
DR GRAEME DAVIS & KARL A. BERNHARDT

PETER LANG

Oxford · Bern · Berlin · Bruxelles · Frankfurt am Main · New York · Wien

Christopher Beedham, Warwick Danks
and Ether Soselia (eds)

RULES AND EXCEPTIONS

USING EXCEPTIONS FOR EMPIRICAL RESEARCH IN THEORETICAL LINGUISTICS

PETER LANG

Oxford · Bern · Berlin · Bruxelles · Frankfurt am Main · New York · Wien

Bibliographic information published by Die Deutsche Nationalbibliothek
Die Deutsche Nationalbibliothek lists this publication in the Deutsche National-
bibliografie; detailed bibliographic data is available on the Internet at
http://dnb.d-nb.de.

A catalogue record for this book is available from the British Library.

Library of Congress Control Number: 2014930604

ISSN 1660-9301
ISBN 978-3-0343-0782-6

© Peter Lang AG, International Academic Publishers, Bern 2014
Hochfeldstrasse 32, CH-3012 Bern, Switzerland
info@peterlang.com, www.peterlang.com, www.peterlang.net

This publication has been peer reviewed.

Printed in Germany

Contents

vi

Figures

Tables

Preface

The papers in this volume are revised and updated versions of papers delivered at the Summer School and Conference on the Method of Lexical Exceptions held from 2 to 8 September 2007 at the University of St Andrews, Scotland, organized by myself and Warwick Danks.[1] From the publication of this volume the above mentioned method is now called the method of exceptions and their correlations, for reasons which are given in my paper. Appended to each paper is an extract from the discussion which followed the paper, as transcribed at the time, with updates where necessary.

I am especially grateful to Prof. Thomas V. Gramkrelidze, University of Tbilisi, Georgia, for recommending the Summer School and Conference to his colleagues and students and facilitating their attendance, and for giving permission to publish here slightly revised versions of two papers first published in the *Bulletin of the Georgian National Academy of Sciences*. The contribution of the Georgian participants was invaluable, both quantitatively and qualitatively. I am grateful to all those who attended and gave papers at the Summer School and Conference, making it such an interesting and fruitful event. Thanks also to my colleagues, students and the secretarial staff in the School of Modern Languages and in SAILLS (St Andrews Institute of Language and Linguistic Studies) for their help, advice and support. I am grateful also to the Russell Trust and to the Carnegie Trust for the Universities of Scotland for their financial support.

Christopher Beedham
St Andrews
21 November 2013

---

[1] See <http://www.st-andrews.ac.uk/modlangs/research/conferences/pastevents/>, accessed 21 November 2013.

CHRISTOPHER BEEDHAM

1 Exceptions and their Correlations: A Methodology for Research in Grammar

ABSTRACT

A method of empirical research is described in which unexplained exceptions to a rule and their correlations are used in a systematic way to lead the researcher to a revised version of the rule which explains and removes the rule's anomalies, especially the exceptions which one started out with. Two rules and their exceptions in English, German, and Russian are presented as case studies in the method: the passive and non-passivizable transitive verbs; tense formation and irregular verbs. It is hoped that other linguists will try out the method on their own chosen constructions in their own languages.

Introduction

In this paper we will look at how unexplained exceptions to a rule and their correlations can be used in a systematic way to lead the researcher to a revised version of the rule which explains and removes the rule's anomalies, especially the exceptions which one started out with.[1] We will examine two constructions and their exceptions as case studies in the method – the

---

1   This paper was written in 2013 and is an updated summary of the summer school part of the Summer School and Conference on the Method of Lexical Exceptions held at the University of St Andrews, Scotland, from 2 to 8 September 2007. Hitherto I have referred to the method as 'the method of lexical exceptions'. I now – i.e. from this volume – refer to it as the method of exceptions and their correlations. It is the same method, but called by a name which goes more to the heart of how the method works.

rule of passive and non-passivizable transitive verbs, tense formation and irregular verbs – in English, German and Russian. The examination of these two areas will be brief, because the paper is about method, not about the passive or irregular verbs, but references will be given to enable the reader to follow up the analyses presented. Because the reason for writing the paper is to encourage other linguists to try out the method on their own chosen constructions in their own languages some detail of the history of the method, how it developed over time, how long it took to carry out the data collection, is included in order to give the reader an idea of the timescale involved if he or she decides to try it out. For the same reason some further practical details about using reference works, native speaker informants, and research assistants are also included. (For further details on all these matters – the method, the passive, and irregular verbs – see Beedham 2005b; Danks 2011, this volume. On exceptions in general see Simon and Wiese (eds) 2011, Corbin and Dessaux-Berthonneau 1985.)[2]

Theoretical background

The approach taken by the method of exceptions and their correlations is descriptive (as opposed to generative) and based on Saussurean structuralism (Saussure 1983). The term 'descriptive' is used here despite the fact that it is misleading in that some linguists claim that descriptive linguistics merely describes, without explaining. However, in our view 'descriptive' linguistics is indeed analytical – it produces analyses – and explanatory, i.e.

---

2   On the approach of the *Junggrammatiker* to exceptions see Bassac, this volume. Helbig (1973: 34) says that understanding and recognition of Saussure's work was impeded by the dominance of the *Junggrammatiker*, especially in Germany, during Saussure's lifetime. In the approach suggested here to exceptions the opposite is the case, in that the suggested way of dealing with exceptions is part and parcel of the Saussurean approach. On the relationship between Saussure and the *Junggrammatiker* see Joseph 2012.

theoretical (in the pre-Chomskyan sense of 'theoretical'): the explanation is in the description. There is a link with pedagogical grammars and language teaching: the areas of grammar and lexis which descriptive grammarians choose to examine are usually the ones which foreign learners of a language find difficult. And for descriptivists the ultimate test of a new theoretical analysis is whether it is taken up in pedagogical grammars.

It is useful though not essential when using the method of exceptions and their correlations to investigate the same formal construction in two or more languages, because it gives you two or more different angles on the same construction. It is also helpful if one of your languages is a foreign language, i.e. not your native language, because you then automatically have the psychic distance necessary to carry out an objective, scientific analysis. It is all too easy when analysing one's native language to fall into the trap of thinking that the categories and rules one sees there are natural and logical and based on the way the world is, rather than the language-specific, idiosyncratic and arbitrary (in the Saussurean sense) categories and rules which they, in fact, are. You should be an advanced learner of the foreign language in question and hence speak it reasonably fluently: this is necessary to enable you to adjudicate the grammaticality judgements of your native-speaker informants. On the other hand, if one of your languages is your native language that is also handy because of the greater intuitive insights you have for that language. For both foreign language and native language the researcher is actually trying to bring out his or her native speaker(-like) intuitions into an explicit, scientific analysis. Having said it is best to investigate your chosen construction in two or more languages, of course the arguments in support of an analysis in a given language have to come from the structure of that language, one cannot argue across languages and say, for example, because the situation in Russian is this I want to analyse a construction of English like this. The arguments for English have to come from the structure of English.

The passive and non-passivizable transitive verbs

One of the problems we face in theoretical linguistics is how to make the discipline empirical. Some would say it does not need to be empirical, it just is a theoretical discipline, but every theory needs a practice; theory and practice go together. Others would say that linguistics is already empirical, e.g. through the use of computer corpora, and that is true, but there is another, *langue*-oriented and grammar-based way in which we can make it empirical, and that is through the use of unexplained exceptions to grammatical rules. Let us take non-passivizable transitive verbs as an example. The traditional and still widespread rule of passive says that every transitive verb can form a passive, but it is well known that there are a small number of transitive verbs in English, German and Russian which do not form a passive, despite being transitive, e.g. 1 in English, 2 in German and 3 in Russian below (on the passive in English see Quirk et al. 1985: 159–71; in German see Durrell 2002: 307–22, and Helbig and Buscha 1989: 161–88; in Russian see Borras and Christian 1971: 165–73, and Грамматика русского языка 1960: 504–15):

(1) a. James knows Fiona.
     b. ?Fiona is known by James.
(2) a. *Er mag Käse.*
         'he likes cheese'
     b. ?*Käse wird von ihm gemocht*
         cheese is   by him liked
         'cheese is liked by him'
(3) a. *Predsedatel'   poblagodaril Ivana*
         the-chairman thanked   Ivan
         'the chairman thanked Ivan'
     b. **Ivan byl poblagodaren predsedatelem*
         Ivan was thanked   by-the-chairman
         'Ivan was thanked by the chairman'

Identifying the exceptions

A common approach in descriptive grammars and theoretical-descriptive accounts is to view these unexplained exceptions, the non-passivizable transitive verbs, as part of the sometimes wilful nature of language and simply to list them, without even attempting an explanation; or else to give a separate semantic reason almost for each sentence, e.g. the agent is not sufficiently agentive, the patient is not sufficiently patient-like, the verb is stative, relational, psychological, etc., such that so many different reasons are given, and all of them semantic, that one realizes that no genuine explanation in terms of a significant generalization is being given at all. But firstly, there must surely be some reason for the aberrant behaviour of the exceptions – we just have to look for it and find it. Secondly, surely the first question we need to ask is exactly how many verbs like that – not able to form a passive, despite being transitive – are there in a given language, and which verbs are they? Instead of theorizing in a vacuum one needs to carry out some empirical work, some work with dictionaries and native speaker informants. That is what this author did for his PhD in the period 1976–1979 (published as Beedham 1982); he trawled through dictionaries of English, German and Russian and got sentences tested for their grammaticality by native speakers, and in the space of about 6 months[3] an exhaustive and finite list of every non-passivizable transitive verb in English, German and Russian was produced. The dictionaries used were for English the *Oxford Advanced Learner's Dictionary of Current English* 1974; for German, Mater 1971 and Klappenbach and Steinitz 1977; and for Russian, the 17 vol. Словарь современного русского языка 1951–1965. The most useful dictionaries were those which give plenty of example sentences showing

---

3   As stated in the first section, some practical details of the method such as the time-scale involved will be provided in this paper to help those who wish to try out the method for themselves. The practical details are intended to give substance to the point that an exhaustive investigation of lexical exceptions is manageable within a reasonable time frame.

how a word is used.[4] Of course, there are always grey areas, in this case to do with what exactly is a transitive verb, what do you do with verbs which passivize in one meaning but not another, some verbs form a passive in one sentence but not another, etc. But in essence it was possible to extract an exhaustive and finite list of more or less non-passivizable transitive verbs in the three languages within a reasonable space of time, some examples of which are given in 4 for English and 5 for German below:

(4) some English non-passivizable transitive verbs:[5]

become	dread	involve	marry	remind
boast	dream	know	near	resemble
contain	exceed	lack	need	stall
cost	get	live	possess	walk
cross	have	love	regret	want

(5) some German non-passivizable transitive verbs:

anheimeln	freuen	schmerzen	übersteigen
'make feel at home'	'please'	'hurt'	'exceed'
anwidern	haben	spüren	verdienen
'nauseate'	'have'	'feel, sense'	'deserve'
bekommen	kennen	tragen	verdrießen
'receive'	'know'	'bear (fruit)'	'annoy'
besitzen	kosten	träumen	wiegen

---

4   The best online dictionary available today that I know of which gives example sentences is Linguee: <http://www.linguee.com/>, accessed 21 November 2013.

5   That is, transitive verbs with a tendency not easily to form a passive in at least one of their main meanings. Note that even the most recalcitrant non-passivizable transitive verb can be made to passivize with sufficient ingenuity, because the passive is an aspect and aspect is compositional (see below). In fact, the blunt truth of the matter is that there is no such thing as a non-passivizable transitive verb, only non-passivizable transitive sentences (again, because aspect is compositional). Nevertheless, we speak about non-passivizable transitive verbs because it is a useful abstraction and generalization of the kind which all grammarians and scientists make. The examples given here are taken from Beedham 1982: 59–81, which contains a list of non-passivizable transitive sentences, each one with a different transitive verb.

'possess'	'cost'	'dream'	'weigh'
enthalten	kriegen	treffen	wissen
'contain'	'get'	'meet'	'know'
erforden	mögen	überkommen	wundern
'require'	'like'	'overcome'	'surprise'
ergötzen			
'enthrall'			

That in itself, acquiring the complete set – or at least a tentatively complete set, given the caveats expressed above and in fn. 5 – of the verbs which present the problem is worth more than endless theorizing about two or three well-worn examples. It is pointless to postulate and hypothesize endlessly on the basis of a tiny number of examples, when you can produce in a relatively short space of time a substantial amount of data, hard facts, which can serve as a sound basis for analysis. Of course, you still need to carry out a theoretical analysis, we are not collecting data instead of doing analysis, but now one has an empirical basis on which to do it. It took six months to produce the data but it was six months well spent, since it was the new data which led to the new analysis which will be presented below.

Conducting 'experiments'

We have the data, i.e. the finite and exhaustive list of non-passivizable transitive verbs, but what do you do with them? Our working hypothesis is that the exceptions are not really there in the actual structure of language, standing completely outside the system, but are there by dint of an incorrect analysis, they are an artefact of a mistake by the grammarians. The grammarians must have come up with an incorrect rule to have produced so many unexplained exceptions. The exceptions must fit into the system somewhere, because a language is a system whose elements are determined by their place in the system (Saussure 1983) – all of whose elements, not just some of them. So what you do is you examine the exceptions in minute detail, bringing out their properties – syntactic, morphological, semantic, everything you can think of – to try to see what it is that is special about

them, what is it about them that makes them resist a construction which by
rights they ought to undergo, what is it that makes them non-passivizable.
In 1976–1979 the author had no idea where to look or where to start, so
he cast around fairly randomly and blindly, testing the verbs and sentences
he had for the effects of questions, negation, the absence of a passive *by*-
phrase, the presence of an adverb, etc. on their passivizability. This part
of the exercise took about a year, and all the afore-mentioned avenues of
research drew a blank. Then, completely out of the blue, on a hunch, he
tested them for their ability to form a resultative perfect.[6] A resultative
perfect is a sentence in the perfect which expresses an action and the result
which ensues from that action, as in 6 below (Leech 1971):

(6) She has broken the doll.

In 6 the subject carried out an action in the past, breaking a doll, which led
to a result, the result being that the doll is now (at the moment of speech)
broken. The result meaning is not just implied or pragmatically deducible,
it is formally realized in the perfect. To the author's surprise two-thirds of
the non-passivizable transitive verbs were unable to express a resultative
perfect, as illustrated by 7 for English and 8 for German:

(7) James has known Fiona. (Cf. 1)
(8) *Jetzt hat er Käse gemocht. (Cf. 2)
     now has he cheese liked
     'now he has liked cheese'

In 7 the sentence could only be understood as an experiential perfect – in
which James has experienced knowing Fiona at some point in the past –
but never as a resultative perfect. In 8, in which a resultative interpretation

---

6   The resultative perfect test was applied only to the English and German data, it
     cannot be applied to Russian, because Russian does not have a formally realized
     perfect, i.e. a construction structurally equivalent to *have* + 2nd participle. In fact,
     it turned out that the Russian participial passive displays an even more interesting
     correlation than the passive-perfect correlation of English and German – see below.

is forced by starting the sentence with *jetzt* 'now' (see Gelhaus and Latzel 1974: 228–9), the sentence is ungrammatical.

Thus we have established a correlation between the passive and the perfect. The passive and the perfect have something in common, viz. they are both unexpectedly incompatible with the same set of verbs. Of course, it could be an accidental, purely statistical correlation. But we suspect not, we suspect that if we dig deeper we will find a structural reason behind the correlation. Notice that the correlation is unexpected, i.e. we did not expect to find it. And of course we did not expect to find it. We are dealing with a bizarre set of unexplained exceptions (non-passivizable transitive verbs) and of course you do not expect such randomness to tie in with anything, because they are just that, random, bizarre, unexplained and exceptional. In that sense the name of the method described here – the method of exceptions and their correlations – is on the face of it a contradiction in terms. A set of random exceptions is not expected to correlate with anything. But if they do, if you find that they do correlate with another construction, then you may be on to something. Dig deeper and see what you find, if you are lucky – or if your hunch is right – you may find other characteristics linking your two constructions, in this case the passive and the perfect. You may find that your exceptions are the consequence of the grammarians' mistake in their analysis of your construction. In this sense the phrase 'exceptions and their correlations' is not a contradiction in terms, the phrase aims precisely to expose incorrect analyses by discovering correlations which are not supposed to be there, going by our current knowledge.

The crucial methodological point here of exploring different avenues which may or may not lead somewhere does not come across in Waltisberg's 2012 otherwise excellent review of Danks 2011. Waltisberg (2012: 634) writes:

> Already in this chapter, D makes extensive use of the chi-square test, a statistical hypothesis test ... Although this methodology yields interesting results, its complexity may not be readily comprehensible to many readers unfamiliar with mathematical statistics. Considering the complexity of this methodology, D's statistical results seem overall a bit meagre (... for example, 'one-quarter of pattern III and one-third of pattern VI verbs do not conform to these dominant meanings' ...).

I am not sure here to what extent Waltisberg is referring to the use of the chi-square test and to what extent to the method of exceptions and their correlations.[7] As regards the latter, it is important to realize that, with reference to Waltisberg's statement that 'D's statistical results seem overall a bit meagre', the method works by trying out different avenues which inevitably initially do not lead anywhere but then eventually, hopefully, the researcher does hit on an avenue which leads to a significant correlation, as happened to Danks. And Waltisberg does indeed speak elsewhere in the review of Danks 'presenting valuable statistical data'. The point is that without going through the counts which do not end up producing valuable data you wouldn't do the counts which (unexpectedly) do lead to valuable data and correlations (see also Danks, this volume, footnotes 6 and 11). The 'unexpectedly' here is crucial. What you expect is based on your current knowledge. But scientific research is about expanding our knowledge. If you restrict yourself to what your current knowledge leads you to expect you will be trapped within the confines of that knowledge, you will never discover anything new empirically and thus will never come up with any new ideas. The only route to new knowledge is through empirical exploration, data collection and experiments. People associate experiments with physics and chemistry, not with grammar, but the method of exceptions and their correlations allows you to do just that, to carry out experiments in grammar which lead empirically to new insights and knowledge.

Interpreting the data

Returning to the passive-perfect correlation, the question then was, why? Why was it that such an unexpectedly large proportion[8] of non-passivizable

---

7   I myself do not use the chi-square test, though Danks 2011 does. See Danks 2011: 32–7, this volume: 44, 46, 49.

8   Given that there was no known connection between the passive and the resultative perfect in English and German, what was expected was that a few of the non-passivizable transitive verbs might for various chance reasons be also not susceptible to a resultative perfect – say, anything up to 50 per cent – but that as many as two-thirds

transitive verbs did not form a resultative perfect? When the test or 'experiment' was carried out there was no reason, given our state of knowledge then, to expect that that would be the case. There was no reason to expect that the passive had anything to do with the resultative perfect. What had been discovered – note 'discovered', not assumed or hypothesized – was a syntactic correlation between the passive and the perfect (syntax in the sense of combinatorial possibilities (not word order)). The passive and the perfect are exhibiting the same behaviour vis-à-vis the same set of verbs, viz. they will allow them to form neither a passive nor a resultative perfect. In other words, the passive is behaving like the perfect. The inference which was drawn from this correlation – taken together with numerous other arguments, e.g. the formal differences between active and passive when they are supposed to be (cognitively) synonymous, the fact that four-fifths of passives occurring in texts are without a realized agentive *by*-phrase, etc. (see Beedham 2005b: 33–60 for details) – was that the passive is the same construction as the perfect, viz. an aspect of the type Auxiliary + Participle, with its own meaning, 'action + state', i.e. a new state is expressed (on the subject) as the result of a preceding action (hence the subject is patient), which is similar to the perfect meaning 'action + result'. To form a passive – and a resultative perfect – a verb or a sentence has to be telic, i.e. it has to have a built-in potential end-point in its semantics, an end-point which becomes the end-state of the meaning 'action + state' (on telicity see Comrie 1976: 44–8). The non-passivizable transitive verbs do not have a built-in end-point, they are atelic. That is why they do not form a passive (for further details see for English Beedham 1987a, Tobin 1993: 280–313; for German Beedham 1987b, Abraham 2000; for Russian Бидэм 1988, Schoorlemmer 1995, Beedham 1998, Poupynin 1999). The formal evidence for the idea that non-passivizable transitive verbs are atelic is the fact that they do not form a resultative perfect.

---

of them were precluded from the resultative perfect was unexpected and unlikely to be a matter of chance. Having said that, the statistic of two-thirds would not by itself have justified the conclusion that the passive is behaving like the perfect. There have to be other structural and semantic reasons to warrant such a conclusion, some of which are mentioned below.

This last point is the nub of the method of exceptions and their cor-relations. The data which take you to a particular analysis also serve as the syntactic evidence for that analysis. This feature of the method arises from the Saussurean point mentioned above that a language is a structure or system whose elements are determined by their place in the system. Also crucial is the fact that the experiment is repeatable, i.e. it is open to anyone to test non-passivizable transitive verbs – in English, German, or any language which has a (formally realized) resultative perfect, the modern language or a historically earlier stage of a language – for their ability to form a resultative perfect. Such a repeated experiment would confirm or refute the analysis given here.

Within the methodology described here it is important to note that a new rule for the passive and a new meaning for the passive were found at the same time. This fact ties in with the indivisibility of the linguistic sign, i.e. *signifiant* (form) and *signifié* (meaning) are inextricably linked (Saussure 1983, Tobin 1990, Zubin and Köpcke 1984, Köpcke 1982, Beedham 2008). It is also significant that it was a syntactic correlation – the passive-perfect correlation – which led us to both the new rule and the new meaning: it is an example of form determining meaning.

The Russian passive

The analysis of the passive as an aspect works particularly well in Russian. Russian has two passive constructions, one formed with *byt'* 'to be' + pas-sive participle, the other formed with the reflexive clitic *–sja* 'self', as shown in 9 and 10 below:

(9) *Most byl postroen izvestnym inženerom.*
bridge was built by-famous engineer
'the bridge was built by a famous engineer'

(10) *Most stroilsja izvestnym inženerom.*
bridge built-itself by-famous engineer
'the bridge was built by a famous engineer'

The two Russian passives display a well-known aspectual restriction: usually only perfective verbs form a participial passive, whilst only imperfective verbs form the reflexive passive. The question is, why? Under the voice analysis one has no idea, so much so that the question is never asked. But under the aspect analysis the answer is clear. The two Russian passives are two very different animals. The participial passive is an aspect of the type Auxiliary + Participle, with the meaning 'action + state'. One sees immediately from the meaning why the participial passive is confined to the perfective verb only. The perfective verb views an action from the outside, having an overview from the beginning to the end of the action. The imperfective verb, in contrast, views an action from within, from inside. Thus only the perfective verb has sight of the end of an action, thus only the perfective verb can form a construction involving the end-state of an action, i.e. the participial passive. The imperfective verb cannot form it, because it cannot see the end of an action, it is firmly ensconced in the middle of the action. The reflexive passive, on the other hand, is not an aspect of the type Auxiliary + Participle – it has a quite different form, based on the reflexive clitic –*sja* 'self' – and it does not mean 'action + state'. Hence the imperfective verb can form the reflexive passive, despite the fact that it cannot form the participial passive.

The advantage of working on the same formal construction in more than one language can be seen here. With hindsight it was probably the aspectual restriction on the passive in Russian which subconsciously led the author to the passive-perfect correlation in English and German; even though it was not until he discovered the passive-perfect correlation and realized that the passive is an aspect in English and German that he realized that the participial passive in Russian is an aspect. (For an aspectual analysis of the passive in Arabic see Danks 2011, in Spanish see Gregory 2006, and Daniel Honert, Non-Passivizable Transitive Verbs in Spanish, paper given at the Romance Linguistics Seminar, Cambridge, 5–6 January 2012).

Recognizing errors and correcting them

By using a set of unexplained lexical exceptions to a grammatical rule, i.e. transitive verbs which do not form a passive, we have arrived at a new analysis of the construction with respect to which the exceptions were exceptions. We have taken a theoretical and intellectual step forward and made the new insight that the passive is an aspect of the type Auxiliary + Participle, which like all Auxiliary + Participle aspects is sensitive to the lexical aspect of the verb with which it combines and to the compositional aspect of the sentence in which it appears. Compositional aspect is the overall aspect of a sentence, as determined not just by the verb but by the subject, object and adverbials as well (Verkuyl 1972, 1993). This analysis replaces the old voice analysis, under which passives are derived from an underlying active, actives and passives are 'cognitively synonymous', and all and only transitive verbs form a passive. We can see now that the voice analysis was wrong. Actives and passives are not synonymous, passivizability is not determined by transitivity, and the passive is not a 'voice' of the verb. The passive is an aspect of the verb, it has its own meaning, 'action + state', and its syntax is determined by lexical and compositional aspect. Moreover, we have explained the exceptions of the voice rule that we started out with, and rendered them no longer exceptions. We are back again with the nub of the method – the empirical data that you start out with take you to the theoretical analysis which you end up with. If your rule is 'transitive verbs form a passive' you have exceptions, but if your rule is 'to form a passive a verb has to be telic' you do not. This situation is summed up in Table 1.1. (for details see Beedham 2005b: 33–60).

Table 1.1. The voice analysis versus the aspect analysis of the passive
(in English *be* + V-*ed*)

	Old analysis: the voice analysis	New analysis: the aspect analysis
Form*	*be* + V-*ed* is a voice of the verb	*be* + V-*ed* is an aspect of the verb
Meaning	passive is synonymous with underlying active	passive means 'action + state'
Syntax	all and only transitive verbs form a passive	only telic verbs and sentences form a passive

* That is, grammatical form. It is important to distinguish grammatical form – which involves a theoretical analysis – from phonological form (it might be clearer to say shape, rather than form here), which is data and does not involve a theoretical analysis. We have taken a phonological form – *be* + V-*ed* in English – as our data and produced a new grammatical analysis of it, and express that analysis by saying that the (grammatical) form of *be* + V-*ed* is aspect, not voice.

The structuralist tenet that a language is a system whose elements are determined by their place in the system, the idea of syntax as combinatorial possibilities, and the notion of compositional aspect are three different ways of saying what is basically the same thing. They all have their embodiment in the sentence.

The measurement of pro and contra examples

It was said in the section titled 'Conducting experiments' that in the experiment conducted two-thirds of non-passivizable transitive verbs did not form a resultative perfect. So what about the one-third counterexamples, for example many atelic verbs can form a passive, e.g. *to like*? Firstly, the kind of passive sentences which spring to mind with atelic verbs are those with a special compositional aspect, e.g. *John is liked by everyone* (in contrast *John is liked by Mary* is odd). The fact that compositional aspect affects passivizability is entirely to be expected if the passive is an aspect

of the type Auxiliary + Participle (but is not to be expected if the passive
is a voice of the verb). Secondly, to say that some or many atelic verbs form
a passive is an impressionistic and vague statement, whilst the method of
exceptions and their correlations allows or forces you to list the atelic verbs,
using a formal test – we have used the resultative perfect – and then to list
the subset of them which form a passive. This was done in Beedham 1982:
102–6, where under the heading 'Inconsistencies' 27 sentences of English
and 11 sentences of German are given which are atelic – they do not form
a resultative perfect – but which nevertheless form a passive. There then
follows a section headed 'Tentative explanation of inconsistencies' (p. 107).
Out of the 219 transitive sentences of English and German, each one containing a different transitive verb (see fn. 5), given in Beedham (1982:
59–81, 92–107) two-thirds of them support the aspect analysis because
they form neither a passive nor a resultative perfect, and one-third are
counterexamples because they form one but not the other (either a passive but not a resultative perfect, or a resultative perfect but not a passive).
The question arises, do the one-third counterexamples refute the aspect
analysis of the passive? Indeed, if you think of just one counterexample
does it refute the aspect analysis and show that it is wrong? The answer is
no. In grammar you will never get 100 per cent support from the data for
any analysis, because any scientific analysis is only ever an approximation
to the truth, it is never the whole and absolute truth; because language is
a complex system of sub-systems, and some of the smaller sub-systems are
bound to bump up against the bigger sub-system that you are explaining;
and because the number of sentences in a language is infinite, you can
never list them all, not the ones in support of your analysis and not the
ones which contradict your analysis. If we reject the aspect analysis because
of the one-third counterexamples we would have to return to the voice
analysis. And the voice analysis cannot explain the two-thirds of examples
which are explained by the aspect analysis (ignoring for the moment the
numerous other anomalies of the voice analysis which are explained by
the aspect analysis). Moreover, for each counterexample there are special
circumstances which plausibly explain their counterexample status, which
are discussed in the above-mentioned section 'Tentative explanation of
inconsistencies', e.g. the 2nd participle of *to marry* is also an adjective,

married, indicating that the verb has a special lexical aspect which allows it to form a resultative perfect – *John has married Mary* – but not a passive – **Mary was married by John* (assuming John is not the church minister who performed the ceremony). There will always be counterexamples, but the method of exceptions and their correlations allows you to see the proportion of pro examples to contra examples, in order to put the contra examples in perspective. By squaring up to the existence of exceptions and the complex interaction of the sub-systems of a language the method of exceptions and their correlations brings precision, explicitness, exhaustiveness, repeatability and a systematic approach to linguistics, in place of vague impressions. The one-third counterexamples in the passive-perfect correlation point the way towards where more work needs to be done but they do not refute the aspect analysis of the passive.

Time-scale

In terms of the debate between rationalism and empiricism, we have come to a rationalist conclusion – a new analysis – on the basis of empirical groundwork. We have combined theory and practice. We have engaged in data collection, but it is smart data collection. After spending about 6 months isolating the problem, i.e. identifying all the non-passivizable transitive verbs, and a further year testing those verbs for their compatibility with a wide range of different constructions, it took another six months thinking through theoretically the implications of the data, to arrive at the insight that the passive is an aspect, and that the voice analysis – the tradition of deriving passives from an underlying active – was wrong. It then took another year, i.e. a third year,[9] writing up the results of the previous two years' work, in a PhD thesis which was published as Beedham 1982. The 18 months spent collecting and analysing data was a hard slog, and it was risky, because it was entirely possible that the series of experiments

---

9   The three years which the author spent researching on the passive was full-time, i.e. during that time he had no other duties to interrupt that research.

carried out would all be negative, entirely possible that a pattern would never emerge. But it was worth it in the end, since it was primarily the empirical correlation discovered – the passive-perfect correlation – which led to the realization that the passive is an aspect.

In Beedham 2005b: 163–4 I summarized the work of the method in six phases. I would like now to put a time-scale on those six phases, assuming a full-time British PhD of three years – see Table 1.2.[10] Obviously, the period allocated here to each phase is approximate, it will vary from project to project.

Table 1.2. A proposed schedule of phases for using the method of exceptions and correlations in a PhD

	Phase	Length of time in months
1	choose a (formal) construction	2
2	identify the problems, anomalies etc., especially semantic ones	3
3	identify and list the (unexplained lexical) exceptions	3
4	identify the properties of your exceptions	}
5	look for a correlation between your exceptions and one of your exceptions' properties identified in phase 4. At this stage it can be a purely statistical correlation, roughly at least two-thirds.	} 14
6	can the meaning associated with the property discovered in phase 5 be found in your construction? Is it a meaning in your construction which no one has ever noticed before? Is it a meaning which could explain the semantic anomalies found in phase 2? If so, you have made a crucial empirical discovery and come up with a new and better analysis of your construction.	2
	writing up	12

---

10   I am grateful to P. Sreekumar for help in drawing up Table 1.2.

The link with language teaching

The methodology described here is a mixture of theory and practice and is closely associated with language teaching. According to this approach the ultimate test of a new grammatical analysis is for it to be accepted into pedagogical grammars, as mentioned above. Despite the fact that the aspect analysis of the passive was first published in 1981 and 1982 it still remains true today that no language course-book or pedagogical grammar, of English, German, or Russian, has been published which incorporates it. Why? The aspect analysis of the passive seems to me to be eminently applicable in language teaching, and this view was reinforced recently, in 2011, when a second-year student of German at my University, Ashley Husband Powton, having read Beedham 2005b, was rather miffed to find that the passive in her German language classes was taught as a voice of the verb (related to an underlying active), and she asked her tutor to teach it as an aspect. She then went further, and sent an e-mail, signed by all nine members of the German Society (student) Committee, to the Head of the German Department, again asking that the German passive be taught in language classes as an aspect, in all its relations to and affinity with the German perfect, not as a voice of the verb. This episode raises the question, if a second-year modern languages student, albeit a particularly talented one, is able to understand the aspect analysis of the passive and see immediately that it is begging to be applied in the language teaching classroom, why have professional applied linguists not incorporated the aspect analysis of the passive into their course-books and grammars for language students? In my view it is because the link between theoretical and applied linguistics has been broken by the dominance in theoretical linguistics of the formalistic model-building approach known as generative grammar (see Chapter 4 of Beedham 2005b, and Beedham 2002b). I hope that language teachers will eventually take on board the aspect analysis of the passive, and if and when they do I hope they reflect on why it took so long.

Tense formation and irregular verbs

After completion of the passive research the next set of exceptions chosen
to work on was irregular verbs, again in English, German, and Russian. The
term 'irregular' verb is used here to mean all those verbs whose conjugation
in the modern language differs from the regular (in English and German
'weak', in Russian 'productive') verbs, so in English and German modal
and mixed verbs are included and in Russian the fact that one can identify
sub-regularities amongst the non-productive verbs does not make them any
the less irregular in comparison to the regular/productive verbs. For this
project it was not necessary to spend time identifying the exceptions, as had
had to be done for the passive, since every grammar book and dictionary of
English and German lists the irregular verbs (known as 'strong' verbs), and
the irregular verbs of Russian (known as 'non-productive' verbs) are quite
well picked out and described in some grammars of Russian. The reason for
the difference is that for the passive the exceptions were syntactic exceptions – i.e. is this verb transitive, and if so, does it form a passive? – and as
such they were quite difficult to identify, whereas the irregular verbs are a
morphological question, much easier to identify and isolate.

Working with informants

When working with native speaker informants the difference between
syntax and morphology takes on a new significance in a highly inflecting language like Russian. With syntax one is more likely to present a
sentence to a native speaker and ask is it correct. With Russian, because
it is so highly inflecting – e.g. most verbs have about 45 different possible
forms – it makes more sense to present a single verb form, not in a sentence,
completely devoid of any context whatsoever, to informants and ask is it
correct. Of course, one does not take the response entirely at face value,
the responses of informants have to be viewed critically and evaluated, not
least because informants often disagree; this applies both to judgements
of sentences and of isolated morphological forms.

The way a researcher handles informants differs from language to language, depending on the structure and sociolinguistic variety of the language concerned, and from culture to culture, depending on the education system and the attitude to language in that culture. Danks (2011, this volume) had to cope with the fact that the language he was investigating, Modern Standard Arabic, is the high form in a diglossic relationship with a range of national and local Arabic dialects. Thus, while Arabs may be native speakers of Egyptian Arabic, Moroccan Arabic, etc., Modern Standard Arabic is used primarily as a written language and spoken only in formal and pan-Arab contexts. Moreover, the structure of Arabic vocabulary – most often three root consonants fitted into a finite number of patterns to derive different words – is such that it is difficult to draw a line between words or forms which actually exist and those which are theoretically possible but are not attested. Both these factors made Danks' task of identifying unexplained exceptions and getting words and sentences evaluated by native speaker informants extremely difficult.

Mohawk is a polysynthetic language which uses long, polymorphemic words where English would use a clause consisting of several words. According to Marianne Mithun, the Mohawk speakers she works with are unable to look inside a word of Mohawk and perceive and talk about its constituent morphemes.[11] This would make a study of Mohawk grammar using the method of exceptions and their correlations extremely difficult indeed.

The situation is also intriguing when one considers that the method of exceptions and their correlations should certainly be usable on an earlier synchronic stage of a language, e.g. Old English, Middle High German, whereby there are no longer any native speaker informants alive to obtain grammaticality judgements from. Again, anyone attempting to carry out such research would be faced with a challenging new set of circumstances within which to work. On using informants to obtain grammaticality judgements

11 Mithun, M., Rhetorical Prosody and Polysynthesis, paper given at the 39th Annual Meeting of the Societas Linguistica Europaea (SLE), Bremen, Germany, 2006.

see Schütze 1996, Kepser and Reis (eds) 2005, Cornips and Poletto 2005, Sorace and Keller 2005, Cowart 1997, Quirk and Svartvik 1966.

Identifying the exceptions

Returning to the irregular verbs, the English and German irregular verbs are irregular in terms of preterit tense and participle formation, whilst the Russian irregular verbs are irregular in respect of the present tense paradigm. The overwhelming majority of English verbs form their preterit and 2nd participle with –*ed*, e.g. *walk walked walked* – these are the regular verbs. But a substantial minority of verbs form their preterit and 2nd participle with ablaut (and some with the ending –*en*) instead, e.g. *break broke broken* (Quirk et al. 1985: 96–120) – these are the irregular verbs, of which there are 126 in our data. Turning to German, most German verbs form their preterit with -*te* and their 2nd participle with *ge-* + -*t*, e.g. *sagen sagte gesagt* 'to say'. A substantial minority of verbs, however, form their preterit and 2nd participle with ablaut and the ending –*en*, e.g. *gehen ging gegangen* 'to go' (Durrell 2002: 231–60, Helbig and Buscha 1989: 34–49) – these are the irregular verbs, of which there are 169 in our data. Moving to Russian, most verbs ending in -*at'* form their present tense by retaining the –*a*- in the stem and by not undergoing consonant interchange, e.g. *čitat'* 'to read' *čitajut* 'they read' – these are the regular or 'productive', as they are usually called, verbs. But again a substantial minority of Russian verbs ending in –*at'* form their present tense differently, they form it by dropping the -*a*- in the stem and by undergoing consonant interchange in all persons, e.g. *pisat'* 'to write' *pišut* 'they write' (Pulkina and Zakhava-Nekrasova 1960: 226–44, Грамматика русского языка 1960: 531–76)[12] – these are the

---

12 All productive verbs in –*it'* undergo consonant interchange, but only in the 1st pers. sing. Another contrast of non-productive verbs in -*at'* with the productive verbs in –*at'* concerns the distinction between 1st conjugation and 2nd conjugation. Most non-productive verbs in -*at'* are 1st conjugation (like the productive verbs in -*at'*; productive verbs in -*it'* are 2nd conjugation), but a small number of non-productive verbs in -*at'* (about 17 per cent) are 2nd conjugation, like verbs in -*it'*.

non-productive verbs in *–at'*, of which there are 132 simplex such verbs in our data.[13] This situation is summarized in Tables 1.3, 1.4 and 1.5. Having explained the exceptions to the passive rule, viz. some transitive verbs do not form a passive because they are atelic, the hope now is to explain the exceptions to the rule of tense formation, i.e. to explain (synchronically, structurally) why it is that some verbs for example in English form their preterit and 2nd participle with ablaut instead of with *–ed*.

Table 1.3. The basic morphology of English irregular verbs

	Regular verbs		Irregular verbs	
Grammatical form	Phonological realization	Example	Phonological realization	Example
infinitive	Ø	walk	Ø	break
preterit	-ed	walked	ablaut	broke
2nd participle	-ed	walked	ablaut (and *–en*)	broken

Table 1.4. The basic morphology of German irregular verbs

	Regular verbs		Irregular verbs	
Grammatical form	Phonological realization	Example	Phonological realization	Example
infinitive	-en	sagen 'to say'	-en	gehen 'to go'
preterit	-te	sagte	ablaut	ging
2nd participle	ge- + -t	gesagt	ablaut and *-en*	gegangen

13   Russian verbs in *–et'* were also included in the research project adumbrated below, but will not be mentioned here for reasons of space. Our research was confined initially to verbs in *–at'* and *–et'* only, because their irregular verbs are easiest to identify (Бидэм 2004). Verbs ending in *–it'* and verbs with a miscellaneous infinitive ending have now also been studied, and revealed similar patterns (Бидэм forthcoming).

Table 1.5. The basic morphology of Russian irregular verbs ending in *-at'*

	Regular verbs		Irregular verbs	
Grammatical form	Phonological realization	Example	Phonological realization	Example
infinitive	-at'	čitat' 'to read'	-at'	pisat' 'to write'
present tense	retains –a-, no consonant interchange	čitajut' 'they read'	drops –a-, consonant interchange	pišut 'they write'

Once again, the standard approach in grammars of English, German and Russian is not to attempt to explain the existence of these irregular exceptions, but rather to view them as synchronically inexplicable irregularities. Historical explanations are given – the irregular verbs are a historical vestige – or psycholinguistic explanations are given – the irregular verbs are easy to remember because they are very common – but no synchronic, purely grammatical or structural explanation is ever attempted. But again, that approach is misguided in our view. If a language is a Saussurean system such fairly substantial numbers of verbs, even if they are in the minority, cannot stand outside the system, isolated, in a vacuum, not part of the system. They must fit in somehow. Moreover, forms do not exist synchronically in a language for no reason, they are there for a reason, basically to carry meanings. It follows that the irregular verbs, with their own special and indeed very striking forms, must have a meaning of their own which those forms carry. The fact that we cannot say now what that meaning is speaks of our ignorance and the research still to be done but it does not follow that the forms do not have a meaning. Remember, under the voice analysis of the passive *be* + V-*ed* did not have a meaning, but thanks to the aspect analysis we now know that it does have a meaning, viz. 'action + state'. Quirk 1970 suggested that a subset at least of the English irregular verbs are perfective, viz. the irregular *burnt, dreamt* etc., in contrast to the regular *burned, dreamed* etc., which are durative. Tobin 1993 suggested that the irregular verbs of English, Hebrew, and the Romance languages are resultative, in contrast to the regular verbs, which are process-oriented.

And Even-Simkin and Tobin (2013, 2011) have now identified fourteen sub-meanings of resultative which they match up with fourteen phonetically defined sub-groups of irregular verb in English. Whilst they do not give structural, grammatical evidence for their semantic impressions, I believe that the meaning which Quirk and Even-Simkin and Tobin suggest will turn out to be correct, but we must have synchronic, structural, lexico-grammatical evidence for it.

It is that structural evidence which we are looking for. The aim is to find a rule or rules by which one can derive the forms *drank, hit, left*, etc., i.e. the forms which at the moment are irregular. As happened with our research on the passive we expect to find a new rule and a new meaning at the same time. For this project, the irregular verbs, we seem to have an indication of the meaning – resultative – before we have found the rule, which is the other way round to what happened with the passive, where we found first the rule – the passive is an aspect – and then the meaning – the passive (in English *be* + V-*ed*) means 'action + state'. But in both cases the indivisibility of the sign still holds, and our assumption is that we won't really know what the irregular verb forms mean until we know the rule(s) by which they are derived.

Conducting experiments

VCs of irregular and regular verbs

So again, the question arises, what do we do with the irregular verbs, these lexical exceptions? The answer is the same as before, for the non-passivizable transitive verbs. We examine them in great detail, to try to find out what is special about them, what is it about them that makes them behave differently in terms of their tense formation. We look at their morphological, syntactic, semantic, etc. properties, to see if we find anything odd, i.e. odd in terms of our current state of knowledge. We look for a formal correlation between the irregular verbs and something else in the lexico-grammar of the languages concerned, some still to be identified thing. The author has been working on the irregular verbs since about 1981 – in contrast to the passive project described above, for part of the time only, not full-time – and tested them, using native speaker informants, for their ability to form an imperative, an actional passive, a statal passive, an attributive 2nd participle, an expanded attributive 2nd participle, and for many other properties. Again, as happened at first with the passive, all of these avenues of research drew a blank. It was then decided to change tack and in 1992 the phonotactic properties of the irregular verbs were examined, and here at last something came to light.[14] Again, it is a question of finding something which marks out the irregular verbs as different, i.e. different from the regular verbs. In order to make it easier to spot the difference an exhaustive list of all the regular verbs in the relevant languages was compiled. As with the passive it is important that the list be exhaustive. That was not as difficult as it might sound, because you only need to compare those regular verbs which are structurally comparable with the irregular verbs, since obviously one wants to compare like with like. Since nearly all the (stems of the) irregular verbs are monosyllabic, the first restriction is that you only need to look at regular verbs which are monosyllabic or which have a monosyllabic stem. Again, standard dictionaries and other reference works were used to facilitate the task: for English the *Oxford Advanced Learner's Dictionary of Current English* 1989, for German Mater 1967a, for Russian Daum and Schenk 1971, and the *Обратный словарь русского языка*. Together with the effects of other restrictions arising from structural comparability – see Beedham 2005b: 107–33 for details – the final numbers in our data were 1,768 English regular verbs, 1,467 German regular verbs, and 891 Russian regular verbs in *–at'*. Thus the relative proportions are that one had 14 times as many English regular verbs as irregular verbs, 9 times as many German regular verbs as irregular verbs, and 7 times as many Russian productive verbs in *-at'* as non-productive verbs in *–at'*. This situation is summarized in Table 1.6.

---

14   Phonotactics is the study of the permissible combinations and order of vowels and
       consonants in a language.

Table 1.6. Numbers of irregular verbs and structurally comparable regular verbs in English, German and Russian

	Irregular verbs	Structurally comparable regular verbs	Proportion of regular to irregular verb
English	126	1,768	14:1
German	169	1,467	9:1
Russian	132	891	7:1

It was now a question of laying out the two lists for each language side by side, and trying to spot the difference. What was the difference between the verbs in the irregular list and the verbs in the regular list? On the face of it there was no difference, at first glance there appeared to be no significant difference between the infinitives of the irregular verbs and those of the regular verbs. Might the irregular verbs contain more high front vowels? No, an examination of the lists soon showed that this was not the case. Might the irregular verbs contain more voiced consonants? Again no, they did not. Then, with the help of a research assistant, Uwe Junghanns, bearing in mind that the overwhelming majority of the (stems of the simplex) irregular verbs are monosyllabic, the vowel + consonant sequences (VCs, in which C stands for consonant or consonant cluster) were examined and here a difference became apparent. We noticed that the list of irregular verbs contained a large number of certain VCs, VCs which occurred in only small numbers in the regular verb list.[15] At this point the irregular verb forms themselves were added to the infinitive forms, e.g. not just (*to*) *drink* but also *drank* and *drunk*. To give an example from English, there were 11 irregular verbs with [ɪŋ] (e.g. *bring, cling*) but only 4 regular verbs with [ɪŋ] (e.g. *to wing*). Given that the regular verb list was 14 times longer than the irregular verb list this was surprising. To give an example

15   The consonant + vowel sequences (CVs) also played a similar role, but will not be described here for reasons of space. See Beedham 2005b: 107–33. For an analysis of German strong verbs which takes account of the consonant following the vowel see Köpcke 1998.

from German, there were 11 irregular verbs with [iːs] (e.g. *fließen* 'to flow')
but only 1 regular verb with [iːs] (viz. *spießen* 'to skewer'). Again, given that
the German regular verb list was 9 times longer than the irregular verb list
this was surprising. To give an example from Russian, *-ot* appeared in 13
non-productive verbs (e.g. *bormotat'* 'to mutter') but in only 4 productive
verbs (e.g. *rabotat'* 'to work'). Once again, given that the Russian regular
verb list was 7 times longer than the irregular verb list this was surprising.

Moreover, many of the regular verbs containing an irregular verb VC
had special reasons for doing so. The overwhelming majority of irregular
verbs are base verbs, i.e. not derived (synchronically). But many of the
regular verbs containing an irregular verb VC were derived verbs. Either
they were derived from a noun, and had to conjugate regularly so as to
retain the VC of the noun from which they derive in order to maintain
that derivational link, e.g. going back to verbs in English with [ɪŋ] *to wing*,
from the noun *wing* (in other words, if it went *wing wang wung* the derivation of *wang* from the noun *wing* would no longer be discernible). Or else
they were phonaesthetic verbs designating a sound, i.e. the pronunciation
of the verb imitates the sound it designates, which again have to conjugate
regularly in order to maintain their phonaesthetic effect, e.g. returning again
to verbs with [ɪŋ] the verbs *to ping, to ting* (on phonaesthemes see Hinton
et al. (eds) 1994, Gamkrelidze 2006). Thus we see that were it not for the
special circumstances of derived verbs and phonaesthetic verbs there would
be no (monosyllabic) regular verbs whatsoever with [ɪŋ], and we would be
looking at a statistical difference of 11:0, not 11:4.

So the initial answer to the question, how do irregular verbs differ
from regular verbs, is that they differ in terms of their VCs: the irregular
verbs contain VCs which tend not to occur on the regular verbs. Thus the
VCs serve as phonotactic markers of strong conjugation in English and
German and non-productive conjugation in Russian. Although this is
not so much an analysis as an initial observation, it is worth pointing out
that once again, using the method advocated here, it is not a hypothesis
or assumption but a discovery. Once again the data have taken us to an
analysis, or here rather an initial observation on the way hopefully to a full
analysis. Once again, as with the passive, the experiment is repeatable, i.e.
other linguists can explicate and compare the VCs of the irregular verbs

and regular verbs of English, German, Russian, and any language which has irregular verbs, either the modern language or a historically earlier stage of a language, to confirm or refute the findings described here.

The findings described here are similar to those given in Pinker 1999 (see also Pinker 1994: 138–45; see Beedham 2002a; see also Bybee and Slobin 1982). Firstly, Pinker notes the role of the consonant or consonant cluster following or preceding the vowel of the irregular verb in the structural sustainability of irregular conjugation:

> The verbs undergoing a given irregular change are far more similar than they have to be. If you are a verb and want to undergo the *i-a-u* pattern, all you really need is an *i*. But the verbs that do follow the pattern (*drink, spring, shrink,* and so on) have much more in common; most begin with a consonant cluster like *st-, str-, dr-, sl-,* or *cl-,* and most end in *-ng* or *-nk.* ... Imagine a rule that said, 'If a verb has the sound *consonant-consonant -i-ng,* change *i* to *u*'. (Pinker 1999: 91)

Secondly, he notes that verbs which one would expect to be strong because of the vowels and consonants in them are prevented from undergoing strong conjugation because they are derived from a noun or adjective: 'Verbs that are recognized as thinly disguised nouns or adjectives don't accept irregular forms, even when they sound like an irregular verb', e.g. the verb *to ring* as in *Powell ringed the city with artillery* (Pinker 1999: 158). Thirdly, he notes the way in which phonaesthetic or onomatopoeic verbs are prevented from being strong by their onomatopoeia:

> Onomatopoeic verbs ... need past tense ... forms, but because they are not canonical roots, they cannot tap into the lexicon of roots and linked irregular forms that encourage irregular analogies. Onomatopoeic forms therefore are regular, even when their sound would otherwise tempt people to borrow an irregular pattern:
> The engine *pinged* [not *pang* or *pung*].
> (Pinker 1999: 155)

Irregular verb VCs and function words

The next obvious question to ask was, do the VCs of the irregular verbs, now shown to be characteristic of the irregular verbs, crop up elsewhere in the grammar or vocabulary of the languages concerned? To find out the answer to this question, in 1999 with the help of research assistant Wendy Anderson and in 2002 with the help of research assistant Albina Ozieva[16] another experiment was conducted in which all the monosyllabic[17] function words (pronouns, conjunctions, etc.) were extracted from dictionaries of English, German, and Russian, and their VCs examined. The dictionaries used were for English the *Oxford Advanced Learner's Dictionary of Current English* 1989, for German the *Duden Bedeutungswörterbuch*, for Russian the *Словарь структурных слов русского языка* (Морковкин 1997). It was found that for all three languages the VCs of the irregular verbs had a surprisingly high rate of occurrence there: 72 per cent of English monosyllabic function words contained a strong verb VC, 64 per cent of German monosyllabic function words contained a strong verb VC, and 79 per cent of Russian monosyllabic function words with a VC contained a nonproductive verb VC.[18] Once again, these experiments are repeatable, i.e. other linguists can identify the VCs of irregular verbs and look for them in monosyllabic function words, either in English, German and Russian or in any other language which has irregular verbs, the modern language or a historically earlier stage of a language, to come up with their own results which will either confirm or contradict the findings given here.

16   Research assistant Noel Brackney was of the opinion that the Russian verbal system is so complex that only a native speaker could do the work required. It was then that Albina Ozieva was appointed, who is a native speaker of Russian – and a Germanist, Anglicist and lexicographer – and who used her native speaker knowledge of Russian to great effect on the project.

17   The investigation was restricted to monosyllabic function words only because, as mentioned above, the overwhelming majority of irregular verb stems are monosyllabic.

18   The figure of 79 per cent for Russian is taken from Бидэм forthcoming and is based on verbs ending in -*at'*/-*jat'*, -*et'*, -*it'* and with a miscellaneous infinitive ending. Furthermore, 80 per cent of Russian inflectional endings with a VC contain a nonproductive verb VC (my German data do not reveal a similar correlation for German inflectional endings). (NB The percentages given in Beedham 2005: 132 are lower than those given here because the former are based on verbs ending in -*at'*/-*jat'* and -*et'* only).

Working with research assistants

As has been noted, research assistants play an important role in the data collection which is the day to day work of any project involving the method of exceptions and their correlations. Having the services of a research assistant at your disposal is useful because the work with dictionaries and native speaker informants is time-consuming and the tasks involved are often rather mechanical (though never entirely mechanical, they all require a great deal of knowledge, sensitivity and skill). If you are working by yourself you start down various avenues and there is simply not the time to pursue them all fully, so by having research assistants you get more done. However, a word of caution here. You do still have to work closely with your research assistant, you cannot give them some tasks to do and let them get on with it for several months. You have to consult with them regularly, several times a week for hours at a time, to learn from them what they have discovered and where they should go next in the light of their discoveries. Moreover, you yourself still have to do some of the legwork, because it is precisely during explorations of the data that you yourself both acquire conscious new knowledge of what is going on and an intuitive, subconscious awareness of what is going on which will surface in time one way or another into conscious knowledge. For that reason having a full-time research assistant will only work if you yourself have either a full-time research post or temporary research leave and can devote all your time to the project in hand. If you are carrying out the research alongside teaching and administrative duties it is better to have a part-time research assistant.

Irregular verb VCs and prefixes in German

How does one interpret this latest discovery, that the irregular verb VCs have an unusually high rate of occurrence in function words? That is difficult to say at the moment, but there is one area where an explanation does readily suggest itself for German. A study was conducted in which the 7,290 separable verbs listed in Mater 1970 were examined for the VCs in their prefixes. It was found that 74 per cent of the separable prefixes[19] listed contained a strong verb VC, and 79 per cent of the verbs listed had a prefix with a strong verb VC.[20] Prefixes in German have a perfectivizing function,[21] many of them add an element of result to a verb, which matches Tobin's resultative meaning for the English irregular verbs, and indeed Quirk called a subset of the English irregular verbs perfective, as was pointed out earlier. In other words, in German, verbal prefixes tend to be resultative, the strong verbs have probably a resultative meaning,

19   In contrast to the function words, where only monosyllabic function words were taken, this time both monosyllabic and polysyllabic prefixes were examined, whereby the stressed syllable of polysyllabic prefixes was taken as the source of the VC. The motivation for this change of tack was simply to see what would happen. Fortunately, it was a move which turned out to be fruitful.

20   See Beedham 2012; Eine phonotaktische Korrelation und semantische Verbindung zwischen starken Verben und trennbaren Präfixen der deutschen Gegenwartssprache [A phonotactic correlation and semantic link between strong verbs and separable prefixes in modern German], paper given at the University of Bonn and the University of Münster, June 2010.

21   Helbig and Buscha 1989: 73, *Duden-Grammatik* 2006: 415, Flämig 1965: 8, Fleischer 1976: 326–8. Helbig and Buscha define *perfektiv* for German as follows: '*Perfektive Verben* grenzen den Verlauf des Geschehens zeitlich ein oder drücken den Übergang von einem Geschehen zu einem anderen Geschehen aus' (*Perfective verbs* place a temporal limit on the course of an event or express the transition from one event to another event) (Helbig and Buscha 1989: 72). Like Russian there is a link in German between perfective verbs and resultative meaning, expressed in the fact that in German only perfective transformative verbs form a statal passive (whereby the statal passive, which in German has its own auxiliary *sein* 'to be' in contrast to the auxiliary *werden* 'to become' of the actional passive, expresses the result of a process): 'Das Zustandspassiv kann ... nur gebildet werden von solchen transitiven Verben, die perfektiv und transformativ sind, die einen solchen starken Grad der Affizierung des Akkusativobjekts ausdrücken, daß ein zeitweilig bleibendes Resultat ... überhaupt ermöglicht wird' (The statal passive can only be formed from those transitive verbs which are perfective and transformative, which express such a strong degree of affectedness of the accusative object that a temporarily lasting result is made at all possible) (Helbig and Buscha 1989: 181–2).

and they share the same VCs.²² So if this correlation is to be believed, we have formal confirmation of the idea that the German strong verbs have their own meaning, different from that of the weak verbs, and that meaning is resultative, in contrast to the process meaning of the weak verbs, as predicted by Tobin and Quirk. Strong verbs and separable prefixes in German tend to contain the same VCs because they both mean resultative/perfective.²³ The meaning proposed here illustrates a link between form (ablaut and –*en*, and VC) and meaning (resultative), it illustrates the indivisibility of the linguistic sign, it corroborates the view being advocated here that the apparently bizarre and senseless forms of the irregular verbs are the grammarian's mistake, that those forms must fit in somewhere in the verbal system of English, German, and Russian, and that they must convey meanings, in the usual way in language. If it does turn out that the VCs of the strong verbs are meaningful in the manner indicated above we will have to recognize a new level of language, between morphology and phonology, a variant of phonaesthemes which are more clearly meaningful than the familiar phonaesthemes. However, there is no point in tackling that question until we have greater clarity on whether the strong verb VCs are indeed meaningful in the manner indicated above. That clarity will only emerge from further empirical research, from more experiments (for further details on the phonotactics of irregular verbs see for English Beedham 1994, forthcoming, Tobin 1993: 315–54; for German Beedham 1994, 2005;²⁴ for Russian Бидэм 2004, forthcoming).

22 Interestingly, Wegener (2007) says that the irregular verbs are more prone to take a prefix than the regular verbs.
23 The parallel place to look in English is the particles and prepositions of phrasal verbs. I have not checked them out yet, but certainly Bolinger (1971: 96–110) discusses the perfective characteristics of phrasal verbs in English.
24 See also Beedham, Eine phonotaktische Korrelation und semantische Verbindung zwischen starken Verben und trennbaren Präfixen der deutschen Gegenwartssprache [A phonotactic correlation and semantic link between strong verbs and separable prefixes in modern German], paper given at the University of Bonn and the University of Münster, June 2010.

Be that as it may, the point is – granted the ongoing nature of the work on irregular verbs presented above – once again we have used unexplained lexical exceptions to a grammatical rule to empirically investigate that rule and to come up with pointers to a new explanation of how it works.[25]

Turning briefly again to typology, in exemplifying the method of exceptions and their correlations two examples have been used which show that apparently diverse languages and language families are more similar in their structure than is usually thought. Taking two Germanic languages, viz. English and German, and a Slav language, viz. Russian, we have seen that in all three languages, in both language families, Germanic and Slav, the passive is the same construction, viz. an aspect of the type Auxiliary + Participle, subject to the same aspectual constraints, viz. lexical and compositional aspect – to form a passive a verb must be telic;[26] and the irregular verbs again in all three languages, in both language families, Germanic and Slav, display similar phonotactic patterns concerning their vowel + consonant sequences. Beneath apparent linguistic diversity lies uniformity, if we dig deep enough.

Conclusion

In the course of the last thirty-five years the author has used the method of exceptions and their correlations twice, on the passive in English, German and Russian to produce a complete new analysis, the aspect analysis, and on the irregular verbs of English, German and Russian in ongoing research

---

25 To give an idea of the time-scale involved, the author has probably spent part-time over the last thirty years slightly longer than he spent on the passive full-time, viz. the equivalent of roughly four years full-time.

26 Furthermore, as mentioned above, Danks (2011) shows that one formal realization of the passive in Arabic is an aspect, governed by telicity, and Gregory (2006) shows that the passive in Spanish is an aspect, thus adding Semitic and Romance languages to the list of different language families with an aspectual passive.

which has so far unearthed some hitherto unnoticed phonotactic patterns which it is hoped will lead eventually to a new account of the tense systems of those languages, rendering the irregular verbs regular. David Crystal has described the method as being like detective work,[27] and the comparison is entirely apt. The method is empirical, and allows the researcher to sift through large amounts of data in a systematic and reasoned way, using research assistants where appropriate. It encourages the grammarian to work systematically through dictionaries, thus uniting grammar and the lexicon, grammarians and lexicographers. Yet this highly empirical method sits squarely in the middle of a *langue*-oriented, theoretical linguistics in which one produces new analyses of grammatical phenomena. The method is practical, in that the new analyses produced, if they are correct and therefore persuasive, will be taken up by language teachers in their pedagogical grammars. By the same token the analyses are easily understood, and can be summarized in a sentence and explained fairly successfully to the non-specialist. It is an interesting and exciting method to use, partly because one works a lot with native speaker informants, and partly because one goes down various avenues of research, looking and probing, any one of which could produce a discovery leading to a new analysis. The method allows you to follow up your hunches, and to discover something by accident. It is hoped that other linguists will try out the method to see if they can use it on their own chosen area of grammar in their own language or languages.[28]

27 On the website of Beedham 2005b: <http://www.benjamins.com/#catalog/books/sfsl.55/main>, accessed 21 November 2013.

28 By way of further illustration of what can be done with the method, the following students at the University of St Andrews have tried out or are trying out the method on the following topics and languages, supervised by the author and a co-supervisor where specified: Warwick Danks on pattern III and pattern VI verbs in Arabic in his PhD thesis of 2010, supervised by the author and Catherine Cobham, Dept. of Arabic (published as Danks 2011, reviewed in Waltisberg 2012; see also Danks, this volume). Samirah Aljohani on negated passive participles in English and Arabic in her ongoing PhD, supervised by the author and Kirill Dmitriev, Dept. of Arabic. Natalia Szczepanska on the Polish passive in her MLitt dissertation of 2012. Michelle Leese on the impersonal passive in German of the type *Es wurde getanzt* in her MLitt dissertation of 2013. Michael Carswell on phrasal nouns (formed from phrasal verbs,

Bibliography

Abraham, Werner. 2000. Das Perfektpartizip: seine angebliche Passivbedeutung im Deutschen. *Zeitschrift für germanistische Linguistik* 28/2.141–66.

Beedham, Christopher. 1981. The passive in English, German and Russian. *Journal of Linguistics* 17.319–27.

Beedham, Christopher. 1982. *The passive aspect in English, German and Russian.* Salford University PhD thesis, 1979. Narr, Tübingen.

Beedham, Christopher. 1987a. The English passive as an aspect. *Word* 38.1–12.

Beedham, Christopher. 1987b. Das deutsche Passiv: Aspekt, nicht Genus verbi [The German passive: aspect, not voice]. *Deutsch als Fremdsprache* 24.160–5.

Beedham, Christopher. 1994. The role of consonants in marking strong verb conjugation in German and English. *Folia Linguistica* XXVIII.279–96.

Beedham, Christopher. 1998. The perfect passive participle in Russian. Review of Schoorlemmer 1995. *Lingua* 105.79–94.

Beedham, Christopher. 2002a. Irregularity in language: Saussure versus Chomsky versus Pinker. Review of Pinker 1999. *Word* 53.341–67.

Beedham, Christopher. 2002b. Über die Anwendbarkeit der theoretischen Grammatik in pädagogischen Grammatiken: Saussure, das Passiv und starke Verben. *Akten des X. Internationalen Germanistenkongresses Wien 2000: 'Zeitenwende – Die Germanistik auf dem Weg vom 20. ins 21. Jahrhundert'*, ed. by Peter Wiesinger, Band 4, 37–42. Bern: Peter Lang.

Beedham, Christopher. 2005a. Eine phonotaktische Verbindung zwischen starken Verben und grammatischen Wörtern der deutschen Gegenwartssprache [A

---

e.g. *a buyout*) in English in his Honours (= undergraduate) dissertation of 2013. Francesca White on gender of the noun in Russian in her Honours dissertation of 2013, supervised by the author and Nadezda Bragina, Dept. of Russian. Claire Rampen on teaching the passive as an aspect to learners of English as a foreign language in her Honours dissertation of 2013. Emily Sheppard on gender of the noun in French in her URIP (Undergraduate Research Internship Programme) project of 2011, supervised by the author and David Evans, Dept. of French. As happened in some of the above cases, if you are familiar with the method of exceptions and their correlations and you want to supervise a student on a language which you do not know it is entirely viable to have a co-supervisor who is an expert in the language but not necessarily in theoretical linguistics.

phonotactic link between strong verbs and function words in modern German].
Deutsch als Fremdsprache 42.167–72.

Beedham, Christopher. 2005b. *Language and meaning: The structural creation of reality*. Benjamins: Amsterdam.

Beedham, Christopher. 2008. La méthode des exceptions lexicales et la relation entre la langue et la réalité [The method of lexical exceptions and the relationship between language and reality]. *Res per nomen*, ed. by Pierre Frath, Christopher Gledhill and Jean Pauchard, 215–29. Reims: Editions et Presses universitaires de Reims.

Beedham, Christopher. 2012. Starke Verben: Deutsche Morphologie in Harmonie mit Englisch und Russisch [Strong verbs: German morphology in harmony with English and Russian]. *Akten des XII. Internationalen Germanistenkongresses Warschau 2010: Vielheit und Einheit der Germanistik weltweit*, ed. by Franciszek Grucza and Jianhua Zhu, Band 15, Mitherausgeber: Horst J. Simon, J.P. Darski, K. Ezawa, S.J. Schierholz and P. Colliander, 27–31. Frankfurt am Main: Peter Lang.

Beedham, Christopher. Forthcoming. A phonotactic link between strong verbs and function words in English. *Word*.

Bolinger, Dwight. 1971. *The Phrasal Verb in English*. Cambridge, Mass.: Harvard University Press.

Borras, F.M., and R.F. Christian. 1971. *Russian syntax: Aspects of modern Russian syntax and vocabulary*. London: Oxford University Press.

Bybee, Joan L., and Dan I. Slobin. 1982. Rules and schemas in the development and use of the English past tense. *Language* 58.265–89.

Comrie, Bernard. 1976. *Aspect: an introduction to the study of verbal aspect and related problems*. Cambridge: Cambridge University Press.

Corbin, D., and A.-M. Dessaux-Berthonneau. 1985. L'exception. *Langue Française* 66.

Cornips, Leonie, and C. Poletto. 2005. On standardising syntactic elicitation techniques (part 1). *Lingua* 115.939–57.

Cowart, Wayne. 1997. *Experimental syntax: applying objective methods to sentence judgments*. Thousand Oaks, California: Sage.

Danks, Warwick. 2011. *The Arabic verb: form and meaning in the vowel-lengthening patterns*. St Andrews University PhD thesis, 2010. Amsterdam: Benjamins.

Danks, Warwick. This volume. Evaluation and adaptation: applying the method of exceptions and their correlations to Modern Standard Arabic.

Daum, E., and W. Schenk. 1971. *Die russischen Verben*. Mit einem Aufsatz zur Syntax und Semantik der Verben des modernen Russisch von Prof. Dr. R. Růžička. Leipzig: Enzyklopädie.

Duden 10: *Das Bedeutungswörterbuch*, 1985. 2. Auflage. Mannheim: Dudenverlag.

Duden 4: *Grammatik der deutschen Gegenwartssprache*. 2006. 7. Auflage. Mannheim: Dudenverlag.

Durrell, Martin. 2002. *Hammer's German grammar and usage*. Fourth Edition. London: Arnold.

Even-Simkin, Elena, and Yishai Tobin. 2011. Common semantic denominators of the internal vowel alternation system in English. *Poznan Studies in Contemporary Linguistics* 47/2.308–30.

Even-Simkin, Elena, and Yishai Tobin. 2013. *The Regularity of the 'Irregular' Verbs and Nouns in English*. Amsterdam: Benjamins.

Flämig, Walter. 1965. Zur Funktion des Verbs. III. Aktionsart und Aktionalität. *Deutsch als Fremdsprache* 2.4–12.

Fleischer, Wolfgang. 1976. *Wortbildung der deutschen Gegenwartssprache*. 4. Aufl. Leipzig: Bibliographisches Institut.

Gamkrelidze, Thomas V. 2006. The problem of 'L'arbitraire du signe'. *Gamkrelidze, Th.V., Selected writings: linguistic sign, typology and language reconstruction*, ed. by I. Hajnal, 56–64. Innsbruck: Institut für Sprachen und Literaturen der Universität Innsbruck.

Gelhaus, Hermann, and Sigbert Latzel. 1974. *Studien zum Tempusgebrauch im Deutschen*. Tübingen: Narr.

Gregory, Amy E. 2006. Review of Beedham 2005b. *LINGUIST List* 17.3168.

Helbig, Gerhard. 1973. *Geschichte der neueren Sprachwissenschaft. Unter dem besonderen Aspekt der Grammatik-Theorie*. Leizpig: Bibliographisches Institut.

Helbig, Gerhard, and Joachim Buscha. 1989. *Deutsche Grammatik: Ein Handbuch für den Ausländerunterricht*. Berlin: Langenscheidt/Enzyklopädie.

Hinton, Leanne; Johanna Nichols; and John J. Ohala (eds). 1994. *Sound symbolism*. Cambridge: Cambridge University Press.

Joseph, John E. 2012. *Saussure*. Oxford: Oxford University Press.

Kepser, Stephan, and Marga Reis (eds). 2005. *Linguistic evidence: empirical, theoretical and computational perspectives*. Berlin: de Gruyter.

Klappenbach, Ruth, and Wolfgang Steinitz. 1977. *Wörterbuch der deutschen Gegenwartssprache*. Berlin: Akademie-Verlag.

Köpcke, Klaus-Michael. 1982. *Untersuchungen zum Genussystem der deutschen Gegenwartssprache*. Tübingen: Niemeyer.

Köpcke, Klaus-Michael. 1998. Prototypisch starke und schwache Verben der deutschen Gegenwartssprache. *Variation und Stabilität in der Wortstruktur*, hg. von M. Butt und N. Fuhrhop, 45–60. Sonderheft *Germanistische Linguistik*.

Leech, Geoffrey N. 1971. *Meaning and the English verb*. London: Longman.

Mater, Erich. 1967a. *Deutsche Verben 2: Grundwörter und deren Zusammensetzungen*. Leipzig: Bibliographisches Institut.

Mater, Erich. 1967b. *Deutsche Verben 3: Gesamtverzeichnis der Grundwörter, Stellung der Kompositionsglieder*. Leipzig: Bibliographisches Institut.

Mater, Erich. 1970. *Deutsche Verben 9: Trennung der Kompositionsglieder; Wortlänge der Grundwörter.* Leipzig: Bibliographisches Institut.

Mater, Erich. 1971. *Deutsche Verben 6: Rektionsarten.* Leipzig: Bibliographisches Institut.

Oxford Advanced Learner's Dictionary of Current English. 1974. By A.S. Hornby, with A.P. Cowie and A.C. Gimson. Third Edition. Oxford: Oxford University Press.

Oxford Advanced Learner's Dictionary of Current English. 1989. By A.S. Hornby, Chief Editor A.P. Cowie. Fourth Edition. Oxford: Oxford University Press.

Pinker, Steven. 1994. *The language instinct: the new science of language and mind.* London: Penguin.

Pinker, Steven. 1999. *Words and rules: the ingredients of language.* London: Weidenfeld & Nicolson.

Poupynin, Youri A. 1999. *Interaction between aspect and voice in Russian.* München: Lincom Europa. [Translation of Пупынин 1980].

Pulkina, I., and E. Zakhava-Nekrasova. [No date given; c. 1960]. *Russian (A practical grammar with exercises).* Moscow: Progress.

Quirk, Randolph. 1970. Aspect and variant inflection in English verbs. Language 46.300–11.

Quirk, Randolph; Sidney Greenbaum; Geoffrey Leech; and Jan Svartvik. 1985. *A comprehensive grammar of the English language.* London: Longman.

Quirk, Randolph, and Jan Svartvik. 1966. *Investigating linguistic acceptability.* The Hague: Mouton de Gruyter.

Saussure, Ferdinand de. 1983. *Course in general linguistics.* Ed. by C. Bally and A. Sechehaye, translated from the French and annotated by R. Harris. London: Duckworth.

Schoorlemmer, Maaike. 1995. *Participial passive and aspect in Russian.* OTS Dissertation Series. Utrecht: OTS [Onderzoeksinstituut voor Taal en Spraak/Research Institute for Language and Speech].

Schütze, Carson T. 1996. *The empirical base of linguistics: Grammaticality judgements and linguistic methodology.* Chicago: University of Chicago Press.

Simon, Horst, and Heike Wiese (eds). 2011. *Expecting the unexpected: exceptions in grammar.* Berlin: Mouton de Gruyter.

Sorace, Antonella, and Frank Keller. 2005. Gradience in linguistic data. *Lingua* 115.1497–524.

Tobin, Yishai. 1990. *Semiotics and linguistics.* London: Longman.

Tobin, Yishai. 1993. *Aspect in the English verb: process and result in language.* London: Longman.

Verkuyl, H.J. 1972. *On the compositional nature of the aspects.* Foundations of Language, Supplementary Series, Volume 15.

Verkuyl, Henk J. 1993. *A theory of aspectuality: the interaction between temporal and atemporal structure*. Cambridge: Cambridge University Press.

Waltisberg, Michael. 2012. Review of Danks 2011. *Language* 88.634–6.

Wegener, Heide. 2007. Entwicklungen im heutigen Deutsch – wird Deutsch einfacher? *Deutsche Sprache* 35.35–62.

Zubin, David A., and Klaus-Michael Köpcke. 1984. Affect classification in the German gender system. *Lingua* 63.41–96.

Бидэм, Кр. 1988. Видовое значение конструкции "быть + срtadательное причастие" [The aspectual meaning of the construction *"byt'* 'to be' + passive participle"]. *Вопросы Языкознания* 6.63–8.

Бидэм, Кристофер. 2004 Последовательности гласный + согласный в простых непродуктивных глаголах на *-ать/-ять* и *-еть* в русском языке [Vowel + consonant sequences in Russian simplex non-productive verbs ending in *-at'/-jat'* and *-et'*]. *Язык и Речевая Деятельность* 7.9–38.

Бидэм, Кристофер. Forthcoming. Фонотактика непродуктивных глаголов русского языка: глаголы на *-ить* и с разными суффиксами инфинитива [The phonotactics of Russian non-productive verbs: verbs ending in *-it'* and with a miscellaneous infinitive ending]. *Язык и Речевая Деятельность*.

Грамматика русского языка, Том I: Фонетика и морфология. 1960. Москва: Академия Наук.

Морковкин, В.В. 1997. *Словарь структурных слов русского языка*. Лазурь.

Обратный словарь русского языка. 1974. Москва: Советская Энциклопедия.

Пупынин, Юрий Алексеевич. 1980. *Функционирование видов русского глагола в пассивных конструкциях (К проблеме взаимосвязей категорий вида и залога)*. Канд. дисс., Ленинград. [Translation into English: Poupynin 1999].

Словарь современного русского языка. 1951–1965. Т. 1–17. Академия Наук СССР.

WARWICK DANKS

2   Evaluation and Adaptation:
    Applying the Method of Exceptions and their
    Correlations to Modern Standard Arabic

ABSTRACT

Application of Beedham's method of exceptions and their correlations to researching a grammatical puzzle in Modern Standard Arabic is described and evaluated. A three-year period of research for a PhD from 2006 to 2009 is documented having the method as its starting point and culminating in formulation of an apposite solution to the research problem. It is shown how Beedham's principles are examined, applied and adapted, together with other methodologies, in pursuit of a grammatical formulation which is almost exception-free. Valuable insight provided by examination of exceptions is acknowledged, whilst proving Beedham's original methodology capable of modification and adaptation to grammatical problems in a language substantially dissimilar and unrelated to the Indo-European languages on the basis of which the method first developed.

Introduction

Modern Standard Arabic (MSA) is notable for its high degree of regularity.[1] Word formation follows a typically Semitic root-and-pattern morphology[2] which is highly systematized according to a finite set of patterns. However, despite a rich and ancient tradition of grammatical introspection,

---

1   This is a completely revised and updated (in 2013) version of a paper given at the Conference on the Method of Lexical Exceptions held at the University of St Andrews from 2 to 8 September 2007.

2   Though see also Danks 2011: 39–55.

the language still offers many puzzles for the contemporary linguist. In Danks (2011), I pursue the meaning of two related verbal patterns (III and VI), in research inspired by the application of Beedham's (2005, this volume) 'method of exceptions and their correlations'.[3] In this paper, I will highlight the method's strengths and weaknesses in the light of my own research and suggest extensions and adaptations, with a view to making this investigative tool more accessible and relevant to those wishing to study exceptions wherever they are found in language systems.

The specific challenge of MSA

In the traditional grammatical view, the verbal patterns are foundational, so it is perhaps surprising that elucidation of the meanings of this restricted set of patterns constitutes 'a problem that has been considered previously, but never adequately addressed' (Watson in Danks 2011: back cover).

The majority of Arabic roots are triliteral sequences,[4] consisting of three-letter combinations of the 28 consonants. Each root can give rise to a base pattern (I), in which only short vowels are inserted, and up to 14 morphologically-derived patterns. Although all patterns are morphologically possible for each root (with some phonotactically motivated exceptions), no root exhibits all patterns. Following earlier studies by Al-Qahtani (2005) and McCarthy and Prince (1990), I obtain my data from Wehr's widely respected *Dictionary of Modern Written Arabic* (1994).

Wehr records 2963 triliteral roots which give rise to a total of 7981 verbs. In Table 2.1, which also lists frequency data, note that C_1, C_2 and C_3 represent the three consonants comprising the root and V represents any one of the three vowels a, i, o; 'ā' is the long vowel equivalent of a.

---

3   Formerly known, prior to this volume, as the 'method of lexical exceptions'.
4   For simplicity, we will ignore the less common quadriliteral roots here.

Table 2.1 Verbal patterns and lexical frequencies (Danks 2011: 20, 28)

Pattern	s-stem*	Lexical frequency
I	$C_1aC_2VC_3$	2523
II	$C_1aC_2C_2aC_3$	1416
III	$C_1\bar{a}C_2aC_3$	465
IV	$'aC_1C_2aC_3$	938
V	$taC_1aC_2C_2aC_3$	953
VI	$taC_1\bar{a}C_2aC_3$	389
VII	$(i)nC_1aC_2aC_3$	267
VIII	$(i)C_1taC_2aC_3$	606
IX	$(i)C_1C_2aC_3C_3$	19
X	$(i)staC_1C_2aC_3$	395
XI	$(i)C_1C_2\bar{a}C_3C_3$	2
XII	$(i)C_1C_2awC_2aC_3$	7
XIII	$(i)C_1C_2awwaC_3$	0
XIV	$(i)C_1C_2anC_3aC_3$	1
XV	$(i)C_1C_2anC_3\bar{a}$	0

* Also commonly known as the perfect stem.

Three possible types of exceptionality, if not irregularity, suggest themselves, formulated here as three questions:

Is the Arabic verb really this regular?

To consider it completely regular is an oversimplification. It is necessary to modify the paradigm to account for certain special conditions in the root. Hence Reig (1983) lists 164 'conjugations' and this is not exhaustive. However, provided that any relevant special conditions in the root are considered, these are almost completely predictable from the basic paradigm for the given pattern. Minor exceptions consist generally of alternative treatments of weak consonants, thus all variations on the basic paradigms are explicable by phonotactic considerations and do not constitute unexplained exceptions; i.e. Arabic has no irregular verbs in the generally accepted sense and this consequently provides no input to Beedham's 'method of exceptions and their correlations'.

How are the verb patterns distributed in the lexicon – is it random?

Given the clear morphological relationships between certain patterns, it would be surprising if the distribution were random. In order to obtain evidence which transcends the anecdotal, a full table was prepared, listing each root combination together with the verb patterns which arise, from which the excerpt in Table 2.2 is taken. Using the tabulated data, co-occurrences for pairs of verb patterns were examined. Figure 2.1 shows selected data for co-occurrences for the same root sequence of patterns I to VIII and X with patterns III and IV only. The y-axis scale has been adjusted such that 1.00 represents chance co-occurrence. It is clear that the distribution of patterns is not random, as exemplified by patterns III and VI occurring together with almost four times chance frequency. Chi-squared tests for statistical significance were used to confirm the observations, using the null hypothesis of random distribution. Table 2.3 shows the results of chi-squared testing on the co-occurrence of patterns III and VI: the Φ value indicates a high correlation between the patterns and the extremely low value of p indicates a high probability that this correlation is statistically significant.

Table 2.2 Extract from data tabulated by root and pattern

C_1	C_2	C_3	I	II	III	IV	V	VI	VII	VIII	X	Other patterns
q	b	l	✓	✓	✓	✓		✓		✓	✓	
q	b	n		✓								
q	b	w	✓	✓								
q	b	t	✓							✓		
q	t	r	✓	✓		✓						
q	t	l	✓	✓	✓			✓		✓	✓	
q	t	m	✓									IX

Pattern III Co-occurrences　　　　Pattern IV Co-occurrences

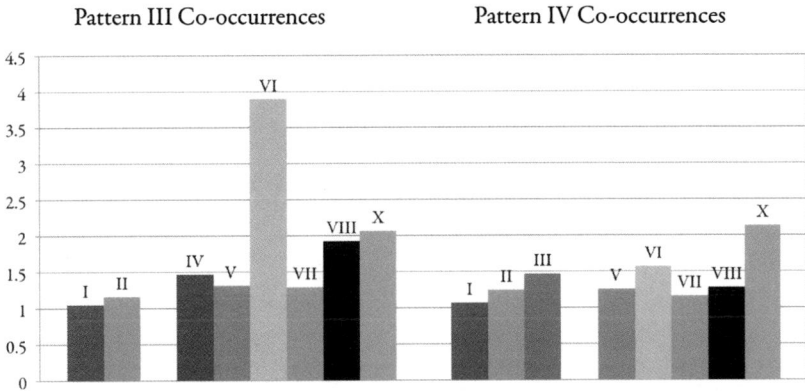

Figure 2.1 Selected data for co-occurrences of verbal stems.

Table 2.3 Co-occurrence of Patterns III and VI

	+Pattern III	−Pattern III
+Pattern VI	238	151
−Pattern VI	227	2347

Chi-square = 700
$p < .001$ Phi coefficient $(\Phi) = 0.49$

The striking co-occurrence between patterns III and VI is of particular interest, since they bear a clear morphological relation, which may be represented as:

(1)   [ta-] prefix + $C_1\bar{a}C_2aC_3$ (III) → $taC_1\bar{a}C_2aC_3$ (VI)

It is therefore suggested not only that the distribution of patterns in the lexicon is not random, but that co-occurrence of patterns is implied by morphological derivation and that the converse also holds. This hypothesis leads to two potential sets of lexical exceptions for each pair of patterns linked by secondary derivation. These sets comprise those roots which display either the primary derivative or the secondary but not both, i.e. there are lexical gaps in the morphological system which may provide sets of exceptions. However, whilst co-occurrence is a parameter which subsequently proves significant on occasion when analysing my data, there is no *a priori* reason why the lexical gaps should not exist and no existing hypothesis concerning their distribution which may be tested.

To what extent are the syntactic and semantic properties of verbs predictable from their morphology? Does formal similarity imply semantic similarity?

Arabic grammarians have, with varying degrees of success, attempted to explain the meanings and functions of the verb patterns in order to bring a degree of systematicity to the lexicon. For pattern III, the most common property cited is mutuality or 'implied reciprocity' (Wright 1967. I: 31–8), with many also pointing to conativity or attempted action (e.g. Holes 2004: 101–3). Although there is a measure of agreement, some grammarians overgeneralize in favour of one meaning to the exclusion of alternatives, while others include a range of possibilities at the risk of blurring the predominant meaning. Schulz (2004: 28) is not alone in concluding that '[a] functional-semantic description ... provides little benefit for language practice'. However, with mutual meaning dominant for pattern III and reciprocal for pattern VI, it is apparent that the relationship between these two patterns may offer a set of exceptions which is suitable for study. Thus, categorization of patterns III and VI by semantic function constituted my initial investigation by the method (Danks 2011: 83–102).

Foundations of the method of exceptions and their correlations

Let us first examine Beedham's (2005) foundational principles as they apply to the problem in hand.

From form to meaning

The selected data set, comprising all verbs in patterns III and VI, is morphologically distinct and complete, characterized by vowel-lengthening between C_1 and C_2. It is therefore consistent with the method of exceptions and their correlations to proceed from this unique form to elucidate its meaning. This elucidation therefore constitutes my research goal.

Synchronicity

Inasmuch as any dictionary can be synchronic, Wehr (1994) may be deemed suitable.[5] However I am not as convinced as Beedham that any living language, let alone one as diverse and widely dispersed as Arabic, can ever be free of synchronic anomalies. It would be unwise to infer from a still image of a charging elephant that the subject of the photograph itself was motionless at the time of the snapshot. Likewise even a perfectly synchronic sampling of language is actually capturing a moving target, whilst any real data collection will necessarily involve blurring of certain features, analogous with the finite shutter speed of a camera. Moreover, following centuries of relative equilibrium, Arabic is presently undergoing rapid change affecting its grammar in ways as fundamental as its inflections and word-order and it may well be that a degree of systematization is still in progress. At the risk of accusations of Saussurean heresy, could it be that MSA is at present *un système où tout* ne *se tient* pas? Thus I will tolerate a certain minimal incidence of unexplained exceptions, though I am sufficiently committed to the Saussurean ideal that I would expect the language to eventually either shift to systematically accommodate the exceptions or to expel them from use. Hence, whilst primarily committed to synchronic analysis, I remain open to being informed by a diachronic perspective.

Unexplained exceptions are indicative of incorrect analysis

For the purposes of my initial investigation, the analysis is that vowel-lengthening in the verbal patterns (specifically long $\bar{a}$ between C_1 and C_2) has the meaning of mutuality/reciprocity of action. I categorize the 465 pattern III and 389 pattern VI verbs according to semantic function and, despite allowing a verb to be categorized as mutual or reciprocal if at least one of its meanings conforms to this analysis, the success rate is only

---

5   Lexicological issues are explored in Danks 2011: 24–7.

77.6 per cent for pattern III and 64.0 per cent for pattern VI. I have thus convincingly demonstrated that the conventional analysis is inadequate.[6]

The Hegelian triad and scientific method

The existing analysis provides me with the thesis required by Beedham's application of Hegelian principles, while the exceptions I have discovered provide the antithesis. Furthermore, Beedham's (2005: 155) aspirations for his methodology include '[rendering] theoretical linguistics an empirical science' and I suggest that application of chi-squared testing takes Beedham's commitment to scientific method a stage further. It is not sufficient to look at a set of data and identify trends and correlations by eye, but rather numeric data by their very nature lend themselves to statistical testing which can elevate the status of the linguist's findings beyond the level of reasonable doubt.

What is lacking thus far is synthesis: I have successfully dispensed with conventional analysis but have nothing with which to replace it. This appears to be the point at which grammarians of Arabic have tended to conclude that satisfactory analysis of the functional meanings of the verbal patterns is unattainable. However, I am hopeful that, like Beedham (2005: 160), I am making 'new observations' and discovering 'new facts, which lead to new insights and new analyses'.

6   In commenting that '[c]onsidering the complexity of this methodology, [the] statistical results seem overall a bit meagre', Waltisberg (2012: 634) appears to miss the point that the percentages at this stage of my research (Danks 2011: 102) highlight the inadequacy of the very analysis which poses the research question, not of the method.

Adapting the method of exceptions and their correlations

I am now aware that the method of exceptions and their correlations can lead one down the occasional blind alley. In retrospect, it becomes obvious that if it is not just the existing analysis of a formal property which is incorrect, but a more fundamental issue with the category of the property being examined, these blind alleys are inevitable. In this case, I have been categorizing verbs according to a partial analysis of their semantic components, using the presence or absence of the mutual/reciprocal property as the starting point. I therefore decided to take a sideways step into the realm of syntax.

Revisiting the data

At this point, my task is rendered less onerous by the fact that I was recording transitivity data at the same time as semantic functional categories. Thus I now effectively repeat phases two and three of Beedham's methodology[7] (2005: 164), except that this time I have set up a new thesis that derivation of pattern III from pattern I, by inclusion of a long vowel, is a process of transitivization, analogous with that attested for pattern II, as suggested by Wright (1967. I: 33) and consistent with the prosodic templatic analysis of McCarthy and Prince 1990.

Developing analytical tools

Transitivity in Arabic is more nuanced than can be represented by a binary opposition of transitive/intransitive and if I am to apply a method of analysis, it must be fit for purpose. I therefore first develop a hierarchical

---

7   Phase 2: 'identify the problems, anomalies, contradictions, etc.'. Phase 3: 'identify and list the unexplained lexical exceptions'.

approach to Arabic valency by investigating the *ta-* prefix which pattern VI shares with other paradigms, described by Watson (2002: 139–42) as 'detransitivizing' and involving 'a reduction or minimization of the valence [sic] of the underlying verb'. The hierarchy I propose, which takes account both of numeric valency and the directness or indirectness of the object elements contributing to that valency, succeeds in identifying valency reduction or minimization in 83.2 per cent of the 238 pattern III/pattern VI pairs (i.e. co-occurrences for the same root). I now employ a 'method within a method', identifying lexical exceptions to *ta*-prefixed valency reduction and reconciling those which are amenable to explanation, finally arriving at only nine unexplained exceptions, equivalent to a 96.2 per cent success rate. Confident that my hierarchical valency approach is effective, it becomes a tool to investigate the original problem of establishing whether vowel-lengthening in pattern III derivation is transitivizing/valency-increasing. However it becomes clear that there is no evidence that this conclusion can be drawn, with only 26.7 per cent of pattern III verbs conforming to it. Nevertheless, this excursion into transitivity has demonstrated that new insights and new analyses can indeed be inspired by careful and methodical examination of exceptions.

Lateral thinking and an intuitive leap

I have had moderate success in determining what vowel-lengthening in the verbal patterns does *not* mean, but it seems that I am no closer to establishing what it *does* mean. It is time for lateral thinking, as I reconsider the formal properties of the verbs in my data set. My thinking has been confined to the verbal system, but the formal property which most characterizes patterns III and VI is not exclusively found within those verbs and I proceed to investigate two avenues: broken plurals and nominal templates. Although the notion of verbal plurality proposed by Benmamoun 2003 and others is initially promising, it still relies on the initial flawed semantic analysis. However, long vowel insertion into template forms also characterizes certain classes of noun and, whilst it is not surprising that nominal forms derived from patterns III and VI contain a long vowel, it is remarkable how frequently it occurs in unrelated paradigms. Table 2.4 shows selected forms characterized by the presence of a long vowel, after exclusion of those unambiguously derived from the pattern III and VI $C_1\bar{a}C_2$ sequence.

Table 2.4 Selected forms with $C_1\bar{a}C_2$ or $C_2\bar{a}C_3$ sequence

Description	Paradigm form	CV template
active participle [I]	فاعِل	$C_1\bar{a}C_2iC_3$
noun of instrument	فاعِلة	$C_1\bar{a}C_2iC_3a$
noun of instrument	فاعول	$C_1\bar{a}C_2\bar{u}C_3$
broken plural of verbal noun [IV]	أفاعِيـل	$'aC_1\bar{a}C_2\bar{\imath}C_3$
verbal noun [II]; broken plural	تَفاعِيـل	$taC_1\bar{a}C_2\bar{\imath}C_3$
verbal noun [I]; broken plural	فَعال	$C_1aC_2\bar{a}C_3$
verbal noun [I]; broken plural	فَعالة	$C_1aC_2\bar{a}C_3a$
broken plural	فَعـالى	$C_1aC_2\bar{a}C_3\bar{a}$
verbal noun [I]; verbal noun [III]; noun of instrument etc.; broken plural	فِعال	$C_1iC_2\bar{a}C_3$
verbal noun [I]; broken plural; noun of occupation	فِعالة	$C_1iC_2\bar{a}C_3a$
verbal noun [I]	فُعال	$C_1uC_2\bar{a}C_3$
verbal noun [I]; noun of fragmentation	فُعالة	$C_1uC_2\bar{a}C_3a$
broken plural	فُعـالى	$C_1uC_2\bar{a}C_3\bar{a}$
verbal noun [I]	فَعالية	$C_1aC_2\bar{a}C_3iya$
verbal noun [III]	فِيعـال	$C_1\bar{\imath}C_2\bar{a}C_3$
verbal noun [III]	فِعّال	$C_1iC_2C_2\bar{a}C_3$
noun of occupation / intensity	فَعّـال	$C_1aC_2C_2\bar{a}C_3$
noun of instrument	فَعّالة	$C_1aC_2C_2\bar{a}C_3a$

verbal noun [II]; verbal noun [III]; verbal noun [VIII]	فِعَّال	$C_1iC_2C_2\bar{a}C_3$
broken plural	فُعَّال	$C_1uC_2C_2\bar{a}C_3$
broken plural	أفعال	$'aC_1C_2\bar{a}C_3$
verbal noun [IV]	إفعال	$'iC_1C_2\bar{a}C_3$
noun of instrument etc.	مِفعال	$miC_1C_2\bar{a}C_3$
active participle [XI]	مُفعالّ	$muC_1C_2\bar{a}C_3C_3$
verbal noun [II]	تَفعال	$taC_1C_2\bar{a}C_3$
verbal noun [II]	تِفعال	$tiC_1C_2\bar{a}C_3$
verbal noun [V]	تِفِعّال	$tiC_1iC_2C_2\bar{a}C_3$
verbal noun [VII]	انْفِعال	$(i)nC_1iC_2\bar{a}C_3$
verbal noun [VIII]	افْتِعال	$(i)C_1tiC_2\bar{a}C_3$
verbal noun [X]	استِفْعال	$(i)stiC_1C_2\bar{a}C_3$

Most prominent among these forms is the pattern I active participle, though there are also numerous verbal noun templates and several specialized noun classes. I note in Danks (2011: 145–56) that all these nominal forms[8] typically display agency rather than patiency, process rather than result and, crucially, they represent situations as being temporally complex. I now make the intuitive leap which provides the key: the evidence from the nominal templates which share the formal property of a long vowel with patterns III and VI is that the meaning is aspectual and specifically that it is atelic.

8   I have not dealt here with the issue of the pattern III and pattern VI passive participles, which might be thought to constitute counterexamples. However, I present evidence in Danks 2011: 154–5, 241–5 that verbs in these patterns strongly resist use of their passive participles, which I explain in terms of their aspectual properties.

Reiteration

I now repeat the relevant phases of the method of exceptions and their correlations, with atelic meaning within the category of lexical aspect as my thesis. Because I have once again switched category, I find this testing iteration of the method both helpful and necessary, even though I am convinced that I am close to reaching my goal of relating form and meaning. Although Beedham does not explicitly state the need to examine one's 'synthesis' in this way, it seems to me that if it is to possess integrity, it must be subjected to the same scrutiny as the original thesis it has displaced and indeed it must fare better.

Again, I must fashion a diagnostic tool, this time to systematically examine verbs according to their aspectual properties and I elect to use a scheme devised by Olsen (1997) on principles established by Vendler (1967), adapting it to the specific requirements of Arabic. I identify 83.2 per cent of verbs in patterns III and VI as either ACTIVITY or STATE[9] verbs, designations which in accordance with Olsen's privative feature marking are unmarked for telicity. This is already considerably more promising than the conventional mutual/reciprocal analysis.

Corpus data and examples

In common with Beedham, I make some use of native-speaker informants to test my analysis of specific verbs. However, I also use a corpus (*arabiCorpus*) for quantitative analysis and as a source of real language examples, together with web pages and other texts. I refine the verb counts according to their relative type and token instances in *arabiCorpus*,[10] which effectively excludes verbs which are archaic and gives more weight to verbs in common

9   Lexical aspect designations are henceforth capitalized to distinguish specialized usage of these terms.
10   The type count includes all verbs which are attested in the corpus at least once, whereas the token count sums the total instances of the verbs. For full methodology, see Danks 2011.

usage. Since the form/meaning relationship is mediated through the minds of native speakers, it seems reasonable that commonly used words most strongly evoke the associations of meaning reported by these informants. Thus using *arabiCorpus* in this way is more likely to mirror such data. Initial analysis of the counts reveals that 91.0 per cent of pattern III and 92.4 per cent of pattern VI tokens are of ACTIVITY/STATE verbs and hence conform to atelic meaning.

I proceed to demonstrate by reference to real language examples that two small sets of verbs having meanings related to either surprise or giving are in fact also atelic. There is, however, a substantial set of 118 verbs with inceptive meanings, contributing 6.8 per cent to the token count, which are potentially exceptions to the atelic hypothesis. Of the remaining 15 verbs, only 10 are attested in *arabiCorpus*, of which two have long vowels which are analysed as non-derivational, and only one of the remainder is positively identified as telic. Were it not for the inceptive verbs, the new synthesis would therefore be almost free of exceptions.[11]

Adequacy of methodology

Careful examination of the set of exceptions, in this case the inceptive verbs, may reveal that it is the methodology, not the synthesis which is at fault. I discover that a new aspectual designation of INCEPTIVE is required, as the verbs in question strongly resist categorization according to Vendler and Olsen. I therefore extend Olsen's scheme to encompass this category and in doing so discover that there is a discrete set of English verbs which are also INCEPTIVE (Danks 2008). I demonstrate that the INCEPTIVE category must be unmarked for telicity and thus these verbs are not exceptions to the new synthesis.

---

11 Waltisberg (2012: 635), in contrast to his earlier criticism, acknowledges that the methodology has now produced 'valuable statistical data'. See also the tables in Danks 2011: 211, 249, which demonstrate progression culminating in a success rate of over 99 per cent for the final synthesis, according to all three measures employed.

Summary

I formulate my synthesis thus (Danks 2011: 250): 'The Arabic vowel-lengthening verbal patterns give rise to atelic meaning.'

However, whilst the end goal of my research was to be able to reach such a formulation, the purpose of this paper has been to more specifically document the process. As to whether I have faithfully followed the method of exceptions and their correlations, I leave the reader and its creator to judge. However, at the very least, I believe I have demonstrated that application of the method is not necessarily a linear process. For me, it took many twists and turns and involved some detours which eventually led nowhere, despite being highly instructive. Should the reader decide to use the method of exceptions and their correlations, the kind of adaptations and extensions I outline above may prove directly useful. It may be that another puzzle in another language will require different modifications to the methodology. My primary hope is that the reader will be inspired to take lexical exceptions seriously.

Bibliography

Al-Qahtani, Duleim M. 2005. *Semantic valence of Arabic verbs*. Beirut: Librairie du Liban.

Beedham, Christopher. 2005. *Language and meaning: The structural creation of reality*. Amsterdam: John Benjamins.

Beedham, Christopher. This volume. Exceptions and their correlations: A methodology for research in grammar.

Benmamoun, Elabbas. 2003. Reciprocals as plurals in Arabic. *Research in Afroasiatic grammar II: Selected papers from the fifth conference on Afroasiatic languages, Paris, 2000*, ed. by Jacqueline Lecarme, 53–62. Amsterdam: John Benjamins.

Danks, Warwick. 2008. Standing up to scrutiny: Inceptive verbs in Arabic and English. Paper presented to the Linguistics Institute of St Andrews, 25 November 2008, University of St Andrews.

Danks, Warwick. 2011. *The Arabic verb: Form and meaning in the vowel-lengthening patterns*. Amsterdam: John Benjamins.

Holes, Clive. 2004. *Modern Arabic: Structures, functions and varieties*. Revised edn. Washington, D.C.: Georgetown University Press.

McCarthy, John, and Alan Prince. 1990. Prosodic morphology and templatic morphology. *Perspectives on Arabic linguistics II: Papers from the second annual symposium on Arabic linguistics*, ed. by Mushira Eid and John McCarthy, 1–54. Amsterdam: John Benjamins.

Olsen, Mari Broman. 1997. *A semantic and pragmatic model of lexical and grammatical aspect*. New York: Garland.

Reig, Daniel. 1983. *La conjugaison arabe*. Paris: Maisonneuve et Larose.

Schulz, Eckehard. 2004. *A student grammar of modern standard Arabic*. Cambridge: CUP.

Vendler, Zeno. 1967. *Linguistics in philosophy*. Ithaca, NY: Cornell University Press.

Waltisberg, Michael. 2012. Review of Danks 2011. *Language* 88.634–6.

Watson, Janet C.E. 2002. *The phonology and morphology of Arabic*. Oxford: OUP.

Wehr, Hans. 1994. *A dictionary of modern written Arabic: Arabic – English*. Ed. by J. Milton Cowan. Ithaca: Spoken Language Services.

Wright, W. 1967. *A grammar of the Arabic language*. Cambridge: Cambridge University Press.

Online resource

arabiCorpus. Dilworth B. Parkinson (creator). Brigham Young University. <http://arabicorpus.byu.edu> (accessed June 2007 – Sept. 2009).

Discussion (Extract)[12]

BASSAC: A crucial element in the method of lexical exceptions[13] is the comparison between two or more languages. So obviously the question is: what language do you plan to compare Arabic to? The answer is probably Hebrew or some other Hamito-Semitic language.

DANKS: The only possible languages for comparison would be other Semitic languages, probably Hebrew. However, since the range of verbal forms is not available in other languages, I will probably have to confine myself to Arabic.

BEEDHAM: I looked at non-passivizable transitive verbs in two Germanic languages (English and German) and a Slav language (Russian), and ended up finding that the participial passive in both sets of languages is the same construction (an aspect of the type Auxiliary + Participle), governed by the same syntactic constraint (atelic verbs do not form a participial passive (even if they are transitive)). Whilst Germanic and Slav are both Indo-European – whereas Arabic is a Semitic and non-Indo-European language – they are considered to be a long way apart and very different from each other structurally. Whilst not wishing to understate the very real and quite radical structural differences between Semitic and Indo-European languages is it not possible that one could, in fact, find a construction (formally speaking) and its exceptions in Arabic and English which would lend itself to investigation using the method of lexical exceptions?

---

12   Editors' note: Dr Danks carried out the PhD research described above from 2006 to 2009. The discussion given below is as recorded after his paper, which he gave in 2007, looking mostly ahead to what he was planning to do. The paper published above is a revised and updated (in 2013) version of the conference paper, looking back on what he actually did.

13   Now known, as of this volume, as the method of exceptions and their correlations.

DANKS: It is certainly not inconceivable that one might find such a construction common to both Arabic and English. In Danks (2011: 241–5), I present some preliminary findings and suggest future research on passive participles for verbs in patterns III and VI, observing that the atelicity of these verbs does indeed largely preclude use of these participles. This aspectual constraint has clear parallels with the Indo-European languages studied by Beedham, but non-passivizability was an outcome of my study rather than its starting point.

BEEDHAM: In the aspectual analysis of the (participial) passive in English, German and Russian the fact that the (participial) passive in those languages is formed from the verb *to be* followed by a (passive) participle plays a crucial role, because it is those forms which realize the meaning 'action + state'. You have previously told me that the Arabic passive is not formed from a verb meaning 'to be' and a participle, and that it is generally accepted by Arabic grammarians that the Arabic passive expresses a state resulting from an action. How can that be? For that to be the case there has to be at least one formal item in the construction which realizes the meaning 'state'. But apparently there isn't. How can that be? Where does the 'state' meaning come from?

DANKS: I should probably clarify that there are three distinct ways of expressing passivity in Arabic: vowel melody, use of certain verbal patterns and participial passives. The latter is a passive on the lines of *be* + *V-ed* in English, in which the participle is very much statal, as evidenced by its frequent occurrence as an attributive adjective. Leaving aside verbal pattern passivity (principally pattern VII), which needs further investigation and, I suspect, may be more aligned to middle verbs, I believe you are alluding to passivization by vowel melody, which certainly does not share a *be* + *V-ed* construction. In Danks 2011: 237–41, I again present some preliminary findings and suggestions for further study. My intuition is that the passive formally realized by the *u* vowel in C_1VC_2 position is primarily perceived as actional while the participial passive is primarily statal, though this would be an interesting direction for more specific and thorough research.

Reference to Discussion

Danks, Warwick. 2011. *The Arabic verb: Form and meaning in the vowel-lengthening patterns*. Amsterdam: John Benjamins.

CHRISTIAN BASSAC

3   Rules and Exceptions: Neogrammarians and the Lexicon

ABSTRACT

In the second half of the nineteenth century, a group of German linguists known as the *Junggrammatiker*, or Neogrammarians, firmly expressed the belief that language changes were caused by phonological factors, that they were regular, and consequently could be captured by exception-free rules. Should exceptions to a rule appear, this would be an indication that the rule is inadequate.

After Grimm had established the law codifying the changes from Indo-European to Proto-Germanic, apparent exceptions remained unexplained. This was not a problem for the comparative tradition, but faith in exception-free rules later led Verner, a Danish *Junggrammatiker*, to show that such examples are not exceptions but can be explained by another rule. Verner's law (1875) then states that Grimm's law applies only if some suprasegmental conditions are met, namely if the word in Indo-European received stress on the syllable preceding the consonant. Other apparent exceptions to Grimm's law were explained by laws discovered by Thurneysen and Grassmann, thus completing the demonstration that Grimm's law has no exception. Some hundred years later, however, the belief that lexical change is exceptionless was challenged by the alternative theory of 'lexical diffusion'. This paper is a presentation and assessment of this theoretical journey through the motivations of lexical change and the status of exceptions.

Introduction

In a conference on the method of lexical exceptions,[1] it seems apt to analyse the methodology of the linguistic school known as the *Junggrammatiker*,

---

[1]   Now known, from the publication of this volume, as the method of exceptions and their correlations.

or Neogrammarians. The *Junggrammatiker* is the label given to a group of (mostly) German linguists who, in the second part of the nineteenth century, expressed radical new views on laws and exceptions: these views led them to offer solutions to numerous troublesome problems that had been left unsolved by comparative linguists, and are still methodologically inspiring today.

In the first part of this paper the historical and scientific background in which they worked will be presented, and some of their main principles will be exposed in the second part. The third part will be devoted to a detailed analysis of Grimm's law and to how the *Junggrammatiker* demonstrated that its apparent 'exceptions' were in fact regularities. In the penultimate section, a contemporary alternative theory known as 'lexical diffusion theory' is presented and briefly discussed.

The *Junggrammatiker* and the historical background: Comparative linguistics

It is generally acknowledged that it is Bopp's work on Sanskrit that initiated research in the field of comparative linguistics in the early nineteenth century. Bopp's work was soon followed by other major works by (among others) Grimm and Schleicher, who probably was the last comparative linguist.

The principles that shaped their research are worth stating, at least briefly, and some of their most important results must be sketched out, in so far as they were major results: one of them, Grimm's law, was the starting point of several studies that exemplify the methodology of the *Junggrammatiker*.

The principles

Three basic principles seem to have prevailed in the comparative paradigm. First, for comparative linguists the object of study was the evolution of language (not that of languages), which they thought was undergoing a constant process of decay. Second, they seemed to have been inspired by some kind of Hegelianism: for Schleicher, for instance, the association of a root and a morphological mark was an image of how the human mind manifests itself in a language, an affix being the indication of the relation between man and the object denoted by the root. Last but not least, they believed that Sanskrit was the common source of all the languages they were comparing.

The results

Comparative work has firmly established that there are striking regularities between Gothic on the one hand and Sanskrit, Greek and Latin on the other, as shown in Table 3.1.

Table 3.1 Correspondences between Gothic and Sanskrit, Greek and Latin

Correspondences between:	Gothic	Sanskrit	Greek	Latin
f (Got.) and *p*	*fotus* (Eng: *foot*)	*pad*	*pos*	*pes* (Fr. *pied*)
	faihu (*money*) (Eng: *fee*)	*pasu* (*cattle*)		*pecus*
	fimf (Eng: *five*)	*panca*	*pente*	*quinque< *pinque*

Correspondences between:	Gothic	Sanskrit	Greek	Latin
θ (Got. written þ) and t	Þunnr (Eng: *thin*)	*tanuh*	*tanaos*	*tenuis* (Fr. *ténu*)
	þreis (Eng: *three*)	*trayah*	*treis*	*tres*
	þu (Eng: *thou*)	*tvam*	*su* (*tu* in Doric)	*tu*
	þaursus (Eng: *thirst*)	*trsyati*	*terso* (Eng: *quench*)	*torrus* (Eng: *torrid*)
x (Got. written h) and k	*hairto* (Eng: *heart*)	*hrd*	*kardi* (Eng: *cardiac*)	*cor*
	hunds (Eng: *hound*)		*kunos*	*canis*
	hund (Eng: *hundred*)	*satam*	*hekaton*	*centum*

To account for the above data comparative researchers had first ruled out the null hypothesis, namely that the correspondences observed are accidental, or that there might have been borrowings from one language, Sanskrit, which would be the source of the others, as these languages were too distant in space and time. They also ruled out a possible motivation of the linguistic sign (in different languages identical or very similar 'signifiers' would correspond to the same 'signified'). They thought that the only valid hypothesis was that these languages had a common ancestor, Indo-European. In his comparative research Grimm assumed that the consonant system in Indo-European consisted of the plosives /p/t/k/ (voiceless), /b/d/g/ (voiced) and /bʰ/dʰ/gʰ (voiced aspirated). He then established the following law (Grimm's law 1823), codifying the changes from Indo-European to Proto-Germanic:

p/t/k/ (unaspirated voiceless plosives) in Indo-European → f/θ/x
respectively (voiceless fricatives. Process: lenition)
b/d/g/ (unaspirated voiced plosives) in Indo-European → p/t/k
respectively (voiceless plosives. Process: devoicing)
bʰ/ dʰ/gʰ (voiced aspirated plosives) in Indo-European → b/d/g/
respectively (voiced plosives. Process: loss of aspiration).

The method

Correspondence vs likeness

It must be emphasized here that the correspondence between words is more
significant than likeness: a case in point is Armenian. Taking likeness as
the only factor, the Armenian word for *two* should not be considered as
related to others as might be inferred at first sight from Table 3.2.

Table 3.2 *Two* in Gothic and Sanskrit, Greek, Latin and Armenian

English	Gothic	Sanskrit	Greek	Latin	Armenian
two	*tvai*	*dvau*	*duo*	*duo*	*erku*

Yet if correspondences between forms are taken into account, then some
regularities emerge, as shown by the data in Tables 3.2 and 3.3.

Table 3.3 Correspondences between Indo-European, Greek and Armenian

English	Indo-European	Greek	Armenian
fear	**dwei*	*dedwoike*	*erkwil*
long	**dwaro*		*erkar*

It can then be inferred that *dw* in Indo-European and Greek corresponds to *erk* in Armenian.[2]

A rationale

The main question that must be answered now is the following: why postulate an evolution for instance like t → θ (*þ*) from Indo-European to Germanic (and hence Gothic)? As was shown above, the perception of regularities is of tremendous importance, yet the statistics[3] on the number of cognates in different languages is not the only sign that they are related. The main argument on which the hypothesis of relation and evolution between forms relies is that synchronic models also offer frequent examples of such an evolution. For instance:

- devoicing is known in German (*tag/tak*);
- lenition is a characteristic of Celtic languages;
- Armenian had a consonant shift identical to Grimm's law;
- Tiberian Hebrew has the same, too (partially), in a postvocalic environment (Kenstowicz 1994: 35).
- There was another consonant shift in Germanic (in Old High German (850–1050)), which is another instance of lenition. English kept the Germanic form of voiceless plosives, which shifted to affricates or fricatives in Old High German as shown in Table 3.4.

---

2   For an account of this see Meillet 1925: 46.
3   Lees (1953) established a standard list of words in related languages, unlikely to be borrowings and which are also known not to change much. For any given language, after 1000 years, he found that the number of cognates with its ancestor is constant and ≈81 per cent.

Table 3.4. Old High German consonant shift

Position / Shift	#__	C__	__C	__#	V_V
$p \rightarrow \begin{Bmatrix} p^f \\ f \end{Bmatrix}$	Path Pfad	Carp Karpfen		Sheep schaf	Pope Pfaffe
$t \rightarrow \begin{Bmatrix} t^s \\ s \end{Bmatrix}$	Ten zehn	Salt salz		That das	Hate hassan
$p \rightarrow \begin{Bmatrix} k^x \\ x \end{Bmatrix}$	Corn k^xorn	Thank dank^{x}e		Streak strich	Make machen

Note. Segeral and Scheer (2001) provide an explanation for this phenomenon, using a non-branching syllabic model (CVCV) and comparing the two symmetrical positions: a strong position {C, #}__ and a weak position __{C, #}, the former being called the 'coda-mirror' as it is the mirror image of the coda context.

The *Junggrammatiker*: A radical criticism of the peaceful world of comparative linguistics

The principles that have been presented above were strongly criticized by the new generation of *Junggrammatiker* which followed comparative linguists, among whom the most famous are certainly H. Paul, K. Brugman, K. Verner, H. Grassmann and F. de Saussure.

Creed

The creed of the *Junggrammatiker* can be understood as a point-by-point criticism of the principles of the comparative paradigm just expressed above. They first contended that the object of their study should not be the evolution of language but the history of languages. Second, to the Hegelianism of the comparative tradition they opposed a firm belief in positivism: the object of study must be the objective causes of evolution, one of them being the activity of speakers. Third, the idea that Sanskrit might be the mother tongue was violently rejected (Saussure labelled it a 'glaring mistake') as indicated by this quotation from Saussure (1916: 215):

> Because it is the oldest document of Proto-Indo-European, they promoted Sanskrit to the rank of prototype. To imagine that Proto-Indo-European engendered Sanskrit, Greek, Slavic (...) is one thing; to substitute one of these languages for Indo-European is something else entirely.

Last but not least, the most significant and (for us here) relevant claim they made concerns the nature of rules.

Rules

The new views they formed about the nature of rules are of the utmost interest for us in this conference. They firmly argued that changes were caused by phonological factors, that they were regular, and consequently should be captured by exception-free rules. Should exceptions to a rule appear, this would be an indication that the rule is inadequate. Consequently, a rule does not take the form of 1:[4]

(1) $X \rightarrow Y / A\_\_\_B]_K$ (if X is a K)

---

4   From now on the rules are expressed in the format of Chomsky and Halle 1968.

An example of such a rule would be provided by Turkish, as indicated in 2 below,

(2a) yen + er
     beat + AOR

vs

(2b) ye + n   + ir
     eat + PASS + AOR

As indicated by 2a and 2b, for two identical forms (*yen*) the rule here is sensitive to the morphological nature of the object it applies to: if the object is an unanalyzable whole (in 2a), the aorist allomorph is -*er*. If the morphological object it applies to is made up of two morphemes, like in (2b) (*ye*- and -*n*), the aorist allomorph is -*ir*. For the *Junggrammatiker*, a rule is not a probabilistic statement or implication either (for instance like Greenberg's universals) but a conditional, if P then Q, that is P→Q, for instance:

if /p/ in IE then /f/ in Gothic.

Rules and exceptions: The case of Grimm's law

In this section we first go into some detail about the formulation and motivation of Grimm's law. We then examine phenomena that might be considered as exceptions and how they were accounted for by the *Junggrammatiker*.

Grimm's law

A drag chain

Under the hypothesis that lenition of voiceless plosives initiated the whole process, the various shifts that affected consonants from Indo-European to Germanic can be understood as a drag chain phenomenon and can be summed up as in Figure 3.1.

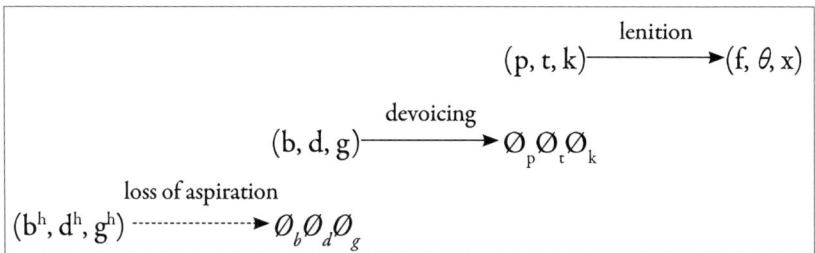

$$
\begin{array}{l}
\text{lenition} \\
(\text{p, t, k}) \xrightarrow{\hspace{2cm}} (\text{f, } \theta, \text{x}) \\[4pt]
\hspace{1cm}\text{devoicing} \\
(\text{b, d, g}) \xrightarrow{\hspace{2cm}} \emptyset_p\,\emptyset_t\,\emptyset_k \\[4pt]
\text{loss of aspiration} \\
(\text{b}^h, \text{d}^h, \text{g}^h) \dashrightarrow \emptyset_b\,\emptyset_d\,\emptyset_g
\end{array}
$$

Figure 3.1 Grimm's law as a drag chain phenomenon.

Motivation

A possible motivation for the set of processes summed up in Figure 3.1 is provided by Fourquet (1948). If we consider lenition, for instance from /p/ to /f/, it can be explained by structural articulatory phenomena, in a three step algorithm:

1) aspiration p^h due to articulatory tension.
2) relaxation of muscular tension, hence $p^h \rightarrow \Phi$: from bilabial plosive /p/ to bilabial fricative /Φ/: they have the same place (bilabial) but different manner of articulation (plosive vs fricative).
3) increase of articulatory energy, then $\Phi \rightarrow f$.

Exceptions?

Cases of unexpected voicing

Grimm's law accounts for most correspondences between classical languages, Sanskrit, and Germanic, including those in Table 3.1. It also accounts for the correspondence between the Gothic word *broþar* (brother) and the word *bhratar* in Sanskrit, (*þ* is the spelling in Gothic for θ). Yet the Gothic forms corresponding to Sanskrit words *pitar* or *mata* (*father* and *mother* respectively) are not *faþar* (and *moþar*) as expected, but *fadar* (and *modar*): *t* has unexpectedly shifted to the voiced plosive *d* instead of the expected voiceless fricative *þ*.[5]

As forcefully claimed by the *Junggrammatiker*, exceptions must be explained by new laws, and this unexpected voicing did receive an explanatory account. Here Verner (1875)[6] had the idea to take into account suprasegmental phenomena and a possible formulation for Verner's law is: Grimm's law applies *only* if the word in Indo-European (as shown by examples in Sanskrit and often in Greek) received stress on the syllable preceding the consonant, which is the case for *bhr'atar* (Sanskrit) and *phr'ater* (Greek). If the stressed syllable follows the consonant, like in *fadar*, or *modar*, as shown by stress on the second syllable in the Sanskrit words *pit'ar*, and *mat'a*, then the fricative is voiced.[7]

5   Later in English the opposition between *mother, father* (Goth *fadar, modar*) and *brother* (Goth *broþar*) was neutralized by assimilation of the voiceless *þ* in *broþar* between the two vocalic phonemes. Also, the voiced plosive in *fadar* and *modar* later became the voiced fricative ð in English.

6   See <http://www.utexas.edu/cola/centers/lrc/books/read11.html>, accessed 21 November 2013.

7   Interestingly, one wonders if the same sometimes does not go in English: *'exit* vs *e'xist*, *'Exeter* vs *e'xhaustive*, *'abscess* vs *a'bsorb*, etc.

Put differently, if stress in Indo-European[8] was on the syllable that follows the consonant candidate to undergo Grimm's law, then this consonant shifts to a voiced fricative.[9]

Hence the representation of Verner's law:

$$(3) \begin{bmatrix} Plosive \\ -voice \end{bmatrix} \rightarrow \begin{bmatrix} Fricative \\ +voice \end{bmatrix} / \begin{bmatrix} V \\ \dots \end{bmatrix} - \left\{ \begin{bmatrix} stress \\ V \\ \dots \end{bmatrix} \begin{bmatrix} V \\ \dots \end{bmatrix} \begin{bmatrix} C \\ \dots \end{bmatrix} \begin{bmatrix} stress \\ V \\ \dots \end{bmatrix} \right\}$$

This forcefully shows that examples such as *fadar* and *modar* in Gothic are not counterexamples or exceptions to Grimm's law but are in fact regularities.[10]

Clusters

Another set of 'exceptions' to Grimm's law is provided by the phenomena presented in Table 3.5.

8   In Indo-European stress was variable and could be either on the root or on the suffix, whereas in Germanic only roots were stressed.
9   It is important to underline that the voiced plosive *d* in *fadar* and *modar* in Gothic was an evolution of the voiced fricative ð in Germanic.
10   From now on in the rules, V is used for vowel and C for consonant. Only relevant features captured by the law are provided, hence the use of suspension points for other features.

Table 3.5 Correspondences between Gothic, Sanskrit, Greek and Latin

Exceptions?	Gothic	Sanskrit	Greek	Latin
Not *f* (Got) vs *p*	*speh-* (Eng: *spy*)	*spa*		*specere* (*see* >-*spec*)
Not *θ/þ* (Got) vs *t*	*ist* (Eng: *is*)	*asti*	*esti*	*est*
Not *x/h* (Got) vs *k*	*skinan* (Eng: *shine*)	*skia*	*skia*	*sciomachia* (*fight against a shadow*)

Contrary to what would be expected by Grimm's law, in these examples the voiceless plosives do not undergo lenition but are conserved. The obvious explanation is that they are parts of a cluster and as expressed by Grammont (1933) the voiceless fricative *s* cannot be followed by an aspirated plosive, hence the first step of the evolution towards a fricative is blocked (cf. algorithm above in 3.1.2) as the air stream needed by /s/ is continuous. The rule that captures this phenomenon can be expressed as 4:

$$(4) \quad \begin{bmatrix} plosive \\ -voice \\ [\ldots]_i \end{bmatrix} \rightarrow \begin{bmatrix} plosive \\ -voice \\ [\ldots]_i \end{bmatrix} \Big/ \left\{ \# \, s \, \underline{\quad} \begin{bmatrix} V \\ \ldots \end{bmatrix} \right\}$$

Grimm's law can now be formulated as the most general statement about consonant shift, after rules whose domains are smaller have been described:

$$(5) \quad \begin{bmatrix} plosive \\ -voice \\ \ldots \end{bmatrix} \rightarrow \begin{bmatrix} fricative \\ -voice \\ \ldots \end{bmatrix} \Big/ \left\{ \begin{bmatrix} stress \\ V \\ [\ldots] \end{bmatrix} \underline{\quad} \begin{Bmatrix} \# \\ V \end{Bmatrix} \right\}$$

No examples of cases such as

$$p \rightarrow f / X\_\_Y \text{ and } p \rightarrow p / X\_\_Y$$
or
$$t \rightarrow \theta \ (\text{\th}) / \ 'X\_\_Y \text{ and } t \rightarrow \eth \ / \ 'X\_\_Y$$
$$t \rightarrow \theta \ (\text{\th}) / \ X\_\_'Y \text{ and } t \rightarrow \eth \ / \ X\_\_'Y$$

can be found: this shows that the rules above are in complementary distribution and consequently that they capture a unique phenomenon.

Residues explained by laws proper to Gothic or Sanskrit

Some problems still remain and some phenomena might still be interpreted as exceptions to Grimm's rule. According to Verner's law a voiceless plosive (p,t,k) in Indo-European should shift to a voiced fricative in Germanic if it is followed by a stressed vowel. The voiceless plosive of the Indo-European stressed suffix *–tu* should then shift to a voiced fricative in Germanic and be realized in Gothic as *–du*. This is exactly what happens for the Gothic word *wratodus* (travel). Yet, in the Gothic word *gabarjoþus* (pleasure), which is derived on the same pattern as *wratodus*, the consonant correlated to *t* is unexpectedly voiceless and we find *þ* instead of *d*.

This is not an exception to Verner's rule either. It is an example of dissimilation proper to Gothic: after an unstressed vowel, voicing in a continuant is dissimilated by the preceding obstruent (minimally a fricative) consonant. This was discovered by Thurneysen, and Thurneysen's law can then be stated as 6 below:

$$
(6) \quad
\begin{bmatrix} fricative \\ ... \end{bmatrix}
\rightarrow [\alpha \ voice] \ /
\begin{bmatrix} C \\ -\alpha \ voice \end{bmatrix}
\begin{bmatrix} -stress \\ V \end{bmatrix}
\_\_
$$

in which α is variable for the Boolean feature (+Feat. or –Feat.). Other examples of this law are found in the following Gothic minimal pairs:

expected *aupida* (desert) vs unexpected *meripa* (rumour),
expected *witubini* (science) vs unexpected *waldufni* (power).

Another dissimilation process in Sanskrit accounts for the last set of
'exceptions' to Grimm's law. All voiced plosives in Gothic do not come from
aspirated plosives in Indo-European: for instance *bind* does not come from
b^handh but from *bandh*. This is another instance of dissimilation, proper
to Sanskrit, in which the last aspirated plosive dissimilates aspiration on
the initial plosive which is consequently unaspirated.[11] This was discovered
by Grassmann and now Grassmann's law can be stated as 7:

$$(7) \quad \begin{bmatrix} C \\ ... \end{bmatrix} \rightarrow [-\alpha \text{ aspiration}] / \quad - \begin{bmatrix} V \\ ... \end{bmatrix} \begin{bmatrix} C \\ \alpha \text{ aspiration} \end{bmatrix}$$

Chronology of rules

So far, we have shown that even the slightest exception to Grimm's law was
accounted for by the *Junggrammatiker*. Nothing has been said, however,
about the chronology of changes captured by Grimm's and Verner's laws.
But one might assume that Verner's law describes phenomena which took
place before those described by Grimm's law, in which case the so-called
exceptions or the 'irregularities' would have preceded the 'regular' phenomena, which raises doubt about the very notion of exception.

Whatever the order in which the phenomena happened, all this shows
that considering that rules have no exceptions but that exceptions are only
unaccounted for regularities, is a viable methodology that simply requires
paying close attention to details that might pass unnoticed. Even though
the results of the research carried out by the *Junggrammatiker* are achieve-
ments of paramount importance, the principle of underdetermination of

---

11   The same phenomenon can be observed in Greek: for instance *tit^{h}emi* (I put) instead
of *t^hit^{h}emi*.

theory by data is still at work: many theories can account for the same set of data, and an alternative theory was developed, starting with Wang 1969.

An alternative theory of sound change: Lexical diffusion

Lexical diffusion

The theory of a sound change that would have affected all candidates indiscriminately has been challenged by various authors, mainly following Wang 1969, Chen and Wang 1975 and all the contributors to Wang 1977, who contend that phonological change occurs first only for a small number of items, then spreads and percolates through a growing number of lexical items.

Definition

In this conception of lexical change known as 'lexical diffusion', of all potential combinations of the feature ±gradual with phonetic and lexical change, that is

a)   phonetic & lexical: -gradual
b)   phonetic & lexical: +gradual
c)   phonetic: +gradual & lexical: -gradual
d)   phonetic: -gradual & lexical: +gradual

sound change as hypothesized by the lexical diffusion theory could be defined by combination b) or d) above, but d) seems more plausible as it tends to make sound change similar to the widely observed diffusion across dialects or languages (Wang 1969: 15). Using the same factors in the description of phenomena, the *Junggrammatiker* conception would be that of the combination of lexical and phonetic factors expressed in c) above. Abundant empirical data collected by Wang 1969 and subsequent works, mainly Chen and Wang 1975, seem to support the lexical diffusion hypothesis.

Data from English

The lexical diffusion hypothesis suggests that several words should have two (or more) pronunciations at any given time. Items with two phonological forms are not hard to find in English, witness the different stress patterns and correlative vowel reduction in *abdomen* (/əbˈdəʊmən/ vs /ˈæbdəmən/) or voicing of intervocalic obstruent clusters as in *exit* (/ˈeksɪt/ vs /ˈekzɪt/) or the presence or absence of the j-glide in *new* (/nu/ vs /nju/) in American English, which can all be readily accounted for by the lexical diffusion hypothesis.

Data from Chinese dialects

Chen and Wang 1975 show that in Chaozhou, a Min dialect spoken on the southeast coast of mainland China, the phonologically conditioned split in the four tones (1, 2, 3, 4) of Middle Chinese into eight tonemes (1a, 1b, 2a, 2b, 3a, 3b, 4a, 4b, the *a* variant for words with a voiceless initial, the *b* variant for words with a voiced initial) of modern Chinese dialects, displays a puzzling result: the vast majority of words with tone 3 which had a voiceless initial in Middle Chinese now have the expected tone 3a, in accordance with the general pattern, whereas the words that had a voiced initial, instead of the expected 3b tone, have either a 3b tone or a 2b tone, the number of words with tone 3b being approximately equal to that of words with tone 2b. After a careful study, the hypotheses of a phonologically conditioned tonal split and that of possible regulation due to paradigmatic pressure[12] or borrowing were ruled out. The only hypothesis left is that of an independent tone shift from tone 3b to tone 2b that took place in the tonal evolution from Middle Chinese to present day Chaozhou, which is further evidence that change spreads gradually across the lexicon in accordance with the lexical diffusion theory.

Data from Dravidian languages

Other data, presented in Krishnamurti 1978, also seem to add strong support to the lexical diffusion hypothesis. Krishnamurti shows that in Proto-Dravidian, alveolar and retroflex consonants <L> in stems of type $^*<(C)V_1L-V_2->$ shifted to a position adjacent to the first optional consonant (a phenomenon that he labels 'apical displacement'), to yield stems of type $(C)L-V_2$ either by the loss of V_1 weakened by a stress shift to the following non-root V_2, or by metathesis of $<V_1L>$ resulting in $<LV_1>$ followed by contraction of V_1 and V_2. This phenomenon, which affects stems of the south central subgroup (Telugu, Gondi, Konda, Kui, Kuvi, Pengo, and Manda) of the Dravidian languages spoken in the sub-continent of South Asia, started some two thousand years ago and is still active in some dialects and languages of the sub-group. A computer analysis of data showed that the change initially affected less than a dozen lexical items and then gradually spread over the centuries to affect the languages of the group in various proportions, ranging from only about 20 per cent in Gondi for instance, to 72 per cent in Kui. This obviously adds strong support to the lexical diffusion hypothesis, but does not put to rest other possible explanations. This is precisely what Kiparsky (1995) shows.

---

12   Chinese is a language with no conjugation or declensions, hence the lack of paradigmatic pressure.

Kiparsky (1995): Lexical diffusion and Lexical Phonology

The framework: Lexical Phonology

Kiparsky's analysis is cast in the framework of Lexical Phonology (Kiparsky 1985, Mohanan 1986). In Lexical Phonology, phonological and lexical rules interact at several strata of representation and each stratum is the locus of morphological output: for instance, irregular derivations and inflexional processes result from rules of stratum i, regular derivations are processed at stratum $i+1$, and regular inflexions at stratum $i+2$. Postlexical rules are rules that can have access to the phrasal status of words. In the framework of Lexical Phonology, the changes described by the *Junggrammatiker* would then be captured by postlexical rules.

Moreover, Kiparsky adopts a radical underspecification position, in which underlying representations are minimally specified. Consequently redundant information is not provided in the lexicon, it is left unspecified, and then is rule-derived from another feature present in the underlying representation. In addition to this, default rules assign the unmarked feature to each feature. The two rules used are then respectively:

– redundancy rules of type 8

(8) $[\alpha F] \rightarrow [\pm \alpha F']$

– context free default rules of type 9

(9) $[\ ] \rightarrow [\alpha F'']$

For instance /n/ would not be $\begin{bmatrix} + \textit{sonorant} \\ + \textit{voice} \end{bmatrix}$

but the redundant feature <+voice> would be derived by application of the redundancy rule 10, since all sonorants are voiced:

(10) [+sonorant]→[+voice]

When an item has not been marked positively for a feature F, it is then unspecified and by a default rule is marked negatively. This theoretical position of radical underspecification is applied by Kiparsky to an analysis of lexical diffusion.

Lexical diffusion as analogy

Kiparsky defends the *Junggrammatiker* hypothesis that rules are exceptionless and subject to phonetic conditioning, but with the restriction that only some sound changes can be accounted for by such rules. There are other changes that are not exceptionless, and Kiparsky argues that lexical diffusion is actually analogical regularization, which is a case of 'well-behaved type of analogical change' (Kiparsky 1995/2003: 314). An important motivation for this claim is that both analogy and lexical diffusion share the following properties: they both generalize context by context, item by item, their origin is endogenous, their rate is slow, and neither affects the phoneme inventory or adds new words to the lexical stock, contrary to lexical borrowing, for instance, whose rate is rapid, which is exogenous, and which adds new items to the lexical stock.

In the theoretical framework of Lexical Phonology, lexical diffusion can be analysed as an analogical generalization, a simplification and an optimization of lexical rules. An example provided by Kiparsky 1995/2003: 316–17 is that of the shortening of the English phoneme /uː/, which spread from the core context of 11 to contexts expressed by 12 and 13 below, by relaxing its left (in 12) and right (in 13) contexts with idiosyncratic lexical results:

(11) $[\text{-anterior}] — \begin{bmatrix} \text{-anterior} \\ \text{-coronal} \end{bmatrix}$

11 accounts for /ʊ/ in *cook, rook, shook, crook*, etc, basically with no exceptions.

(12) $\quad \_\_ \begin{bmatrix} \text{-anterior} \\ \text{-coronal} \end{bmatrix}$

12 accounts for /ʊ/ in *took, book, look, nook*, vs /u:/ in *bazooka* and /ʊ/ or /u:/ in *boogie* (in American English).

(13) [-anterior] ___

13 accounts for /ʊ/ in *good, could, hood* vs /u:/ in *proof*, and /ʊ/ or /u:/ in *hoof* (in American English).

Lexical items that display environment 14, which is complementary to the core environment 11, have overwhelmingly long /u:/,

(14) $[\text{+anterior}] \_\_ \begin{bmatrix} \text{+anterior} \\ \text{+coronal} \end{bmatrix}$

as shown by *loose, balloon, snooze, tool*, etc.

For lexical items that do not display the core environment 11, phonological change takes place in an apparently erratic way, as some items undergo change and some do not. For lexical items that underwent /u:/ shortening, the process can be analysed as regularization triggered for those items by the application of a default rule. The configuration of the environment of 11 triggers the application of a regular, systematic change in accordance with the *Junggrammatiker* assumptions, whereas changes which seem to be erratic and unmotivated for environments of type 12 and 13, are actual instances of a process of regularization. Contexts most distant from core context 11, for instance 14, are almost immune to shortening. This is summed up and generalized in Figure 3.2, in which E_1 would be the core environment of 11, E_2, E_3 that of 12 and 13 and E_4 the complementary 14 of 11.

First application of rule R

Set of lexical items: $\{I_1 I_2 I_3 ... I_p\}$

Subset of lexical items: $\{I_1, I_2 ... I_n\}$ $\{I_{n-1}, I_{n-2}, ... I_p\}$

Items: $I_{n-1}, I_{n-2}, ... I_{n-k}$ $I_{n-k-1}, I_{n-k-2}, ... I_n$

in environment: E_1, E_2, E_3, E_4

by default rule

acquire αF: $[\ ] \rightarrow [-F]$ by first application of rule R $\rightarrow [+F]$

Extended application of rule R

Now for items: $I_{n-k-1}, I_{n-k-2}, ... I_{n-1}$ $I_{n-h-1}, I_{n-h-2}, ... I_n$

in environment: $E_2 E_3$ $E_2 E_3$

Rule R extends to E_2, E_3.
Some items I_j in E_3 get $[+F]$

by extended application of rule R

items not marked +F are unspecified $\longrightarrow [\ ]$ $[+F]$

items unspecified for F are then marked −F by default rule $\longrightarrow [\ ] \rightarrow [-F]$

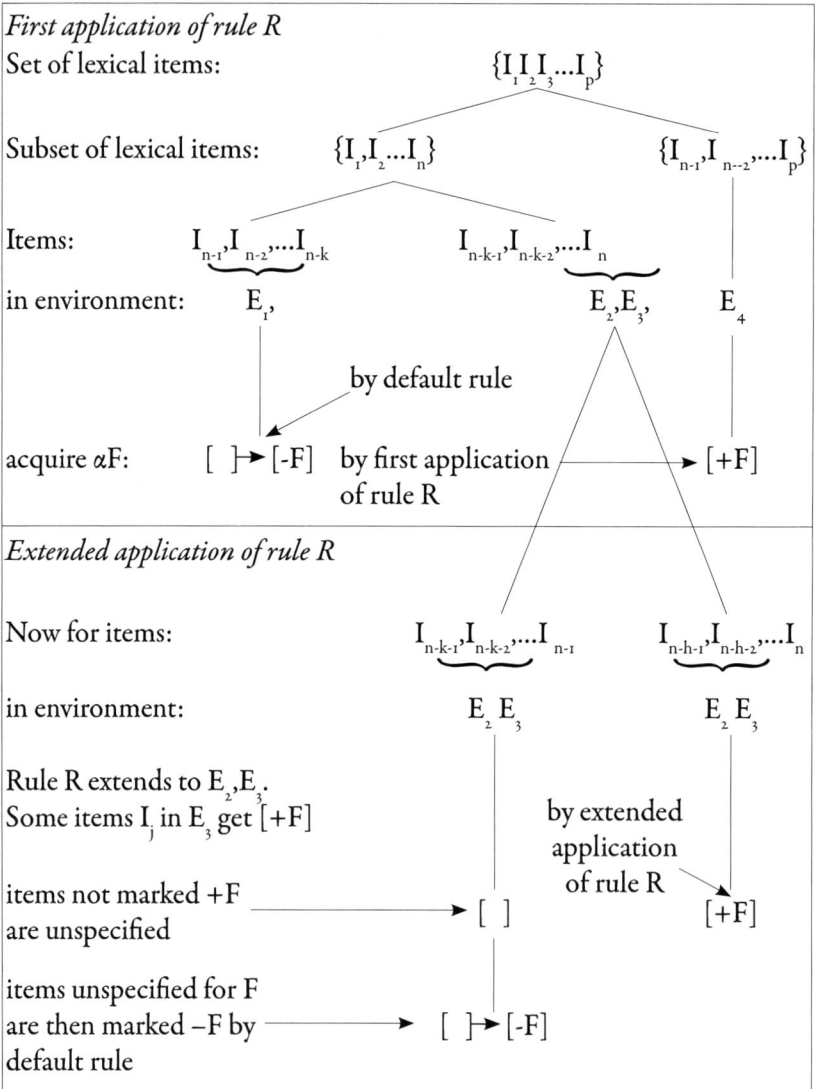

Figure 3.2 Underspecification, default rule application and regularization in Kiparsky 1995.

The regular distribution of long /uː/ and shortened /uː/ in contexts 14 and 11 respectively, results from:

- the application of rule R, which marks items which display 14 as having the feature <+long> and
- the application of the default rule for items which display 11 and marks them with <-long>.

For items that display environment 12 or 13, the extension of the application of rule R specifies some items with long /uː/, and the rest get the feature <–long> by application of the corresponding default rule.

The obvious observation now is that an item with feature +F by application of rule R, can have acquired this feature either by the first application of this specific rule, in which case the rule is 'regular' and exceptionless, or as the result of an extended application of rule R to other different contexts, in which case the results of application of rule R are idiosyncratic. Items targeted in the second application of rule R may (or may not) be regularized and consequently lose their feature +F, in which case they will be reanalysed as unmarked by a default rule. The former case is an example of a *Junggrammatiker* rule, the latter is an example of lexical diffusion. The consequence of this is that in Kiparsky's theory, there is theoretical room both for the *Junggrammatiker* conception and for the alternative model of lexical diffusion.

A rebuttal of Kiparsky: Hale 2003

Methodological flaws

Hale 2003 is a reassessment of the basic claims of Neogrammarian theory and contains a criticism of Kiparsky's analysis of sound change. Firstly, what is difficult to see, Hale argues, is to what extent and in what way, the extension of the rule of /uː/ shortening to contexts defined by [-anterior]_ is more optimal and simpler than a system in which there is only one rule operating in contexts [-anterior]_[-anterior, -coronal] with memorization of a list of lexical exceptions. Second, in Kiparsky's analysis, as is normal in a derivational analysis, the surface form is derived from a change in the underlying process. The problem is that the acquirer of a natural language has no access to these underlying processes, and consequently Kiparsky's theory wrongly suggests that access to the sole output of rules and principles of Universal Grammar would not be sufficient in the acquisition process. Rules such as /u:/ shortening in adequate contexts are descriptions of a diachronic evolution, they are not part of a synchronic linguistic system: consequently, Hale argues, Kiparski's methodological assumptions are flawed.

Moreover, an analysis using underspecification and subsequent feature filling along the lines of what is proposed by Kiparsky cannot be applied to cases of lexical diffusion such as that displayed in dialects of New Caledonia. The empirical data are as follows (Rivierre 1991): in some dialects, word final /k/ is lost; then /p/, and in some dialects all final stops disappear. In Kiparsky's analysis, this final stop deletion would be accounted for by the phonological underspecification of final stops subsequently filled by a zero surface form, which is impossible here as final stop deletion is not a rule in any synchronic system of these dialects.

Diachrony

In any diachronic process an important aspect to take into account is the result of this process: both Kiparsky and Hale agree on the obvious fact that the result of diachronic change must be constrained by the limits of the computational abilities of the human organism. The result of change cannot be a system which violates the basic principles of Universal Grammar. The direct consequence of this is that contrary to the *Junggrammatiker* claim that sound change operates blindly, diachronic events are constrained by output factors. Another consequence is that it is possible to establish a hierarchy between the sets of computationally possible human languages (which we label CG), diachronically possible human grammars (which we label DG), and attested human grammars (which we label AG) represented in 15 below:

(15) $AG \subset DG \subset CG$

Concluding remarks

In this study I have attempted to give a survey of some possible theoretical and methodological approaches to rules and exceptions, starting from the Neogrammarian analysis, for whom this topic was a most basic concern, to recent analyses by Wang and other researchers, which are cast in the lexical diffusion framework.

As this survey shows, the controversy is still simmering in order to accommodate the facts at the core of Neogrammarian concern with the tools of modern linguistics. Kiparsky (1995) tries to save the Neogrammarians' assumption, and argues that at least some types of change are exceptionless, and so does Labov (1981) in his study of sound changes carried out in several communities in Philadelphia. He shows that there is a regular Neogrammarian shift from the original cardinal [ɔ:] to [u:ə] in words like *door, four, more, born forth, fort, horns* or *source*, without lexical exceptions, but that the split of /a/ into tense /a/ and lax /a/ cannot be accounted for in the same way: in environment 15,

$$(15) \quad - \begin{bmatrix} +stop \\ +voice \end{bmatrix}$$

where tense /a/ is expected, some exceptions do exist with lax /a/ in the adjectives *mad* or *glad*. An account along the lines that these are affective adjectives and that their irregular behaviour might be displayed by other affective adjectives would be on the wrong track as shown by the adjective *sad*, which displays lax /a/ as expected. Consequently, Labov argues, this is a case of lexical diffusion.

An intriguing fact, however, seems to have been overlooked in the study of lexical exceptions: Krishnamurti (1978: 17, 11) observes that the early items targeted by the rule of 'apical displacement' (see above 4.1.4) are items that refer to concepts which are basic in the communication and culture of tribal groups, which suggests that frequency effects or lexical

semantics might be relevant factors that at least cooperate with other phonological factors.

Lexical diffusion is a complete reversal of the hypothesis put forward
by the *Junggrammatiker*: for them, phonetic change affects types not tokens,
whereas for Wang and his followers, it first affects tokens. Very interestingly, this view was unambiguously rejected by Saussure, who claimed
that there is no doubt about the answer to the question whether phonetic
change affects words or sounds. For him (Saussure 1916: 94), 'each fact ...
is independent of the words in which the change took place'.

Obviously, the question of lexical change also crucially involves an
analysis of the relationship between diachrony and synchrony, which is at
the core of Hale's rebuttal of Kiparsky's analysis. This is one of the many
theoretical problems raised by the Neogrammarian hypothesis.

Independently of this debate, there is no denying that linguists cannot
dispense with rules: without rules, linguistic description would be but a
list of unrelated facts with no possibility of explanation. This accepted,
rules can only have differently explained residues (in terms of statistics),
but no unaccounted for exceptions: this is the rich and inspiring heritage
left by the *Junggrammatiker*.

Bibliography

For an introduction to Indo-European linguistics including the texts of Grimm's and
Verner's laws, see <http://www.utexas.edu/cola/centers/lrc/books/readoo.html>,
accessed 21 November 2013.

Chen, M.Y., and W.S.Y. Wang. 1975. Sound Change: Actuation and Implementation.
    Language 51.255–81.
Chomsky, N., and M. Halle. 1968. *The Sound Pattern of English*. New York: Harper
    and Row.
Fourquet, J. 1948. *Les mutations consonantiques du germanique*. Paris: Les Belles Lettres.
Grammont, M. 1933. *Traité de phonétique*. Paris: Delagrave.

Hale, M. 2003. Neogrammarian sound change. *The Handbook of Historical Linguistics*, ed. by B.D. Joseph and R.D. Janda, 343–68. Oxford: Blackwell.

Kenstowicz, M. 1994. *Phonology in Generative Grammar.* Oxford: Blackwell.

Kiparsky, P. 1985. Some consequences of Lexical Phonology. *Phonology Yearbook*, 83–138. Cambridge: Cambridge University Press.

Kiparsky, P. 1995. The phonological basis of sound change. *The Handbook of Phonological Theory*, ed. by J.A. Goldsmith, 640–70. Oxford: Blackwell. Repr. in *The Handbook of Historical Linguistics*, ed. by B.D. Joseph and R.D. Janda, 2003, 313–42. Oxford: Blackwell.

Krishnamurti, Bh. 1978. Areal and Lexical Diffusion of Sound Change: Evidence from Dravidian. *Language* 54.1–20.

Labov, W. 1981. Resolving the Neogrammarian Controversy. *Language* 57.267–308.

Lees, R.B. 1953. The Basis of Glottochronology. *Language* 29.113–27.

Meillet, A. 1925. *The Comparative Method in Historical Linguistics*. Paris: Honoré Champion. (English translation 1967).

Mohanan, K.P. 1986. *The Theory of Lexical Phonology*. Dordrecht: Reidel.

Rivierre, Jean Claude. 1991. Loss of final consonants in the north of New Caledonia. *Currents in Pacific Linguistics: Papers on Austronesian Linguistics and Ethnolinguistics in Honour of George W. Grace*, ed. by Robert Blust, 415–32. Canberra: Pacific Linguistics C-117.

Saussure, F. de. 1916. *Course in General Linguistics*. New York: McGraw-Hill. (English translation 1966).

Segeral, P., and T. Sheer. 2001. La coda-miroir. *Bulletin de la Société Linguistique de Paris*, 107–52.

Swadesh, M. 1972. *The Origin and Diversification of Language*. London: Routledge and K. Paul.

Wang, W.S.Y. 1969. Competing changes as a cause of residue. *Language* 45.9–25.

Wang, W.S.Y. (ed.). 1977. *The Lexicon in Phonological Change*. The Hague: Mouton.

Discussion (Extract)

SOSELIA: What is your position on the glottalic hypothesis, and more specifically, to what extent would it affect the various laws presented in the paper?

BASSAC: I'm not a specialist of Indo-European reconstruction, but taking this hypothesis into account would affect only part of the various processes involved in the evolution from Indo-European to Germanic, as only voiced plosives would be excluded from the shift. Consequently, part of Grimm's law and Verner's law would still capture most phenomena, the only problem being for Grassmann's law, which adds the hypothesis that voiced plosives do exist in Indo-European.

JIKIA: If the glottalic hypothesis is accepted, the data concerning Armenian are difficult to interpret and Armenian would be much older than it is admitted here. But even if it is not so, when you are comparing modern Armenian with Sanskrit, Gothic, Greek, or Latin, the problem is that you are comparing states of languages separated by long distances of time.

BASSAC: I agree on this but it is very difficult to decide whether the classical languages have kept the Indo-European system and Armenian had a consonant shift or if it worked the other way round, i.e. Armenian kept the ancient system and classical languages had a consonant shift. As far as the second part of the question goes, comparing languages spanning long distances of time is common practice in historical linguistics.

DANKS: Would it be possible to consider that the English examples provided in the paper are part of Verner's law?

BASSAC: This is very unlikely, but there might be some regularity anyway and the alternations in the voiced and voiceless plosive /b/ versus /p/ in *absorb* and *abscess*, or in the examples of affricates provided cannot be explained by voice assimilation, which would be the most tempting explanation, as the voicing environment is the same in all pairs. Certainly this is not a rule and Juhani Rudanko rightly gives the counterexample of the word *obscene*.

BEEDHAM: Do you think that exceptions in phonology are maybe different to exceptions in grammar, e.g. morpho-syntactic exceptions such as non-passivizable transitive verbs, or morphological exceptions such as strong verbs? For example, perhaps with phonological rules one is more likely to have a rule which applies 100 per cent to every word or morpheme or syllable exhibiting the phonological feature in question. With grammatical rules, in contrast, one is highly unlikely to encounter a rule which applies 100 per cent to every theoretically compatible word or morpheme or clause. If that were true, then the approach to exceptions advocated by the *Junggrammatiker* would not be applicable to language in general, it would only be applicable to phonology. What do you think?

BASSAC: The problem you raise here is the problem of productivity of the rules. So is productivity in phonology different from productivity in morphology, for instance? I would like to answer that this is an old problem and productivity is hard to appreciate. It all depends on the domain on which the rule applies. For instance, it is known that the rule that derives verbs on ADJ+en such as *blacken* does not have a productivity of 100 per cent, witness **yellowen, *ochren, *orangen*. But if you limit the domain to adjectives having a fricative or a plosive in coda, the productivity is probably near 100 per cent (*blacken redden, darken* etc.). The same thing goes for morphology or syntax, I think. Once you have found the right conditions on the domain of application of a rule, then you can expect a high productivity. What makes things different, I think, is the fact that primitives in phonology are well known, they might even be universal, which is not the case for primitives in semantics. Moreover, it seems to me that the interaction between a syntactic object and its environment is much more difficult to grasp in syntax or semantics than in phonology. This is a problem you know well in the domain of passivization: usually most people (maybe not linguists) will tell you that state verbs do not passivize, e.g *resemble* (**he is resembled by his son*). Yet you showed that sentences like *John is not resembled by any of his children* are grammatical (Beedham 2005: 36). So the problem is not so much productivity itself as finding the right constraints on the domain of the rules: this is maybe easier in phonology but the problem is the same.

Reference to Discussion

Beedham, Christopher. 2005. *Language and Meaning: The Structural Creation of Reality*. Amsterdam: Benjamins.

MARINE IVANISHVILI AND ETHER SOSELIA

4 Passive in Georgian

ABSTRACT

The category of voice is one of the main verbal categories in Georgian. There are three kinds of voice: active, passive, and neutral (or medium). The goal of our paper is to discuss the issues raised by the passive voice in Georgian.

It seems that passive in Georgian is quite different from the same category presented in many languages, such as English, German, French, etc., where passive constructions are derived from the corresponding active by conversion. In Georgian in many cases it is difficult to speak about conversion. Verb forms are only regarded as passive voice according to their morphological structure. There are several different markers of passive: the prefixes *e-* and *i-*, the suffix *–d*, and the zero (Ø) marker: *i-xat-eb-a* '(it) is (being) drawn'; *e-ker-eb-a* '(it) is (being) sewed (to him/her)'; *šen-d-eb-a* '(it) is (being) built'; *dn-eb-a* '(it) is being melted'.

Despite the common morphological formal ground, semantic diversity is characteristic for the Georgian passive voice forms: some of them are so-called deponents (*i-mal-eb-a* '(he/she) is hiding'), some of them are called passive of mood (*e-cekv-eb-a* '(he/she) is in the mood of dancing'), some are called passive of opinion (*e-p'at'ar-av-eb-a* '(it) seems small to (him/her)'), etc. All the forms mentioned here could be regarded as lexical exceptions, and due to them the question arises: Is it correct to call this category passive? It is clear that the answer is negative, but the final interpretation of those forms has not yet been reached.

The category of voice has been widely discussed in the linguistic literature (Haspelmath 1990, Langacker and Munro 1975, Perlmutter 1978, Perlmutter and Postal 1977, Comrie 1980, Shibatani 1985, and others). It is one of the important verbal categories, being quite complex, involving forms at syntactic, semantic and morphological levels. Nowadays the voice category, like some other grammatical categories, is considered to be a continuum (Shibatani 1985), as opposed to the traditional view, where it was considered to be discrete. But we do not discuss theoretical problems connected to voice here, our main goal is to present analyses of Georgian data, in the hope that it will prove helpful in solving theoretical problems.

The voice category in Georgian linguistic literature is defined as based on the relation between the action, on the one hand, and subject and/or object, on the other. Such a definition is characteristic of relational grammar, where the essential thing for the definition of voice is so-called conversion, where an argument corresponding to the direct object in a transitive verb construction is converted into the subject in a semantically corresponding intransitive verb construction. So in the passive, object promotion takes place alongside subject demotion (Comrie 1980), or in other terms, defocusing agent and focusing patient are characteristic features for passive.

It seems that passive in Georgian is quite different from the same category presented in many languages, such as English, French, German, etc. In Georgian there are three kinds of voice forms: active, passive, and medium (or medial). Each of them has its own model of conjugation, and only passive has its own marker. Passive formants in Georgian are: suffix –*d*, prefixes *i*-, *e*- and no marker (so called non-marked passive):

i - *xaṭ* - *eb* - *a*   (active: *xaṭ* - *av* - *s*)
PASS.-draw-THEMATIC-S3   draw-THEMATIC-S3
'(it) is (being) drawn'   '(he/she) draws/is drawing'

e - *ḳer* - *eb* - *a*   (active: *u* - *ḳer* - *av* - *s*)
PASS.-sow-THEMATIC-S3   VERSION-sew-THEMATIC-S3
'(it) is (being) sewed (to him/her)' '(he/she) sews/is sewing (it to him/her)'

šen - *d* - *eb* - *a*   (active: *a* - *šen* - *eb* - *s*)
build-PASS- THEMATIC-S3   VERSION-build -THEMATIC-S3
'(it) is (being) built'   '(he/she) builds/is building (it)'

dn - *eb* - *a*   (active: *a* - *dn* - *ob* - *s*)
melt-THEMATIC-S3   VERSION-melt -THEMATIC-S3
'(it) is (being) melted'   '(he/she) melts/is melting (it)'

It is clear even from the small number of forms presented here that in spite of different markers they have a common characteristic – the ending –*eb-a* (for S3 sing. in present tense), or -*eb-i* (for S1/S2 sing. in present tense).

The forms above are enough to see that passive in Georgian is not always derived from a corresponding active by simple conversion. In the last pair of forms above the passive form seems morphologically simpler than the active one, and here it is hard even semantically to regard passive as derived from active. Differences between *i*- and *e*- prefixes are reflected in the first two pairs of forms above: forms with *i*- prefix usually are absolutive (unipersonal), while those with *e*- prefix as a rule are bipersonal:

i- xaṭ- eb- a	*e- xaṭ- eb- a*
PASS.-draw-THEMATIC-S3	PASS.-draw-THEMATIC-S3
'(it) is (being) drawn'	'(it) is (being) drawn (to him/her)'
i - ḳer - eb - a	*e - ḳer - eb - a*
PASS.-sew-THEMATIC-S3	PASS.-sew-THEMATIC-S3
'(it) is (being) sewed'	'(it) is (being) sewed (to him/her)'

As can be seen, when the tripersonal active is converted into the passive with a prefix the prefix is usually *e*.

As for the passive with a suffix, the suffix -*d* is very common for verbs derived from a noun, adjective or numeral:

tetr- i	*tetr- d- eb- a*
white-NOM	white-PASS-THEMATIC-S3
'white'	'(it) gets/is getting white'
mxec- i	*mxec- d- eb -a*
beast- NOM	beast- PASS-THEMATIC-S3
'beast'	'(he/she/it) acts like/is acting like a beast'

These forms hardly could be regarded as converted from a corresponding active (*a-tetr-eb-s* 'he/she makes it white', *a-mxec-eb-s* 'he/she makes him/

her/it like a beast'); *tetr-d-eb-a, mxec-d-eb-a* are passive only due to their morphological structure (compare *a-šen-eb-s, šen-d-eb-a* above).

Prototypically the patient of an intransitive verb is a thing (inanimate), so it means that the prototypical subject of passive is inanimate too. However, in some cases, when the subject of the passive form is animate, the semantics of passive gets closer to active forms:

simartle	*i-*	*mal-*	*eb-*	*a*	*monadire*	*i-*	*mal-*	*eb-*	*a*
truth	PASS-hide-THEMATIC-S3				hunter	PASS-hide-THEMATIC-S3			
'(the) truth is hidden'					'a hunter hides'				

The passive forms presented here make it clear that their semantics often moves away from the usual semantics of passive forms, and they are only called passive because they share morphological structure with the definitely passive forms. From this point of view, and much more from the point of relations between active and passive, so-called unmarked passive forms are quite interesting, as was mentioned above. Here are some more examples:

tb-	*eb-*	*a*	(active: *a-*		*tb-*	*ob-*	*s*)
warm-THEMATIC-S3			VERSION-warm-THEMATIC-S3				
'(he/she/it) gets warm'			'(he/she/it) warms (him/her/it)'				

kr-	*eb-*	*a*	(active: *a-*		*kr-*	*ob-*	*s*)
disappear- THEMATIC-S3			VERSION-disappear-THEMATIC-S3				
'(he/she/it) disappears'			'(he/she) makes (it) disappear'				

We cannot say that the subject of these forms is fully affected; it is affected to some degree, but it is active as well to some degree. Semantically these forms are between prototypical passive and prototypical active in the semantic space of verb; the Georgian language mapped them on the morphological level close to the passive forms.

We would like to mention additionally the semantic diversity of so-called passive forms, and divide them into main semantic groups:

1. Passive of potentials – some forms of passive express the possibility of a corresponding action. Possibility here means whether the action is acceptable, allowed, forbidden, etc. As a rule, negative potentials are frequent, but positive ones are quite usual too:

zogi	*soḳo*	*ičmeva*	– 'some mushrooms are edible'
some	mushroom	passive, root	
		čm-/čam 'eat'	

aḳ	*ar*	*icxovreba*	– 'it is impossible to live here'
here	negative	passive, root	
	particle	*cxovr-* 'live'	

ar	*gatetrdeba*	*qorani*	– 'it is impossible to whiten a raven'
negative	passive, root	a raven	
particle	*tetr-* 'white'		

mas	*daežereba*	– 'him you may trust'
he (dat.	passive, root	
case)	*žer-* 'trust'	

2. Passive of consideration – some forms of passive express how the subject perceives the object of a corresponding verb. Usually these forms are bipersonal with the prefix *e-* as a passive marker, and they are derived from a noun or adjective:

mas	*me*	*vepaṭaravebi*	– 'he considers me to be small'
he (dat.	I	passive, root	
case)		*paṭara* 'small, little'	

mas	*es*	*čanta*	*emžimeba*	– 'he considers this bag to be heavy'/
he (dat.	this	bag	passive, root	'this bag seems heavy to him'
case)			*mžime* 'heavy'	

3   Passive of mood – some forms of passive express the mood of the
subject in carrying out the action denoted by the verb. These forms
are bipersonal with the prefix *e-* as a passive marker; most of them are
derived from a noun:

memɣereba   *da*   *vmɣeri*   – 'I am in the mood for singing and
I am in the   and I am singing   'I am singing'
mood for singing

sul   *ar*   *mecineba*   – 'I am not in the mood for laughing at all'
at all   negative I am in the mood for laughing
         particle

neṭa   *ra*   *melekseba*   – 'I wonder why I am in the mood for poems'
particle   what I am in the
of interest   mood for poems

There is a special group of passive forms (so-called deponents), which
despite their morphological structure have active meaning:

peṭre   *imukreba*   – 'Peter threatens'
Peter   threatens
es   *ʒaɣli*   *ar*   *iḳbineba*   – 'this dog doesn't bite'
this dog   negative bites
          particle

After our description it is clear why the passive in Georgian is called a
morphological passive. It has been shown that passive forms cover a wide
range of semantic diversity, and the only semantic property that is common
to all of them is, according to Shibatani's approach (Shibatani 1985), agent
backgrounding. And here arises a question: Is it enough reason to call all
those forms passive? In the light of Beedham's method of exceptions and

their correlations[1] (Beedham 2005) it is clear that the answer is negative. But here we have to note that there is the other type of passive in Georgian, the so-called stative passive, opposed to the forms looked at above, which are called dynamic passive. To solve the problems of the voice category in Georgian we have to study the forms of the stative passive, and the method of exceptions and their correlations offers great promise here.

Bibliography

Beedham, Christopher. 2005. *Language and Meaning*. Amsterdam: Benjamins.

Comrie, Bernard. 1980. Agreement, Animacy, and Voice. *Wege zur Universalienforschung: Sprachwissenschaftliche Beiträge zum 60. Geburtstag von Hansjakob Seiler*, ed. by Gunter Brettschneider and Christian Lehmann, 229–34. Tübingen: Narr.

Haspelmath, Martin. 1990. The grammaticalization of passive morphology. *Studies in Language* 14.25–72.

Jorbenadze, Bessarion. 1975. *Zmnis gvaris pormata c̣armoebisa da punckiis sak̇itxebi kartulši* [The issues of the derivation and function of the voice forms of the verb in Georgian]. Tbilisi: Tbilisi University Press.

Langacker, Ronald W., and Pamela Munro. 1975. Passives and their meaning. *Language* 51.789–830.

Perlmutter, David M. 1978. Impersonal passive and the unaccusative hypothesis. *Berkeley Linguistics Society* 4.157–89.

Perlmutter, David M., and Paul M. Postal. 1977. Towards a universal characterization of passivization. *Berkeley Linguistics Society* 3.394–417.

Shanidze, Akaki. 1953. *Kartuli gramatikis sapudzvlebi* [Fundamentals of Georgian Grammar]. Tbilisi: Tbilisi University Press.

Shibatani, Masayoshi. 1985. Passive and related constructions: A prototype analysis. *Language* 61.821–48.

---

1   Formerly known as the method of lexical exceptions.

Discussion (Extract)

BEEDHAM: I think it's important for any of us to make clear what we mean when we speak of 'passive'. Do we mean by passive 'any sentence in which the subject is patient' (Halliday 1976: 161–2 calls such sentences 'receptive')? Or do we mean 'in English *be* + V-*ed*'? etc., etc. From what you have told us about what is called in grammars of Georgian 'passive' it is clear, and you have made it clear, that the term 'passive' applied to Georgian involves far more than what is usually meant by passive in other languages. The broadest definition of passive I had encountered before hearing your paper was one which defines passive as 'any sentence in which the subject is patient', and this is an incredibly broad, semantic notion of passive which is so all-encompassing that it is useless. The notion of passive you have given us today is also broad, but in a different way. Moreover, you have given us a formal definition of passive as your starting point, viz. the prefixes *e*- and *i*-, the suffix -*d*, the zero marker, and the endings –*eb-a* and –*eb-i*, which I applaud. However, having started with that starting point the range of meanings which those forms cover is remarkable, as you have said, especially when you get to 'passive of mood' and 'passive of opinion'. I agree with you entirely that it hardly seems correct to call this huge diversity of meanings 'passive'.

SOSELIA: Yes. One of the things we want to look at it in more detail is the frequency of the passive. My impression is that in Georgian the passive appears well over 50 per cent of the time.

BEEDHAM: That is a very important statistic. In English for most text types the occurrence of the passive is something like 5 per cent, if I remember rightly (it is about 30 per cent for some science texts, but that is very much register-specific).

As you know, I have claimed that the Auxiliary + Participle passive in English, German and Russian means 'action + state' and is an aspect of the verb, not a voice of the verb. The meaning 'action + state' is very much tied to the forms auxiliary and participle, and since I see no indication of auxiliaries and participles in the Georgian passive I would not expect the meaning 'action + state' to be found there. Warwick Danks and I have been discussing the same issue for Arabic. The construction in Arabic which is called 'passive' is also formed by the addition of a morpheme to a word – the vowels *u* and *i* – it is not formed with an auxiliary and a participle, and I would expect the same thing there, i.e. I would not expect it to mean 'action + state'. I was therefore quite surprised when Warwick Danks told me that there are Arabic grammarians who believe that the Arabic passive does express a state, e.g. Hallman 2002. On the other hand, a few months ago I heard a paper by Aleksander Wereszczynski[2] in which he acknowledged the claim that the Arabic passive expresses a state but disagreed with that claim. Since I do not know Arabic or Georgian it is impossible for me to be certain or to produce internal evidence (i.e. evidence internal to Arabic or Georgian) one way or the other, but I can say for certain that as regards a similar situation in a language I do know, viz. Russian, the Russian reflexive passive with *–sja* '-self' (called 'passive' because the subject is patient) definitely does not express a state. How do things look with the Georgian passive to you, do people think it expresses a state?

SOSELIA: All the forms considered here are so-called dynamic passives. As the term itself says, they do not express a state. Those forms are called passive only due to their morphological structure, which is characteristic for the verb forms in the passive constructions, i.e. for the constructions that are derived from transitive active voice constructions by conversion, when the direct object of the active voice construction (semantically usually patient) is converted into subject, and the subject of the active voice construction (semantically usually agent) is converted into the so-called simple object. So those forms are passive only morphologically. But beside those forms there are some forms in Georgian called static passives. They

---

2   Linguistic Relativity and Resultative, paper presented at the Second International Conference of the *Association Française de Linguistique Cognitive*, Université Lille 3, Lille, France 10–12 May 2007.

really expresses a state, and in our opinion they will meet your approach. Now I can see that for the next time we have to analyse those forms to solve the problem of voice in Georgian.

References to Discussion

Halliday, M.A.K. 1976. *System and function in language*. Selected papers. Ed. by G.R. Kress. London: Oxford University Press.

Hallman, Peter. 2002. Passive in English and Arabic. In Sabrina Bendjaballah et al. (eds), *Morphology 2000*, Amsterdam: Benjamins.

ETHER SOSELIA

5 On the Specification of Basic Colour Terms in Georgian

ABSTRACT

The main goal of the paper is to define the type of Georgian colour term system. Firstly, in accordance with Berlin and Kay's theory, the basic colour terms of Georgian have to be established. There are a lot of colour terms in Georgian denoting different hues. The criterion of basicness makes it possible to choose basic terms from this diversity.

It has been found that among Georgian colour terms the following ones meet the four main points of the criterion of basicness: *tetri* – WHITE, *šavi* – BLACK, *c'iteli* – RED, *q'viteli* – YELLOW, *mc'vane* – GREEN, *lurži* – BLUE, *ruxi* – GREY. The fourth, the last point of basicness, says that basic colour terms have to be salient. The best way to check this point is the list test, which was carried out on Georgian data with 38 participants taking part in it.

According to the results of the list test it was shown that the first six terms are salient enough and so they are basic, but as for the term *ruxi* 'grey', it is not salient, and therefore it is excluded from being basic. However, it appears that *q'avisperi* 'brown' meets the same point of the main criterion of basicness, and despite its morphological structure, which is not simple, we came to the conclusion that *q'avisperi* 'brown' has to be regarded as a basic colour term. The basicness of *q'avisperi* is supported by the universal model of colour categorization, which implies that the seventh basic colour term in the colour term system is the one denoting the category BROWN.

Ever since 1969, when Berlin and Kay's theory on colour term systems was published, linguists have more actively paid attention to colour term systems in the world's languages. According to Berlin and Kay's theory (Berlin and Kay 1969), the type of colour term system is defined by the number of basic colour terms in a given language. Why are basic colour terms so important? They are the main structural units in the organization of a colour term system, basic colour terms reflect how colour space is categorized in a particular language.[1]

Berlin and Kay's theory is based on basic colour terms and the authors establish criteria consisting of four main and four additional points to identify basic colour terms (see also Mervis and Roth 1981, Kay and McDaniel 1978). The main points are: 1) basic colour terms are monolexemic, i.e. the meaning of any basic colour term cannot be derived from the meanings of its parts; 2) there is not semantic subordination between basic colour terms, i.e. the meaning of any basic colour term is not contained by the meaning of any other colour term; 3) basic colour terms have an unrestricted set of referents; 4) basic colour terms are psychologically salient. The additional points are: 1) the distributional power of a basic term is the same as that of the already established basic colour terms; 2) the basicness of a term is questionable if it is the name of a thing, or hints at a thing whose colour is encoded by it; 3) loan words are probably not basic; 4) morphological complexity is probably characteristic of non-basic terms.

Berlin and Kay's theory is called a *Universal Model of Colour Categorization*, and the main idea here is that basic colour categories are regarded as universal ones. Their universality means the universality of their foci, and each of them represents the best sample of the corresponding basic colour term.

After the considerable quantity of linguistic data had been analysed Berlin and Kay established 11 universal basic colour categories, i.e. 11 universal foci were defined, and they are the places in the colour spectrum where the best samples of corresponding basic colour categories of English are found: BLACK, WHITE, RED, YELLOW, GREEN, BLUE, BROWN, ORANGE, PURPLE, PINK, and GREY. The foci were defined as primary designates of universal semantic categories. In order to tell apart colour categories and corresponding terms, the categories are written in capital letters, e.g. WHITE is a category, while *white* is a term.

---

1   This is a slightly amended version of a paper which first appeared in the *Bulletin of the Georgian National Academy of Sciences*, vol. 2, no. 1, 2008.

Besides the universality of basic colour terms Berlin and Kay established the universal regularity of colour categorization, which at first had been felt intuitively, but after various linguistic data had been studied the following universals were established:

1. In every language there are basic colour terms for BLACK and WHITE.
2. If there are three basic colour terms, then there is a basic colour term for RED in this language.
3. If there are four basic colour terms, then there is a basic colour term for either YELLOW or GREEN.
4. If there are five basic colour terms, then there are basic colour terms for both YELLOW and GREEN in this language.
5. If there are six basic colour terms, then there is a basic colour term for BLUE in this language.
6. If there are seven basic colour terms, then there is a basic colour term for BROWN in this language.
7. If there are eight or more basic colour terms, then there are basic colour terms for PURPLE, PINK, ORANGE, GREY, or for some other combinations of them in this language.

In order to define the type of the Georgian colour term system we had to establish basic colour terms. There are a lot of colour terms in Georgian, denoting different hues. Georgian data was gathered from the Georgian Explanatory Dictionary in 8 volumes (*Kartuli Enis Ganmartebiti Leksikoni* 1950–1964). The criterion of basicness makes it possible to choose basic ones from this range.

As was mentioned above, the criterion of basicness contains four main points. According to the first point (basic colour terms are monolexemic), the greater part of colour terms are excluded from the above-mentioned range as being non-basic. They are composites with so-called equal parts:

šav-tetri ('black and white')[2]
tetr-c'iteli ('reddish-whitish') and some others like them.

Some other composites are excluded as well, in which the components
are colour terms, but one of them (or both) is like English terms with the
ending *-ish*:

molurǯo-šavi ('bluish-black')
moc'italo-q'viteli ('reddish-yellow')
movardispro-moq'vitalo ('pinkish-yellowish')
motero-monacrispro ('light grey') and some others like them.

The same first point of the criteria excludes terms which are composites as well, but the second component in them is the word *peri* ('colour'),
and the first one is a genitive case form of a noun denoting a plant, fruit,
flower, animal, some mineral, etc. Terms like these are widely present in
the Georgian Explanatory Dictionary:

agurisperi ('colour of brick – yellowish red'),
alisperi ('colour of flame – bright light red'),
gišrisperi ('as black as gagate – very black'), etc.

According to the second point (there is not semantic subordination between basic colour terms), all colour terms with derived stems are
excluded as being non-basic. This kind of colour term is very common in
Georgian. It contains: terms with the suffixes *-ovan*, *-ian*, denoting 'having
s.th.' (*zurmuxt'ovani* – 'having the colour of emerald', *kup'riani* – *'having
the colour of tar'*, ...); terms derived by the circumfix *mo- -o* (*moc'italo* –
'reddish', *moq'vitalo* – 'yellowish', *mošavo* – 'blackish', ...); terms derived by
the circumfix *c'a- -o* (*c'atetro* – 'whitish', *c'amc'vano* – 'greenish', ...).

---

2   Translations here and below are given according to the above-mentioned Georgian
     Dictionary.

After from the first criterion a great number of colour terms have been excluded as being non-basic, the second criterion excludes terms like *bordo* ('colour of comel, dark red'). It is defined by the term *c'iteli* – 'red', but not vice versa, *c'iteli* is never defined by the term *bordo*.

According to the third criterion (basic colour terms have an unrestricted set of referents), the following terms and ones like them are excluded as being non-basic:

talxi – 'black, dark colour of clothes'
kera – 'light yellow, colour of honey, colour of straw (for hair)', etc.

As for the fourth criterion (basic colour terms are psychologically salient), a survey has been conducted, and based on the results and on our own linguistic intuition some terms like the following ones are excluded as being non-basic:

lega – 'dark grey'
mreši – '(old) colour of chestnut', etc.

Finally, it was found that among Georgian colour terms the following ones meet the four main criteria of basicness:

tetra – 'colour of snow, milk (antonym *šavi* – 'black');
šavi – 'the darkest colour, colour of coal, gagate (antonym – *tetri* 'white')';
c'iteli – 'colour of blood, garnet';
q'viteli – 'one of the main seven colours, between orange and yellow in the colour spectrum; golden or amber-coloured';
mc'vane – 'colour of fresh grass, a leaf and so on'; it occupies fourth place in an ordered list of the seven simple colours of the spectrum (red, orange, yellow, green, sky-blue, blue, violet);
lurži – 'one of the main colours of the spectrum, – dark sky-blue';
ruxi – 'black mixed with white, dark grey'.

At a glance the first six terms from the above-mentioned ones certainly seem basic, and therefore they need not to be checked by the additional criteria. Basicness only of the seventh term (*ruxi*) appears doubtful. It could be regarded as a lexical exception because according to Berlin and Kay's universal theory, the categorization of GREY takes place only after the categorization of BROWN. However, the term denoting BROWN is non-basic in Georgian as its morphological structure is not simple; moreover, it contains a root denoting a thing whose colour is encoded by the whole word. This term is *q'avisperi*, the word-for-word translation of which is 'colour of coffee':

q'av-is-per-i
coffee-GEN-colour-NOM

Thus, we need to check the basicness of *ruxi* with regard to the fourth point of the main criteria, i.e. we have to check how salient the given term is. The best way to do this is to carry out a list test, but for a start we would like to emphasize that the term *ruxi* meets all four points of the additional criteria.

So it seems necessary to carry out a list test (Frumkina 1984, Hardin and Maffi (eds) 1997) in order to define clearly the basicness of the term *ruxi*. Moreover, the results of the list test will give more evidence on the basicness of the other six terms.

What is a list test? The participants in the test have to write down all the colour terms (words denoting colour) of a language, and they are given from 3 to 5 minutes to do it. As a rule, salient terms are placed among the first ten ones in the list. All participants in our test were Georgian, there were 38 participants of different age, sex and profession. Usually, people whose professional knowledge is somehow connected with colour do not participate in this kind of test, although two painters, a man and a woman, were included among the participants. In my opinion their attitude to the question seems interesting and they could not affect greatly the results of the test. Before the test started we asked the participants: do you know what a colour term is? – And we named some terms, basic and non-basic ones. After that we spoke to them (about their profession, job, etc.) as we wanted them to forget the terms we had cited.

The goal of the test was to find out whether a term was equally salient for the informants, to define the place of a term in the list, and then based on those characteristics to draw conclusions about the basicness of a term.

There were 38 participants and in total 894 terms were named (including repeated terms). The number of different terms is 112. The average number of terms per informant is 23–24 (to be precise – 23.53). The maximum number of terms named by an informant is 37, the minimum number is 11. It is interesting to note that those data come from the painters: 37 from the woman, 11 from the man. And it is even more interesting that the man added terms for BLACK and WHITE at the very last moment, after much thinking with the following words: OK, I will put them, however, I think that they are not colour terms. We can understand the painter's comment: BLACK and WHITE present achromatic hues and only chromatic ones are considered as real colours. The results of the test are presented in the tables below. Table 5.1 contains 15 terms (it is an extract from the whole table, which contains 43 different terms, but these 15 are quite enough to discuss the results).

Table 5.1. Results of list test: Frequency of terms

No	Colour term	Frequency
1	*c'iteli* 'red'	38
2	*mc'vane* 'green'	38
3	*lurǯi* 'blue'	38
4	*q'avisperi* 'brown'	38
5	*q'viteli* 'yellow'	37
6	*tetri* 'white'	37
7	*šavi* 'black'	36
8	*cisperi* 'light blue, sky-blue'	36

No	Colour term	Frequency
9	*nacrisperi* 'grey'	36
10	*vardisperi* 'pink'	31
11	*narinǯisperi* 'orange'	31
12	*st'apilosperi* 'colour of carrot'	24
13	*iasamnisperi* 'lilac'	21
14	*okrosperi* 'golden'	21
15	*vercxlisperi* 'silver'	19

The tables contain almost all the terms named by the informants (only the terms named by less than five informants are not included). The terms in Table 5.1 are ordered according to the number of their occurrences (frequency) in the lists. The following data are drawn from Table 5.1:

(i)   Frequency reduces evenly from 38 to 36 in the first part of the table: the first four terms (*c'iteli* 'red', *mc'vane* 'green', *lurǯi* 'blue', *q'avisperi* 'brown') occur 38 times; two terms (*q'viteli* 'yellow', *tetri* 'white') occur 37 times; three terms (*šavi* 'black', *cisperi* 'sky-blue', *nacrisperi* 'grey') occur 36 times.

(ii)   After the first nine terms there is a jump in the frequency: from 36 to 31 (two terms, *vardisperi* 'pink' and *narinǯisperi* 'orange', occur 31 times), and then one more jump again – from 31 to 24 (*st'apilosperi* 'colour of carrot' occurs 24 times).

According to the jumps in frequency terms in the table are divided into four groups: group I presumably consists of basic colour terms, group II – of non-basic colour terms, but close to basic ones, groups III–IV – of evidently non-basic colour terms.

We are mostly interested in group I. The above-mentioned six terms defined as being basic are in this group, and in addition it contains the terms: *q'avisperi* 'brown', *cisperi* 'sky-blue', *nacrisperi* 'grey'. We would like to mention that *q'avisperi* 'brown' is the very non-basic term among those three that occurs in the lists of all 38 informants; *cisperi* 'sky-blue' and *nac-risperi* 'grey' are the last terms in the group.

We can define basicness of colour terms more accurately according to the second characteristic of the test – an average place number in the list, which is reflected in Table 5.2. And again, only a part (the first 15 terms) of the table is presented here.

Table 5.2 Results of list test: Average place in the list

No	Colour term	Average place number
1	*c'iteli* 'red'	3.32
2	*q'viteli* 'yellow'	3.89
3	*šavi* 'black'	4.22
4	*tetri* 'white'	4.84
5	*mc'vane* 'green'	5.03
6	*lurǯi* 'blue'	5.05
7	*cisperi* 'sky-blue'	8.22
8	*q'avisperi* 'brown'	9.58
9	*vardisperi* 'pink'	10.87
10	*narinǯisperi* 'orange'	11.42
11	*iasamnisperi* 'lilac'	11.87
12	*nacrisperi* 'grey'	12.39
13	*iisperi* 'violet coloured'	12.73
14	*mec'amuli* 'dark red, purple'	12.80
15	*ruxi* 'grey'	13.28

An average place number is calculated in the following way: n stands for the place number of a certain term in a corresponding list. As the maximum number of terms in a list is 37, $n = 1, 2, 3, …, 37$; k_n stands for the occurrence number of a corresponding term at the nth place in the lists; m stands for an average place number, and $m = \Sigma n k_n : \Sigma k_n$. For example, if a certain term occurs once at the first place in the lists, 3 times at the second place, and 5 times at the third place, then $m = (1 \cdot 1 + 2 \cdot 3 + 3 \cdot 5) : (1+2+3)$ $= 22 : 9 = 2.4$.

There are two groups of colour terms in Table 5.2. The first group consists of the first six terms (*c'iteli* 'red', *q'viteli* 'yellow', *šavi* 'black', *tetri* 'white', *mc'vane* 'green', *lurǯi* 'blue'), where m increases evenly from 3.32 to 5.05.

After the first six terms there is a jump between the values of m, and then m increases more or less evenly. All the remaining terms belong to the second group. The first two terms in the second group (*cisperi* 'sky-blue', *q'avisperi* 'brown') are specific: they have average place numbers 8.22 and 9.58 correspondingly, and the difference between the values is equal to 1.36, while in the other part of the table the difference is less than 1.

What about *ruxi* 'grey', according to the two tables? In Table 5.1 *ruxi* 'grey' occupies 32nd place, it was named by 7 informants, and in Table 5.2 its average place number is 13.28. Thus we can conclude that *ruxi* 'grey' is not a basic colour term.

The basicness of certain colour terms is attested and some interesting information is given in Table 5.3, which actually reflects to what extent the informants were unanimous in placing certain terms in the first part of the list. The first column of the table shows the place number of a term in the list, in the second column there are terms occurring at the corresponding places, and the third column shows a percentage value, more exactly, what percentage of informants named a certain term at a corresponding place.

Table 5.3. Results of list test: Percentage score within a place number

Place number	Colour term	Percentage
I	*q'viteli* 'yellow'	39.45%
	tetri 'white'	36.82%
	šavi 'black'	18.41%

Place number	Colour term	Percentage
II	*q'viteli* 'yellow'	31.56%
	šavi 'black'	21.04%
	tetri 'white'	15.98%
III	*c'iteli* 'red'	21.04%
	mc'vane 'green'	21.04%
	šavi 'black'	18.41%
	lurǯi 'blue'	15.98%
	q'viteli 'yellow'	13.35%
	tetri 'white'	10.72%
IV	*q'viteli* 'yellow'	26.30%
	lurǯi 'blue'	23.67%
	mc'vane 'green'	15.98%
	narinǯisperi 'orange'	7.89%
	c'iteli 'red'	7.89%
V	*mc'vane* 'green'	28.93%
	cisperi 'sky-blue'	15.98%
	lurǯi 'blue'	13.35%
VI	*lurǯi* 'blue'	26.30%
	mc'vane 'green'	26.30%
	q'avisperi 'brown'	10.72%
VII	*q'avisperi* 'brown'	21.04%
	narinǯisperi 'orange'	13.35%

The data of Table 5.3 confirm the basicness of the terms *c'iteli* 'red', *q'viteli* 'yellow', *šavi* 'black', *tetri* 'white', *mc'vane* 'green', *lurǯi* 'blue'. The informants are almost unanimous in putting the terms in places I–III. It is interesting that *narinǯisperi* 'orange' appears in sixth or seventh place, *cisperi* 'sky-blue' is presented in fifth place, and *q'avisperi* 'brown' appears in sixth or seventh place. The informants are relatively more unanimous in naming *q'avisperi* 'brown' in seventh place (21.04 per cent). According to the percentage values the following terms are: *cisperi* 'sky-blue' in fifth place (15.98 per cent), and *narinǯisperi* 'orange' in seventh place (13.35 per cent). Thus according to Table 5.3, *q'avisperi* 'brown' is closer to the basic colour terms than any other one is.

Finally, according to the results of the list test it was shown that the basic colour terms of Georgian are: *tetri* WHITE, *šavi* BLACK, *c'iteli* RED, *q'viteli* YELLOW, *mc'vane* GREEN, *lurǯi* BLUE. The term *ruxi* 'grey' does not meet point 4 of the main criteria of basicness and so is excluded from being basic. However, it appears that *q'avisperi* 'brown' meets the same point of the main criteria of basicness, and we have to clarify whether the term is basic or not.

At a glance, the main obstacle for *q'avisperi* being considered basic is its morphological structure: the term is not monolexemic; furthermore, the term contains the name of a thing whose colour is encoded by the whole word. So the term seems to be non-basic. But if we look at basic colour terms in English (according to Berlin and Kay they are: *black, white, red, yellow, green, blue, brown, grey, purple, pink, orange*), and pay attention to the last two terms, we can see that they are the names of a thing whose colours are encoded, but as they are monolexemic and they meet the remaining three points of the main criteria of basicness, an additional criterion does not need to be applied. However, the monolexemic structure of English terms is due to the general morphological structure of English, where even non-basic terms are monolexemic, as e.g. the term *silver* is. The corresponding term in Georgian is *vercxlisperi*, the word-for-word translation of which is 'colour of silver', and the term has the same structure as *q'avisperi* does. So the complex morphological structure of the Georgian term is only due to the general morphological structure of Georgian, and it must be regarded as a basic colour term just like the English terms *pink* and *orange*. The basicness of *q'avisperi* is supported by the universal model of colour categorization, which implies that the seventh basic colour term in the colour term system is the term denoting the category BROWN.

Thus, a lexical exception found in the Georgian colour term system led us to check the basicness of the terms more carefully, and the conclusion of our research is that the Georgian colour term system is that of the sixth stage having the following basic colour terms: *tetri* WHITE, *šavi* BLACK, *c'iteli* RED, *q'viteli* YELLOW, *mc'vane* GREEN, *lurži* BLUE, *q'avisperi* BROWN.

Bibliography

Berlin, Brent, and Paul Kay. 1969. *Basic color terms: their universality and evolution*. Berkeley and Los Angeles: University of California Press.

Frumkina, Reveka M. 1984. *Tsvet, smysl, skhodstvo: aspekty psikholingvisticheskogo analiza* [Colour, meaning, similarity: aspects of psycholinguistic analysis]. Moscow: Nauka.

Hardin, Clyde L, and Luisa Maffi (eds). 1997. *Color categories in thought and language*. Cambridge: Cambridge University Press.

Kartuli Enis Ganmartebiti Leksikoni [Explanatory Dictionary of the Georgian Language]. 1950–1964. 8 vols. Tbilisi: Georgian Academy of Sciences.

Kay, Paul, and Chad K. McDaniel. 1978. The linguistic significance of the meanings of basic color terms. *Language* 54.610–46.

Mervis, Carolyn B., and Emilie M. Roth. 1981. The internal structure of basic and non-basic color categories. *Language* 57.384–405.

MARINA JIKIA

6   On Compounds in Georgian of the Type *cxenip'aria* 'horse stealer'

ABSTRACT

In contemporary Georgian there are compounds of the type noun + verbal stem + *-ia* (suffix). Different specialists interpret these forms in different ways: the second component, i.e. the verbal stem, semantically approximates to the active participle; the second component is represented by the imperative; the direct object is expressed by the noun, and the second component is a participle which is based on the aorist and has lost its prefix; it consists of a participle with a direct object and an infinitive with the suffix *-a*; the verbal components of these forms are based on the stems of infinitives – they express the 'possession' of the action denoted by the infinitives; the verbal components function as participles, confirmed by the existence of the parallel forms as well, although these forms differ in stylistic nuances. The forms with *-ia* express a state and denote some property as the result of subsequent reinterpretation. The case of the nominal components of these compounds is also differently interpreted – nominative, genitive, and adverbial cases are often mentioned, although the genitive is considered more acceptable.

In our opinion these forms are extended morphosyntaxemes, which seem to be equivalent to compressed sentences. It is the model of the simple non-expanded sentence in which the agent is expressed by the suffix *-ia* and the whole compound represents an agent. Predicate is the verbal constituent, which is manifested by the verbal root without any affixes, and the direct object is expressed by the noun. As for the case of the object, generally it is genitive, implying that it agrees with the infinitive. The dative is obligatory when the nouns with elidable vocal ending do not elide their final vocal (dropping of the dative suffix seems quite natural). In such cases we regard the predicative constituent as the finite form of the present tense. The direct object is in the nominative case when the verbal component is presented by the finite form in the aorist tense. The finite forms corroborate the hypothesis of sentence-compression.

In contemporary Georgian there are compounds of the type noun + verbal stem +*-ia* (suffix). These compound units are of different types going by their content and can be semantically grouped as follows:

Plant names:
k'at'ap'aria 'cat-stealer', *namik'repia* 'dew-collector', *perič'amia* 'colour-eater',
pesvič'amia 'root-eater', *c'q'alik'repia* 'water-collector', etc.

Insect names:
bec'vič'amia 'fur-eater', *teslič'amia* 'seed-eater', *k'vercxič'amia* 'egg-eater',
k'ok'rič'amia 'bud-eater', *lešič'amia* 'carrion-eater', *marcvlič'amia* 'kernel-eater',
nemsip'aria 'needle-stealer', *nemsiq'lapia* 'needle-swallower', *tq'avič'amia*
'leather-eater', *potlič'amia* 'leaf-eater', *kerkič'amia* 'crust-eater', *cilač'amia*
'white-eater', etc.

Names of birds:
bat'knič'amia 'lamb-eater', *baq'aq'iq'lap'ia* 'frog-swallower', *baq'aq'ič'amia*
'frog-eater', *gveliq'lapia* 'snake-swallower', *tavidrek'ia* 'head-bower', *tevzip'aria*
'fish-stealer', *tevziq'lapia* 'fish-swallower', *tvalč'q'etia* 'eye-starer', *lamiq'lapia*
'silt-swallower', etc.

Name of fish:
kariq'lapia 'wind-swallower' (pike)

Name of animal:
č'ianč'velač'amia 'ant-eater'

Toponyms:
cxvarič'amia 'sheep-eater'
t'ašikvria 'applauder', etc.

Some units with the *-ia* ending which are loan-translations (calques) from
Russian were found in a dictionary of technical terms:

    k'auč'xvet'ia < *sk'rebok'-k'rjučok* 'scraper-hook'
    k'irduɣia < *izvest'-k'ipel'ka* 'lime-boiler'
    mic'axap'ia < *zemlečerpalk'a* 'ground-digger'
    tvitgoria < *samokat'* 'bike, scooter'
    tvitxap'ia < *samočerpalk'a* 'self-digger', etc.

The meanings of names with *-c'amia* 'eater', *-p'aria* 'stealer' and *-q'lap'ia* 'swallower' are mostly clear (although *codvic'amia* 'sin-eater' means 'grabber', *azrtq'lapia* 'swallower of ideas' means 'censor' and *xarip'aria* 'bull-stealer' is the name of a star, etc.). But the majority of these compound words with a single notion are widespread in a figurative sense: *doq'lap'ia* 'yoghurt swallower' – 'blockhead', *k'eviyec'ia* 'gum chewer' – 'who bores with long conversations', *karipant'ia* 'wind-spender' – 'thoughtless', *kvaxaršia* 'who boils the stone' – 'skinflint', *cxviribzekia* 'who throws back one's nose' – 'haughty', etc.

The meanings of components everywhere is clear and the words when they functioned as nicknames of human beings (and we should say that most of them are nicknames), they sometimes dominated over the real names of persons.

During research into Georgian anthroponyms we encountered about thirty compounds of this kind used as nicknames or stems of personal or family names. In these words the motivation of choice of nickname is clear, and as most stems of family names are based on nicknames we become witnesses to the creation of family names from real facts.

According to the development of onomastics three main cycles can be distinguished in Georgian fairy tales: 1) anonymous personages, 2) nicknames connected with the traits of personages, and 3) the onomastics of common dissemination. In fairy tales there are plenty of names we are interested in. They penetrated there from the lives of real people. For example, *c'q'aliparia* 'water-stealer' drank a lot of water, *cac'vret'ia* 'skylooker' was looking at the sky all the time, *k'vercxip'aria* 'egg-stealer' was stealing eggs from the nest of a turtle-dove, *nacarkekia* 'ash delver' delved into ashes and got the appropriate nickname.

Specialists have interpreted these forms in the following ways:

(1) the noun is in the genitive case, the second component, i.e. the verbal stem, approximates semantically to the active participle, *-ia* is a suffix (Shanidze 1955: 602–3);

(2) the noun is a direct object in the dative case; the second component is represented by the imperative, the suffix is *-a* (Osidze, 1957: 197);

(3) the direct object is expressed by the stem of the noun (in the absolutive case), and the second component is an active participle which is based on the aorist and has lost its prefix (Mrevlishvili 1957: 180);

(4) in the first part is a noun in the nominative case, and the verbal section is expressed with the finite verb; -*a* is the suffix (Ertelishvili 1959: 257);

(5) the noun is in the genitive, the verbal component as substantive is in the genitive too (with partially reduced suffix), and suffix -*a* as manifestation of auxiliary (Machavariani 2000: 149);

(6) these forms are based on the stems of infinitives. They express the subject's 'possession' of the action denoted by the infinitive (Ialamidi 1977: 158);

(7) they function as participles, confirmed by the existence of the parallel forms as well, although these forms differ in stylistic nuances (Salaridze 1978: 80).

The forms with -*ia* express a state and denote some property as a result of subsequent reinterpretation. The case of the nominal components of these compounds is also differently interpreted – absolutive, nominative, genitive and dative cases are often mentioned, although the genitive is considered more acceptable.

The forms with the -*ia* suffix are easy to distinguish from other derivatives of this polysemic affix. The model seems to be that of a participle, but the type of composition does not coincide with that of a participle. Its specificity, in our opinion, would be conditioned by the -*ia* suffix because we do not encounter it among the prefixes and suffixes which form participles. The subject of a participle of active voice is nomen agentis, a person whose main activity is mentioned. In the case of a derivative with the -*ia* suffix a subject will never say about him/herself that he/she is a *kvac'uria* 'stone sweater', which means 'stingy', or *adlibot'ia* 'who walks awkwardly in great strides', whilst no one would hesitate to say 'I am a builder' or 'I am a manager'. A trait of character in the manner of an accepted habit is noticed by someone who gives it a name, and the person who is named is characterized from a point of view not very pleasant for him/her. That habit or the one already transformed into a trait of character is noticed by a third person and given a name. We have the impression that in the material collected the trait denoted by the name may not be evident but is a nuance of his/her negative habit. So, from *adlibot'ia* 'who walks awkwardly in great strides' to *žamit'lekia* 'dish-licker' there is a range of offensiveness.

This model of composition is also evidenced in some proverbs:

dočamias do agondeboda da q'velič'amias – q'velio
'the yoghurt eater remembers yoghurt and the cheese eater – cheese';
dγisit k'evisγe č'iao, γame – sakmisk'etiao
'in daytime – gum chewer, at night – work worker', etc.

In our opinion, the compounds examined above are equivalent to a simple extended sentence. As a result of the compression of this sentence a lexical unit becomes a substantive. This compound, derived from a sentence containing a verb stem, keeps its predicative character and the traits connected to an object which are expressed by a nominal. The meaning of this compound word makes an adequate idea because of the clarity of its components, and the crucial segmentation appears as a one-notion compound. We can easily consider these words extended morphosyntaxemes which seem to be equivalent to compressed sentences.

To confirm this analysis typologically we will apply it to Russian. In Russian several main types of compound substantives can be distinguished according to the character of the stem and to the syntactic correlation of their parts. Compounds which are formed by means of the binding vowels *o* or *e* and the stem of a substantive in the first part and the root of a verb in the second, with or without a suffix, are categorized as those of the first type. They are divided into the following subtypes:

Substantives of masculine gender, mainly names of persons, devices and more rarely names of actions. The correlation of parts here may be various: the first part may have the meaning of an object of action:

k'onok'rad 'horse stealer'; *volk'odav* 'wolf strangler'; *vet'rogon* literally 'wind driver', figuratively 'empty-headed person'; *p'ylesos*

'vacuum-cleaner'; *svinopʹas* 'swine-herd', *skʹalolaz* 'rock climber', etc
(*Грамматика русского языка* 1960: 271).

Both parts can express the relations between an actor and an act made by
him/her/it. The most productive second parts of the compounds of this
subtype are verbal morphemes:

without suffixes:
-*var* – *pʹivovar* 'brewer',
-*ved* – *yazykoved* 'linguist',
-*vod* – *pčelovod* 'bee-keeper',
-*del* – *vinodel* 'wine-maker',
-*kʹopʹ* – *zemlekʹopʹ* 'navvy',
-*lov* – *pʹticelov* 'bird-catcher', etc (*Грамматика русского языка* 1960:
272).

Only the above mentioned subtype of word formation – a noun + typical
interfix *o* or *e* + root of verb – designating mostly people, is semantically
like the Georgian one. Georgian, as well as Russian, of course, has its own
rules and possibilities. For example, we do not have in Georgian so-called
interfixes, like the Russian *e* and *o* binding vowels. And the Russian inventory of affixes does not have an equivalent to the Georgian -*ia* suffix, etc.
  But this type of compound word in both languages has a common
important trait from the point of view of word formation: though the verb
stem of the compound is common for personal and non-personal para-
digms, e.g. -*var*-, -*ved*-, -*vod*-, -*del*-, -*kʹopʹ*-, -*lov*-, etc., there is no such verbal
form by itself in the language. -*kʹrad*- of *kʹonokʹrad* 'horse stealer' exists in
the form *Ja kʹradu* 'I steal', but *kʹrad* by itself does not exist. There are only
two exceptions: *kʹamenotjos* 'stonemason' – *tjos* 'was hewing' (III person
singular, past tense), and *svinopʹas* 'swine-herd' – *pʹas* 'was looking after the
herd of animals'. It is the same in Georgian: *pʹar*- (root of the verb *pʹarva* 'to
steal'), *qʹlap*- (root of the verb *qʹlapʹva* 'to swallow'), *lokʹ*- (root of the verb
lokʹva 'to lick'), *bertʹqʹ*- (root of the verb *bertʹqʹva* 'to shake out'), *tes*- (root
of the verb *tesva* 'to sow') etc., do not coincide with personal forms, except:
čam- (root of the verb *čama* 'to eat') and *kʹrep*- (root of the verb *kʹrepa* 'to

collect') coincide with the forms of the II person singular of the present tense – (*šen*) *č'am* 'you eat/you are eating' and (*šen*) *k'rep* 'you collect/you are collecting'. So in this model of word formation in Georgian, as well as in Russian, the language activates a form which is used nowhere else.

In our opinion these forms are extended morphosyntaxemes, which seem to be equivalent to compressed sentences. Actually, in Georgian it is the model of the simple non-expanded sentence, in which the agent is expressed by the suffix -*ia* (in the finite forms of the verbs in the Kartvelian languages the agent of the 3rd person is denoted by a suffix) and the whole compound represents an agent. Predicate is the verbal constituent, which is manifested by the verbal root without any affixes and the direct object is expressed by the noun. As for the case of the object, generally it is the genitive, implying that it agrees with the infinitive. The dative is obligatory when the nouns with elidable vocal ending do not elide their final vocal (dropping off the dative suffix seems quite natural). In such cases we regard the predicative constituent as the finite form of the present tense. The direct object is in the nominative case when the verbal component is presented by the finite form in the aorist tense:

> *bart'q'ič'amia* 'nestling eater' < *bart'q'i* (nom. case) *č'ama* 'he/she/it ate a nestling.'
> *baq'aq'iq'lap'ia* 'frog-gulper' < *baq'aq'i* (nom. case) *q'lap'a* 'he/she/it gulped a frog.'

The finite forms corroborate the hypothesis of sentence compression. There are over two hundred such forms in Georgian, and they are increasing in number.

Bibliography

Ertelishvili, Ph. 1959. One Type of Participle in Georgian. *Transactions of Tbilisi State University*, vol. 67.

Грамматика русского языка. Т.I. Фонетика и морфология. 1960. Издательство Академии Наук СССР. Москва.

Ialamidi, G. 1977. Georgian in the Ateni Region. *Pedagogics and Methods*. Tbilisi.

Machavariani, N. 2000. On the Origin of Words like *kvercxip'aria* 'egg stealer'. *Phonetics and the norm*. Tbilisi.

Mrevlishvili, M. 1957. Compound Words in Georgian. *Transactions of Tbilisi State University*, vol. 67.

Osidze, Ek. 1957. Formation of the Participle in Georgian. *Transactions of Tbilisi State University*, vol. 67.

Salaridze, T. 1978. *Algetis xeobis kartluri* [The Kartlian dialect of the Algeti Valley]. Tbilisi: Mecniereba.

Shanidze, Ak. 1955. *Kartuli gramat'ik'is sapudzvlebi*, I: *morfologia* [Fundamentals of Georgian Grammar, I: Morphology]. Tbilisi University.

Discussion (Extract)

BEEDHAM: How old are the compound words you have spoken about?

JIKIA: Historically Georgian is divided into Old Georgian, from the fifth century to the end of the eleventh century, Middle Georgian, from the twelfth century to the beginning of the 19th century, and Modern Georgian, from the beginning of the nineteenth century to the present day. The compound words I have spoken about started to come into the language from the beginning of the nineteenth century, with the new sciences of biology and botany and the names they needed to create for their descriptions and taxonomies of plants, insects, fishes, birds, animals, etc. The compound words I have spoken about must be earlier, I think, because they are fixed as the names of folk tale characters.

BEEDHAM: Are they in the dictionary?

JIKIA: Some of them are, that is, the names of insects, plants, fish, birds, animals, some words with a figurative sense, and so on. But the nicknames aren't.

BEEDHAM: Are they humoristic, or neutral?

JIKIA: The names of the plants, insects, fish, birds, animals are mostly neutral. Some of the words are humoristic, e.g. *sharachvetia* 'road sweeper' in the meaning '(female) loafer (one's time away)'; *doklapia* 'yoghurt swallower' in the meaning 'blockhead'; *adlibot'ia* 'one who walks awkwardly with vast strides, man whose gait is awkward' (*adli* old measure of length, roughly one meter, *bot'* root of the verb 'to stride awkwardly'); *kevigechia* 'gum chewer' meaning 'one who bores with long conversations', etc. Such words have mostly a figurative sense.

RUSUDAN ASATIANI

7 A Cognitive Approach to Exceptional Ditransitive Verb Forms in Georgian

ABSTRACT

Language is a system that is defined by general models of linguistic structuring of the world. Exceptions are outside such prototypical models. They are created by specific cognitive processes developed on the basis of the peculiar restrictions, hierarchical relations, competitive and/or alignment constraints which are characteristic for the language system (LS) as a whole. We assume: the restrictions, relations or constraints are important internal features of the LS; their combinations are complex and specific; this creates an illusion of the exception being 'outside the LS'. In order to understand the logics of the exceptions it seems effective to employ a cognitive approach. We need to build clear conceptual structures for every concrete exceptional pattern. Through such an analysis it can be clarified that the exceptions are regular elements of the LS. The paper examines such a theoretical approach on the analysis of so called exceptional ditransitive verb forms in Georgian.

Introduction: The structure of the Georgian verb

Georgian verb forms represent various grammatical categories. The principle of agglutination along with inflexion builds a string of morphemes and morphology mirrors the system of very complex and complicated verb categories. Structurally a Georgian verb may incorporate the following elements:

(1) PREVERB(S)
(2) S/O AGREEMENT PREFIX (*-v-/-m-/-g-/-gv-/-h-,-s-,-o-*)
(3) VERSION VOWEL (*-a-/-i-/-u-/-e-*)

(4) ROOT
(5) PASSIVE FORMANT (*-d-*) or CAUSATIVE SUFFIX
    (*-in-/-evin-*)
(6) THEMATIC SUFFIX (*-eb-/-ob-/-av-/-am-/-op-/-i-/o*)
(7) IMPERFECT MARKER (*-d-/-od-*)
(8) TENSE/MOOD VOWEL (*-a-/-i-/-o-/-e-*)
(9) SIII AGREEMENT SUFFIX (*-s-/-a-/-o-/-en-/-an-/-n-/-nen-/-es*)
(10) PLURAL SUFFIX (*-t*)

E.g. *da* – *g* –   *a* –   *c'er* –   *in* –   *eb* –   *d* –   *e* –   *s*
     prev – OII – vers. – write – cause – them – imp. – mood – SIII

     da – *g* –   *a* –   *c'er* –   *in* –   *eb* –   *d* –   *a* –   *wt*
     prev – OII – vers. – write – cause – them – imp. – SIII – pl(O)

Although for a theoretically possible string of morphemes in the structural formula for one verb root there are maximally 10 positions (3 for
prefixes and 6 for suffixes), the verb form can consist of not more than 9
morphemes. There are some implicational and/or restrictive rules:

1. Imperfect Marker 7 implies the existence of Thematic Markers 6;
2. Plural Suffix 10 phonetically excludes the appearance of the SIII
    person suffix *-s* (9); it can co-occur only with the SIII person
    suffixes *-a* or *-o* (9);
3. The SIII person suffixes (*-a* or *-o*) phonetically exclude the appear-
    ance of Tense-Mood vowel suffixes 8.

Rules 2 and 3 can be generalized as they reflect a more universal phonetic
tendency: *No vowels or consonants clustering at morpheme boundaries.*
    Thus, the permitted combinations are either 8–10, or 9–10, and the
string 8–9–10 is excluded. All other combinations of positions are possible, and a concrete verb form is defined by the various combinations of
verb categories.

Georgian preverbs

Preverbs, which occupy first position in the structural formula of Georgian verb forms, originally indicated direction (Shanidze 1973). There are 9 simple and 7 complex preverbs. Simple preverbs (SP) show different directions of an action: *a-* 'from down to up', *ča-* 'from up to down', *ga-* 'from inside to outside', *še-* 'from outside to inside', *gada-* 'crossing some obstacles', *mi-* 'from speaker and listener', *mo-* 'to speaker and listener', *c'a-* 'from something or somebody' and *da-* 'above some space'. The simple preverb *mo-* may be added to other simple preverbs for indicating the 'hitherness'. As a result complex preverbs (CP) arise: *a+mo-* 'up to us', *ča+mo-* 'down to us', *ga+mo-* 'out to us' and so on. As *da-* denotes movement over a path without marked directionality, the combination *da+mo-* is logically excluded.[1]

Preverbs have additional functions of grammaticalization of Perfective [+Prev]: Imperfective [-Prev] aspect and Future tense [+Prev]. They often combine the root to change the overall meaning of the verb as well (compare the prepositional elements in English – *look up/back/down/ at/into* etc.).

The conceptual representation of space structuring in Georgian

Semantic and pragmatic analysis of preverbs makes clear that for the structuring of space in Georgian it is important to distinguish between Geographic Space (GS) and Communicational Space (CS). GS is structured due to the abstract relations that have concrete interpretation only

---

1   The sequence /*da+mo-*/ can be found in some frozen Participle or Masdar forms (e.g. *damo=k'id-eb-ul-i* 'dependant'), implying that it was logically possible at an earlier stage of the language, but in Modern Standard Georgian it is not productive and does not exist in verb forms.

on the basis of the Point of View (PV) of a 'teller'. The 'teller' usually coincides with the 'speaker', but this is not always the case: sometimes the 'teller' differs from the 'speaker' and the space is structured according to the teller's and not speaker's PV; e.g. 'Nino says that she is going up'. Although the place where Nino is going to could not be 'up' for the speaker, who is located geographically higher than Nino, the speaker can still structure the space according to the teller's, i.e., Nino's, point of view.

Abstract geographic relations are represented in the linguistic structures of the Georgian language by the so-called simple preverbs (SP). The relations can be described by the following conceptual structures:

a- 'from down to up'	↑
ča- 'from up to down'	↓
mi- 'from speaker/listener'	→
mo- 'to speaker/listener'	←
gada- 'overcoming, across'	⌒↗
še- 'from outside to inside'	→⊙
ga- 'from inside to outside'	⊖→
c'a- 'from something/somebody'	○→
da- 'over a path'	◡

Communicational Space (CS) is further divided into 'Ego Space' (ES) and 'Alter Space' (AS). Differences between ES and AS are represented in linguistic structures of Georgian by the formal opposition Complex Preverbs([SP + *mo*-]) : Simple Preverbs (all SP except *mo*-). The opposition distinguishes the orientation of an action according to the dichotomy: I/II person [action directed/oriented to I/II person (ES)] : III person [action directed/oriented to III person (AS)]. Thus, the adding of *mo*- changes the orientation of an action.

It is a peculiarity of the Georgian language that II person is included into ES, e.g.:

(1) *šen-tan*   *xval*   ***gamo-v-ivli***
    2.DAT-at   tomorrow   PR:FUT-S.1-come:FUT(S.1.SG)
    'I'll come to you tomorrow'

(2) *Mosk'ov-ši*   ***čamo-v-(v)al***
    Moscow[DAT]-in   PR:FUT-S.1-come:FUT(S.1.SG)
    'I'll arrive (to you) in Moscow'

The examples describe a situation where speaker's ES is definitely different from the listener's CS, yet the forms with *mo-* representing the orientation to ES are used. The examples are not exceptional ones and represent the regularity of the usages of *mo-*. Thus, we have to conclude that ES in Georgian includes II person as well.

It must be mentioned that the orientation to the space which belongs to speaker and/or listener is not always regarded by the speaker/teller as included into ES, e.g.:

(3) *saxl-ši*   *gvian*   ***mi-v-(v)ed-i***
    house[DAT]-in   late   PR:PRF-S.1-come-AOR(S.1.SG)
    'I came home late'

(4) *šen-tan,*   *mosk'ov-ši,*   ***ča-val***
    2.DAT-at   Moscow[DAT]-in   PR:FUT-S.1-come:FUT(S.1.SG)
    'I'll arrive to Moscow'

Sentence 3 reflects the following situation: The speaker, A, is referring to his or her own home and is in conversation with somebody, B, who is not at A's home; still A includes B in ES and, consequently, has to exclude A's home from ES, despite the fact that it is the speaker's, A's, own home. Compare the sentence *saxl-ši gvian* ***mo-v-(v)ed-i***, which reflects a situation where both the speaker's home and the addressee are included in ES; presumably, either they live together or the addressee is a neighbour, or the owner of the house, etc.

Sentence 4 mirrors the following situation: Speaker, A, will arrive in Moscow; A knows that the addressee, B, lives in Moscow, but A also knows that B will not be in Moscow when he or she arrives. Compare 2, which shows the speaker's presupposition that the addressee will be in Moscow when the speaker arrives or the speaker is going to visit Moscow when the addressee will be in Moscow.

These examples argue once more that in the structuring of space geographic relations and their inclusion in ES are not decisive in the interpretation of space relations: *Structuring of CS depends mainly on the speaker's attitude.*

On the basis of ES:AS opposition the dynamic conceptual model of SP can be represented by the diagram in Figure 7.1.

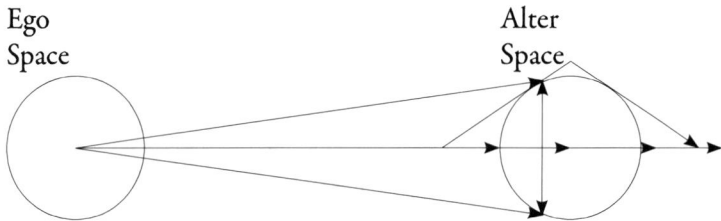

Figure 7.1 A conceptual model of simple preverbs.

Depending on the speaker's attitude, ES can be either compressed or expanded and it can include AS. This is the case when CP with *mo-* arises (see Figure 7.2).

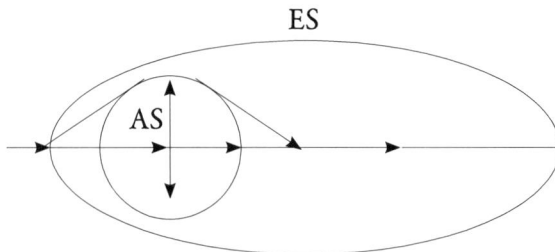

Figure 7.2. Complex preverb with *mo-*: Ego Space includes Alter Space.

ES does not always conform to the semantics of 'Proximate': 'Distal', which is an important feature for structuring of GS according to the concept of 'distance'. The 'distance', like the ES, is relative and is defined by speaker's or teller's attitude, which is different from the opposition ES:AS. Objects near to us are not obligatorily included into ES and vice versa: 'Near' does not always mean 'to us' and 'Far' does not always mean 'from us'. All logically possible cases can be represented by the following figures:

                                                      AS   ES

(5) *ak mo-vid-a* 'S/he came to us (I and/or II) here'
     here PR-come-AOR.S.3.SG

(6) *ik mo-vid-a* 'S/he came to us (I and/or II) there'   ES   AS
     there PR-come-AOR.S.3.SG

(7) *ak mi-vid-a* 'S/he came to III here'   ES   AS
     here PR-come-AOR.S.3.SG

(8) *ik mi-vid-a* 'S/he came to III there'   ES   AS
     there PR-come-AOR.S.3.SG

In Georgian all these possibilities can be realized in linguistic structures, and the most 'unexpected' situations, i.e. 6–7, can be illustrated by the sentences 9–10. The situations corresponding to the cases 6–7 are very specific, of course, and consequently sentences like 9–10 are rare as well:

(9) *ik,*   *tbilis-ši,*   *bevr-i*   *xalx-i*   *mo-di-s*
     there Tbilisi[DAT]-in many-NOM people-NOM PR-come-PRS.S.3.SG
     xolme   *mit'ing-eb-ze.*
     PTC(usually) meeting-PL[DAT]-on
     'There, in Tbilisi, a lot of people are coming to meetings.'

(10) *ak st'undent'-eb-i xšir-ad a-di-an*
      here student-PL-NOM often-ADV PR: up-go-PRS.S.3.PL
      xolme me>sam<e   sartul-ze bibliotek'a-ši.
      usually three<ORD>[DAT] floor[DAT]-on library[DAT]-in
      'Here students often go up to the third floor to the library.'

Sentence 9 corresponds to a situation where the speaker has a conversation far from Tbilisi but still considers the Tbilisi meetings as included in his or her ES. Sentence 10 gives an additional piece of information: the speaker, presumably, works (or, at least, is) in the University, because (s)he uses the adverb *ak* 'here', but does not consider the library as included in his/her ES.

In general, Georgian adverbs and pronouns which represent geographic (and not communicational) relations build tripartite oppositions. They are based on a tripartite opposition of demonstrative pronouns: *es* 'close to I person': *eg* 'close to II person': *is* 'close to III person'. The pronouns have different, suppletive forms for oblique cases: *am : mag : im*. Consequently, adverbs and pronouns mostly have a demonstrative function and distinguish the following space relations: Close to I (forms with vowel *a-*), Close to II (forms beginning with syllable *ma*), and Close to III (forms with vowel *i-*):

(11) *amdeni : magdeni : imdeni* – 'Quantity'
      aseti : maseti : iseti – 'Quality'
      amnairi : magnairi : imnairi – 'Quality' (dialectal)
      ak : mand : ik – 'Place'
      ase : mase : ise – 'Manner'
      amit'om : magit'om : imit'om – 'Reason'
      amdenad : magdenad : imdenad – 'Quantity of manner' and so on.

Semantic and pragmatic analysis of these forms make clear that the geographic feature 'distance' and not the persons' factual inclusion in CS plays an important role in their usages. (See the discussion above concerning the adverbs *ak : ik*).

The main dimensions of space structuring and their various combinations

In line with our analysis, the main dimensions for space structuring in Georgian are the following:

1. Point of view (speaker's and/or teller's);
2. Geographic space (various directions and distance dichotomy);
3. Communicational space (Ego and Alter spaces).

'Point of View', 'Ego Space' and 'Distance' are relative, while abstract relations of 'Geographic Space' are stable. The speaker's or the teller's PV are not always same (cf. section titled 'The conceptual representation of space structuring in Georgian'). Moreover, the speaker's PV is not defined according to his or her position or geographic location and it can be changed for the speaker as well. There are various possibilities: (1) PV conforms with the speaker's position (SP); (2) PV is above the SP; (3) PV is downward from the SP:

When I am on the fourth floor and my friend is going to the third floor I can say:

My friend is going up to the third floor. (3)
My friend is going down to the third floor. (2) or (1)

When I am on the fourth floor and my friend is going to the sixth floor I can say:

My friend is going up to the sixth floor. (3) or (1)
My friend is going down to the sixth floor. (2)

If during the structuring 'my friend's space' is regarded as included into ES a more complex situation arises and the meaning 'to me/you' is added. Such a situation in Georgian is represented by CP. In general, if ES is somehow included during the structuring of a space, CP always becomes relevant.

Preverbs and exceptional ditransitive verb forms in Georgian

Some ditransitive verbs like 'to give' show recipient person suppletion that is a typologically well known phenomenon for some languages. In Georgian such verbs have a specific paradigm where distribution of the preverbs *mi-* and *mo-* is the basis for the suppletion.

Polypersonal verb forms in Georgian incorporate subject markers as well as object markers. A I or II person recipient is represented by object markers. As the semantics of the verb 'to give' (*micema*) implies the meaning of direction, preverbs *mo-* or *mi-* are obligatory and their distribution is in accordance with their conceptual interpretation: *mo-* is used in cases of I/II person recipient and *mi-* in cases of III person recipient. Thus, we have an exceptional suppletive paradigm for this verb; cf. 12.

(12) *mi-v-ec*i   (I gave to him/her)
     mi-eci   (You gave to him/her)
     mi-s-c-a   (S/he gave to him/her)
     mo-m-c-a   (S/he gave to me)
     mo-g-c-a   (S/he gave to you-sg)
     mo-gv-c-a   (S/he gave to us)
     mo-g-c-a-t   (S/he gave to you-pl)

The forms *mi-m-c-a* 'S/he gave me to him/her', *mi-g-c-a* 'S/he gave you to him/her' have different glosses: I/II person markers refer here to the patient (the DO) and never to the recipient (the IO).[2]

The same suppletion according to the preverbs *mi-* and *mo-* is also characteristic for other ditransitive verbs (actually for any of them whose semantics allow differences in orientation): *mic'odeba* 'to send', *mipurtx-eba* 'to spit to', *mipereba* 'to caress', *mikiraveba* 'to hire out', *mitxoveba* 'to marry to', and so on.

---

2   /*mo=s-ca*/ was perfectly acceptable in Old Georgian, but such forms are not possible in Modern Standard Georgian.

Some such ditransitive verbs allow the form *mi-ac'oda* 'S/he gave it to smb.' as well as the form *mo-ac'oda* 'S/he gave it to smb.'. This happens when verb semantics permits the III recipient to be included in ES. But the forms *mi-m-ac'oda, mi-g-ac'oda* where -*m*-, -*g*- could be the markers of I/II person recipient are absolutely excluded.

The cognitive interpretation of semantic roles: Conceptual structures of EDV

To understand the peculiarities of such exceptional ditransitive verbs it might be helpful, first of all, to consider the conceptual structure of the semantic roles. There are various semantic features according to which the roles are defined, but none of them is the decisive one. We are proposing a comprehensive representation for them, which define all other features and helps us to understand the process of the creation of verb forms (Asatiani 2003b).

Every concept has its own space within which 'it stays with itself'. Conceptual space is usually defined according to many features. For the conceptual spaces of semantic roles the most relevant are the features which characterize the noun in relation to the action which is represented by the verb.

In the course of the action described the referents of nouns can: 1) cross space; 2) approach space; 3) stay within space. The three possibilities seem to be decisive for distinguishing between Ag, P and Ad. The Agent (as far as it is active, telic, volitional, dynamic, high in potency, etc) is the referent which crosses (its own or something/somebody else's) space. The Patient (as it is inactive, atelic, non-volitional, static, low in potency) is the referent which stays within its own space; it allows space to be crossed but never crosses space itself. The Addressee is the role which receives something, can be reached but does not allow space to be crossed. Schematically:

Ag   P   Ad

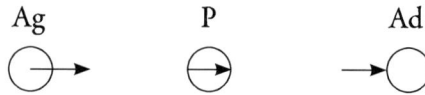

Different combinations of these features construct conceptual structures which mirror the process of the linguistic structuring of extralinguistic situations respective to concrete verb semantics. Some examples:

Ag P: *to build, to write, to paint, etc.*

Ag P Ad: *to build smth. for s.o.,*
to hand over, to do smth. for s.o., etc.

P: *to stand, to lie, to sit, etc.*

Ag: *to live, to dance, to think, etc.*

The strategy of structuring can differ: If the situation implies simple space relations between the nouns only one conceptual structure is constructed. Universally, each linguistic-cognitive system provides for the same conceptual model of structuring of simple relations, i.e. all languages map nouns onto semantic roles similarly. For example, *to build* in almost all languages is structured in the following way:

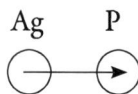

Ag   P

However, if the situation allows different interpretations then languages choose their own specific strategies for structuring. According to these various strategies languages differ in the way of structuring and provide different linguistic structures (Asatiani 2003).

The specific semantics of the ditransitive verb 'to give' (*micema*) can be represented by the following conceptual structure:

Ag   P   Ad (= Rec)

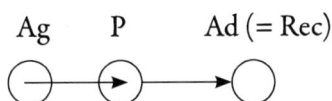

The preverbs *mo-* and *mi-*, as was mentioned above, are elements of the linguistic realization of spatial relations in Georgian, where two dimensions are relevant: 'Ego Space' and 'Alter Space'. The opposition of the preverbs *mo-* : *mi-* is the linguistic representation of the cognitive opposition ES:AS. Thus, *mo-* marks a situation where an action is directed/oriented to I/II persons (ES), whereas *mi-* is the formal representation of a situation with an action directed/oriented to the III person. According to this opposition the conceptual relations involved can be represented by the following schemes:

ES   *mi-*   AS   AS   *mo-*   ES

I and II person recipients are included in ES, while III person recipients are excluded. If we match the two conceptual structures the following complex structures arise:

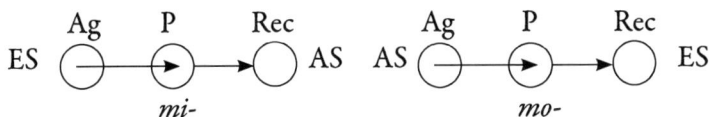

         Ag   P   Rec   Ag   P   Rec
ES   AS   AS   ES
         mi-   *mo-*

We assume that such matching reflects the complex cognitive process of the linguistic structuring of the 'to give'-type ditransitive verb concepts. It clarifies the basis of the 'exceptional', suppletive paradigms in Georgian: the linguistic structures arise in accordance with the conceptual meanings of verb and preverbs, and yield their specific paradigm absolutely logically. Thus they need no longer be qualified as being outside the language system and 'exceptional'.

Bibliography

Asatiani, R. 2003a. Semantics and Typology of Dative Subject (on the Georgian Data). *Proceedings of the 14th Amsterdam Colloquium 2003*, ed. by P. Dekker and R. van Rooy, 69–75. Amsterdam: Amsterdam University Press.
Asatiani, R. 2003b. Conceptual Representation of the Verb Form creation (on the Georgian Data). *Proceedings of the Fifth Tbilisi Symposium on LLC*, 21–9. Amsterdam: Grafisch Centrum Amsterdam.
Chanishvili, N. 2003. Structuring of Space in Georgian. *Proceedings of the Fifth Tbilisi Symposium on LLC*, 51–9. Amsterdam: Grafisch Centrum Amsterdam.
Gärdenfors, P. 2000. *Conceptual Spaces: The Geometry of Thought*. Cambridge, Mass.: MIT Press.
Givon, T. 1979. *On Understanding Grammar*. New York: Academic Press.
Shanidze, A. 1973. *Kartuli enis gramat'ik'is sapudzvlebi* [Fundamentals of the Grammar of the Georgian Language]. Tbilisi: Mecniereba.

Discussion (Extract)

BEEDHAM: You say that we need to 'build' conceptual 'structures' for every exceptional pattern, in other words, for every formal linguistic structure there will be an equivalent in the mind. But what if somebody shows that the exceptions are an artificial by-product of an incorrect analysis, as I have done for non-passivizable transitive verbs, which are exceptions in a voice based rule of passive formation but which are not exceptions in an aspect based rule of passive formation (Beedham 2005: 33–60)? Anyone who has built a 'conceptual structure' to match that set of exceptions, in the belief that the mind has a mental structure reflecting that linguistic structure, has constructed a fiction – or one might say has been sent on a wild goose chase – because the exceptions arise from an incorrect analysis. If you must pursue 'mental structures' then you could build a conceptual structure to match the aspect analysis of the passive, but I don't see the point. As linguists we pursue linguistic structures, not mental structures (Beedham 2002). Is your methodology here not a vicious circle, a self-fulfilling expectation?

ASATIANI: You are right when you say that sometimes exceptions can be an artificial by-product of an incorrect analysis. Sometimes exceptions could be the results of very complex and complicated morphophonological processes as well. Moreover, sometimes exceptions are real 'exceptions' as far as no linguistic or cognitive analysis help us to understand how and/ or why they have arisen. Any linguistic data demand very careful and clear analysis and simple, generalized answers or methodological approaches could not be realistic. Do you agree with me? What I wanted to show by my article is an attempt to make it obvious that sometimes conceptual interpretations make clear the cognitive background to some so called linguistic 'exceptions'.

References to Discussion

Beedham, Christopher. 2002. Irregularity in language: Saussure versus Chomsky versus Pinker. A review of Words and Rules, by S. Pinker. *Word* 53: 341–37.
Beedham, Christopher. 2005. *Language and Meaning: The Structural Creation of Reality*. Amsterdam: Benjamins.

МАНАНА КАРКАШАДЗЕ

8   Грузинский медиоактивный глагол

ABSTRACT

The Georgian Medioactive Verb. Manana Karkashadze, Tbilisi State University, Georgia
Georgian medioactives are intransitive, atelic verbs which express a process or action which
has no other perspective than that of continuous progression. The tense paradigms of
Georgian medioactives are usually regarded as transitive reflexive verbs, and the possessive
prefix *i-* present in the morphological structure of medioactives and transitive reflexives
is likewise regarded as a reflexive prefix. In the present article the structural-semantic features
of Georgian medioactives and transitive reflexives are defined by criteria of Diathesis
Theory. It is shown that medioactives and transitive reflexives are functionally different
linguistic units because of their different relations with lexically correlated active constructions,
and that the prefix *i-* is not a reflexive prefix.

Data from different languages show that one way to represent an atelic process in
the verb is to use a possessive marker to indicate that the process belongs to the subject.
Languages in which adjectives do not constitute an independent lexical class express
attributive meaning by means of an atelic intransitive verb. In such languages the same
constructions have sometimes predicative, sometimes attributive meaning, and only by
looking at the context is it possible to define which meaning it is. If a language expresses
an atelic process and attributive meaning by means of an intransitive verb, then the subject
is to the atelic process as the possessor is to the quality possessed. Therefore the function
of the possessive prefix *i-* in Georgian medioactives is the expression of an atelic process
as 'a thing organically possessed' by the subject.

В современном грузинском языке выделяется класс медиоактивных
глаголов. Эти непереходные глаголы выражают ателиковый (нецелевой)
процесс, не имеющий никакой перспективы, кроме перспективы
монотонной длительности.

В этот класс входят семантические эквиваленты таких русских
глаголов, как: смеяться, плавать, кричать, волноваться, прыгать, думать,

бегать, кипеть, радоваться, блестеть, хромать, царствовать и т.д. Почти треть грузинских медиоактивных глаголов изолирована – не имеет лексически соответствующих активов.

Во временных формах грузинских медиоактивов выделяется префикс i-: i-cinis "смеется", i-mxiarula "повеселилась", i-rbens "побегает" и т.д. Этот префикс функционирует также в транзитивных рефлексивах – в формах субъектной версии, выражая отношение предназначения – принадлежности: xatavs "рисует" (нейтральная версия) – i-xatavs "рисует для себя" (субъектная версия).

В грузинской лингвистической традиции парадигматические формы медиоактивов трактуются как рефлексивные (версионные) формы лексически соответствующих переходных глаголов, которые заполняют дефектную парадигму медиоактивных глаголов, т.е. как заимствованные у активов формы субъектной версии, которые в медиоактивной парадигме теряют свою транзитивность и версионную семантику, а префикс i- в медиоактивах традиционно определяется как маркер рефлексивности (субъектной версии) [Шанидзе, с. 473].

По мнению некоторых авторов версионный префикс i- в медиоактивах марркирует семантику совершенного вида (аспекта) [Меликишвили, с. 123]. "Версионная гипотеза" вызывает довольно серьезные возражения:

1) Медиоактивы нередко изолированы. Глаголы elavs "сверкает молния", davobs "спорит", cruobs "врет", tovs "идет снег" и т.д. вообще не имеют в грузинском соответствующих активов и, следовательно, формы аориста и футурума: i-elva "сверкнула молния"/ i-elvebs "сверкнет молния", i-crua "солгал"/ i-cruebs "будет лгать" не могут быть рассмотрены как рефлексивные формы соответствующих активов по той простой причине, что такие активы не существуют в языке.

2) Не выдерживает критики также точка зрения, согласно которой транзитивные рефлексивные (версионные) формы, заполняя дефектную парадигму медиоактивов, теряют прямое дополнение. Когда предикат, выраженный медиоактивным глаголом, в предложении имеет форму аориста или футурума,

не приходится говорить об эллипсе прямого дополнения, поскольку это структурно полное предложение: gogom i-tira "девочка заплакала". Если эти предикаты не нуждаются в прямом дополнении, то глаголы, выражающие эти предикаты, нельзя считать формами субъектной версии, так как субъектные версионные формы транзитивные глагольные лексемы и префикс i- в медиоактивных глаголах нельзя считать версионным маркером.

3) Противоречивой представляется также "аспектная гипотеза". Префикс i- грузинских медиоактивов встречается во всех временных формах независимо от вида: i-cinis "смеется" / i-cina "посмеялся" / i-cinebs "посмеется". Уже этот факт однозначно указывает на то, что префикс i- в этих глаголах не выражает ни видовую, ни темпоральную семантику.

Если в медиоактивах префикс i- маркер совершенного вида, то в формах аориста и футурума этих глаголов не должны функционировать превербы – выразители совершенного вида в современном грузинском языке: i-cinis "смеется"/ga i-cinebs "рассмеется" (преверб ga -).

Появление преверба рядом с префиксом i- в формах совершенного вида медиоактивного глагола в очередной раз подчеркивает, что префикс i- не является маркером аспектуальной семантики в медиоактивах современного грузинского языка. Кроме того, смена аспектуальной семантики в Грузинском не затрагивает прямой объект. Если допустим, что транзитивный рефлексив в медиоактивной парадигме при выражении аспектуальной семантики становится непереходной рефлексивной формой, мы столкнемся с неразрешимой задачей.

Нетрудно догадаться, что указанные гипотезы опираются только лишь на формальное сходство версионно-рефлексивных форм переходных глаголов и лексически им соответствующих видовременных форм медиоактивов (нецелевых глаголов), не учитывая при этом ни установленный в современной лингвистике принцип дефиниции рефлексивов, ни типологию процессуально-нецелевых глаголов, вследствие чего языковая основа появления в медиоактивах префикса с посессивным значением остается неясной, а функционально-семантические своеобразия грузинских медиоактивов – невыясненными.

Целью предлагаемого доклада является определение специфических особенностей грузинских медиоактивов и транзитивных рефлексивов (форм субъектной версии) на основе концепции диатез с учетом типологии процессуально-нецелевых глаголов.

На базе универсально-типологической концепции диатез возможно осуществить однотипно выполненное, адекватное и, тем самым, сопоставимое описание как отдельных глагольных лексем, так и рефлексивных конструкций разноструктурных языков.

По концепции диатез, семантика рефлексивной или залоговой конструкции – это функция лексического значения и семантики актантов сопоставимого активного глагола.

В грузинском языке медиоактивы и формы субъектной версии, транзитивные рефлексивы (ТР), иногда составляют омонимные пары:

i-duɣebs cqali "закипит вода"
i-duɣebs cqals "кипятит воду для себя"

Во избежание омонимии, анализируемые глаголы будут представлены в сопровождении актантов и, таким образом, объектами нашего исследования станут оппозиций: 1) активная нерефлексивная конструкция (АК) – транзитивная рефлексивная конструкция (РК); 2) активная конструкция (АК) – медиоактивная конструкция (МК).

Диатеза трактуется как соответствие единиц трех уровней [Храковский, сс. 10–19]:

I. Уровень референтов определяется конкретными участниками описываемой ситуации. Эти участники составляют референтную структуру (РефС) в диатезе. РефС уточняется семантикой существительных, обусловленных синтаксической валентностью анализируемого глагола.

Для наших целей необходимо выделить следующие классы референтов: 1) потенты (Pot), т.е. референты, способные совершать действие. Этот класс необходимо разделить на два подкласса: подкласс одушевленных потентов (Anim) и подкласс персон (Pers). 2) Предметы (NonP) и 3) Части целого (Part).

Выделение данного уровня необходимо, так как семантические характеристики референтов (потентность, одушевленность) предопределяют семантику РК. Изменение РефС исходной диатезы происходит как при образовании большей части транзитивных рефлексивов (ТР), так при трансформации МК=>АК.

II. Уровень семантических ролей референтов состоит из единиц, составляющих структуру семантических ролей (СемС) в диатезе. Для наших целей достаточно выделить такие роли, как: субъект (S), объект (O) и место действия (Loc).

Субъект – это тот участник ситуации, из-за которого происходит нечто. Термин "субъект" используется как обобщенное название таких конкретных ролей, как: агенс (Ag), каузатор (Ca) и т.д.

Объект – это тот участник ситуации, с которым происходит нечто. Объект обобщенное наименование таких конкретных ролей, как пациент (Pt), реципиент каузации (Rc), прямой объект (O^d), косвенный объект (O^{ind}).

S и O^{ind}, в зависимости от лексического значения глагола, в СемС совмещают функцию посессора (Pos), бенефицианта (Ben) или реципиента (Rec).

Использование в диатезах обобщенных семантических ролей определяется целевой установкой – иметь сравнительно небольшое число диатез.

СемС не меняется при трансформации АК=>РК, но меняется при МК=>АК. РефС и СемС вместе составляют семантический уровень описания.

III. Уровень актантов (или членов предложения) состоит из единиц, составляющих синтаксическую структуру (СинС) диатезы. СинС представлена единицами: подлежащее (П), прямое дополнение (Д), косвенное дополнение (Дк).

Изменение СинС происходит при образовании определенных ТР, а при МК=>АК – постоянно.

С учетом вышеизложенного, преобразование исходной активной диатезы в транзитивную рефлексивную диатезу может быть представлено следующим образом:

Dedam gogos xelebi dabana => dedam xelebi da-i-bana
"мать девочке руки помыла" => "мать (свои) руки помыла"

(1) $(Pers_1=S=П)$ $(Pers_2=O^{ind}(Pos)=Дк)$ $(Part=O^d=Д_{пр})$ =>
===> (1') $(Pers_1=S=O^{ind})$ $(Pos)=П)$ $(Part=O^d=Д_{пр})$

man aašena saxli => man a-i-šena saxli
"он построил дом" => "он для себя построил дом"

(2) $(Pers_1=S=П)$ $(NonP=O^d=Д_{пр})$ => (2') $(Pers=S$ $(Ben)=П)$ $(NonP=O^d=Д_{пр})$

man čaagona bavšvs siqvaruli => man ča-i-gona siqvaruli
"он внушил ребенку любовь" => "он внушил себе любовь"

(3) $(Pers_1=S=П)$ $(Pers_2=O^{ind}(Rec)=Дк)$ $(NonP=O^d=Д_{пр})$ =>
===> $(Pers_1=S=O^{ind}(Rec)=П))$ $(NonP=O^d=Д_{пр})$

В зависимости от лексического значения АК, производные ТР перераспределяются в разные семантические классы:

I.   da-i bana "помыл/а" (свои) – посессивный ТР
II. a-i-šena "построил/а" (свои) – бенефактивный ТР
III. ča-i-gona "внушил/а" (себе) – реципиентный ТР

Трансформаций: (1) => (1'), (2) => (2'), (3) => (3') представляют собой преобразования семантически простых АК в семантически более сложные рефлексивные (версионные) конструкции. При таких преобразованиях субъект остается в ТР на позицию субъекта; не меняется СемС исходной диатезы; семантически более сложным является ТР, так как в его толкование полностью входит значение активного, лексически соответствующего глагола и, кроме того, семантические компоненты "свой" или "себе", что создает возможность синонимического перифразирования ТР с помощью АК и возвратными местоимениями: "себе" или "свое":

is i-šenebs (ТР) saxls = is ašenebs (АК) tavis saxls = "Он строит свой дом"

Совершенно иная ситуация создается при трансформации МК=>АК:

gogo i-cinis => gogos acinebs is
"Девочка смеется" => "Девочку смешит он"
(4) (Pers$_1$=S =П) => (4') (Pers$_1$=O^d(Rc)=Д$_{пр}$) (Pers$_2$=S(Ca)=П)

Соотношение (4) => (4') есть соотношение семантически простого медиоактива и семантически более сложного актива. При трансформации МК=>АК меняется ролевая структура исходной диатезы, что никогда не происходит при АК=>ТР. Субъект исходной диатезы переходит в трансформе на позицию O^d (Rc), а позицию S в трансформе занимает каузатор (Ca) названной медиоактивным глаголом ситуации.

Если ТР, как более сложного по сравнению с лексически соотносительной АК, можно перефразировать с помощью соответствующей АК, значение МК на толкуется через значения лексически соотносительной АК, так как МК семантически более проста, чем соответствующая АК, в толковании которой полностью входит значение МК. Следовательно, истолковать значение АК мы можем только через лексически соответствующей, семантически простой МК:

is acinebs (АК) gogos = is ikceva ise, rom gogo i-cinis (МК) "Он поступает так, что девочка смеется".

Раз МК исходная конструкция при МК=>АК, раз она непроизводная конструкция, она не может быть транзитивным рефлексивом, так как любой ТР является трансформом, производным глаголом, а префикс i- в медиоактивах не может быть меркером рефлексивности.

В современном грузинском языке медиоактивный глагол и транзитивный рефлексив по-разному соотносятся с активными лексическими коррелятами, поэтому они функционально и семантически разные языковые единицы. В специальной литературе соотношение медиоактив-актив трактуется как соотношение исходный глагол-каузативный глагол и оно никак не сводится к соотношению актив-рефлексив [Иванишвили, Соселия, сс. 135–6].

Медиоактивный глагол выражает нецелевой процесс, для которого субъект является местом, где реализуется этот процесс.

По мнению Э. Бенвениста, индоевропейские медиальные глаголы, в класс которых входят семантические эквиваленты грузинских медиоактивов, выражают процесс, "который развивается в субъекте, субъект является внутренним по отношению к процессу, ... субъект является и центром и производителем процесса; он совершает нечто, что совершается в нем самом" (Бенвенист, сс. 188–9).

Точку зрения Э. Бенвениста поддерживает типология процессуально-нецелевых глаголов.

Особенно значителен тот факт, что во многих языках слова со значением прилагательного, ведут себя как непереходные процессуально-нецелевые глаголы. В языках, в которых прилагательные не образуют самостоятельный лексический класс (языки активной типологии, вьетнамский язык), одна и та же непереходная конструкция с процессуально-нецелевым глаголом может иметь и атрибутивную и предикативную семантику. и только широким контекстом определяется ее значение:

1. "Солнце восходит"
   Вьетнамский Mвt trti lkn =
2. "Восходящее солнце"

1. "Он добр"
   Язык Сенека (Ирокезская группа языков) thaiwai =
2. "Добрый"

В одном из картвельских языков, в сванском, тоже зафиксирован факт выражения атрибутивной семантики ателиковым непереходным глаголом:

1. "Он лучше"
   хоča =
2. "Хороший"

Если один и тот же процессуально-нецелевой глагол может выразить и атрибутивную и предикативную семантику, тогда нужно признать, что этот глагол подразумевает такое же посессивное отношение между субъектом и нецелевым процессом, которое имеется между качеством и его владельцем.

Языковые данные показывают, что присвоение нецелевого процесса субъекту один из словотворческих принципов, действующих в языках при глагольном выражении нецелевых (ателиковых) процессов. Семантическая структура ателиковых непереходных глаголов в языках реализуется по разному, в зависимости от средств выражения посессивности.

В языках активной типологии субъект ателиковых глаголов обозначается инактивными личными аффиксами, тождественными с аффиксами органической принадлежности. Такое тождество определенно сигнализирует "неотчуждаемость" нецелевого процесса от субъекта; указывает на то, что ателиковый процесс является "органической принадлежностью" субъекта, а субъект – посессором процесса.

На основе анализа, проведенного критериями концепции диатез и на основе типологического исследования специфики ателиковых глаголов заключаем: транзитивные рефлексивы (формы субъкетной версии) и медиоактивы разные языковые единицы в современном грузинском; медиоактив выражает нецелевой процесс и пребывание субъекта в нецелевом процессе, а сам этот процесс представляет "органической принадлежностью" субъекта; видовременные формы грузинских медиоактивов органические формы медиоактивной парадигмы, а не заимствованные от активных коррелятов;

бенефактивно-посессивным префиксом i- в грузинском медиоактиве маркируется присвоение ателикового процесса субъекту, этот префикс устанавливает предикативное отношение посессивности между нецелевым процессом и субъектом; префикс i- в медиоактивах функционирует как предикативная языковая единица, указывающая на то, что субъект поссесор названного медиоактивом нецелевого процесса, на то, что "субъект является внутренним по отношению к процессу".

Библиография

Бенвенист Э., Общая лингвистика. М., "Прогресс", 1974.

Иванишвили М., Соселия Э., Некоторые морфо-синтаксические и семантические особенности грузинских пассивных конструкций. Вопросы языкознания, №4, Тб., 2002.

Меликишвили И., Версия, как средство выражения аспекта в грузинском языке. Вопросы языкознания, №4, Тб., 2002.

Шанидзе А., Сочинения в двенадцати томах, т. 3, Тб., 1980.

MARINE IVANISHVILI

9 Lexical Exceptions in the Comparative Reconstruction of the Kartvelian Languages: Words for 'oak'

ABSTRACT

The reason for the breakdown of regular correspondences between daughter languages is generally considered to be the existence of unexplained lexical exceptions. The breakdown consists neither in the deficiency of examples nor in the breach of regularity. Rather, the reason for the breakdown of regular correspondence lies at the intersection of linguistic and extra-linguistic factors.

The study of grammatical, phonological and lexical isoglosses among dialects of a proto-language makes it possible to establish extra-linguistic factors. This trend in linguistics is called 'the linguistic paleontology of culture' (Gamkrelidze 1999), since its object of investigation is not only the proto-language but also the proto-culture of its speakers. What is reconstructed is not so much the language itself as the extra-linguistic world reflected in the linguistic data.

Reconstructing the elements of the extra-linguistic world of the daughter language speakers gives in turn a clearer picture of the linguistic affinities among the daughter languages and their development over time, i.e. of the purely linguistic factors. This is particularly true of the semantic structure of languages. Semantic structure cannot be studied in isolation from the external world that is reflected in the content plane of language. This approach explains lexical exceptions on the proto-level and gives an adequate semantic reconstruction of the archetypes. However, some problems arise in the case of genetically isolated language groups.

The paper presents the etymology and reconstruction of exceptions to the different roots of words for 'oak' in the Kartvelian languages, which remain at first sight unexplained:

Proto-Kartv. *ʒₗel- 'tree, oak', Georg. ʒel- 'tree, board, pillar, post, column, base, foundation': Megr. Laz. ʒa(l)- 'tree': Svan. ǯih-ra || ǯīra || ǯi-ra 'oak'.

Interestingly, from the typological point of view there is a similar picture as regards the semantic reconstruction of 'oak' in the Proto-Indo-European languages.

> Sprachforschung, der ich anhänge und von der ich ausgehe, hat mich
> nie in der Weise befriedigen können, daß ich nicht immer gern von den
> Wörtern zu den Sachen gelangt wäre; ich wollte nicht bloß Häuser bauen,
> sondern auch darin wohnen.
>
> — J. GRIMM

> All trees are oak trees …
>
> — J. BARTH

A language system can be analysed on the basis of different methodologies.
The comparative historical method seems to be the classical one which has
not lost its actuality to the present day.[1]

The study of grammatical, phonological and lexical isoglosses among
the dialects of a protolanguage makes it possible to establish extra-linguistic
factors. This trend in linguistics is called 'the linguistic paleontology of
culture', since its object of investigation is not only the protolanguage but
also the proto-culture of speakers. What is reconstructed is not so much
the language itself as the extra-linguistic world reflected in the linguistic
data (Gamkrelidze 1999).

Reconstructing elements of the extra-linguistic world of the daughter
language speakers gives in turn a clearer picture of the linguistic affinities
among the daughter languages and their development in time, i.e. of purely
linguistic factors. This is particularly true of the semantic structure of language. Semantic structure cannot be studied in isolation from the external
world that is reflected in the content plane of language (Gamkrelidze 1999).

The reconstructed forms and meanings may be grouped into lexical-
semantic fields, which designate extra-linguistic classes such as animals,
handicraft tools, and others. Such a proto-linguistic lexical-semantic
system can give historical reality through typological comparison with the
actual culture of the past and the present and especially by archeological

---

1   This is a slightly amended version of a paper which first appeared in the *Bulletin of
     the Georgian National Academy of Sciences*, vol. I, no. 2, 2008.

facts, in verifying a reconstructed culture and particularly its material side (Gamkrelidze and Ivanov 1995).

Today it is widely agreed that 'culture' does not consist of things, people, behaviour or emotions, but of the forms or organization of these things in the minds of people. How can the organization of 'things' in people's minds be discovered? The best way of discovery lies in the area of language, and there is a whole battery of linguistic tests which can be put to use to reveal different aspects of the organization of the universe in the minds of people (Wierzbicka 1996).

Scholars today pay great attention to semantic problems and questions concerning language and thought: *Weltanschauung* created by language, the mental construction of 'things' (reification), 'language intuition' crop up again and again, i.e. the manner of investigating the semantic level of language moves from formal linguistics to content research.

We can get complete information about various aspects of given objects only through studying them cross-linguistically, on the basis of a comparison of different languages, which is used to solve not only linguistic but also cultural-anthropological issues.

The semantic and pragmatic levels of a language system are the most complex and complicated from the point of view of understanding. We can analyse them only on the basis of the investigation of surface linguistic forms. Theoretically, different semantic interpretations of a language system can be achieved through the use of various algorithms. We must not forget that every language system builds its own world picture specifically and the strategies of structuring and algorithms defining the conceptualization processes are different for them. (Cf. colour terms and corresponding various linguistic models of the colour terms system).

Let us assume a language system (L) and an α-element of it: L ($\alpha \in L$) in a $[t_1, t_2]$ time segment. If we denote the meaning of the α-element by $m(\alpha)$, theoretically there would be the following possible meaning-changes:

$$L(t_1) \,\underline{\hspace{4cm}}\, L(t_2)$$

$$\begin{array}{cccc} \alpha & & \alpha \quad \alpha & \alpha \quad \beta \\ \updownarrow & & \updownarrow \quad \updownarrow & \updownarrow \quad \updownarrow \\ m(\alpha) & & m(\alpha) \;\; m(\alpha)' & \varnothing \;\; m(\alpha) \end{array}$$

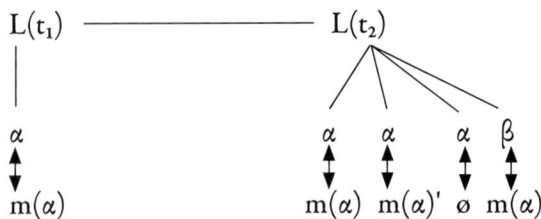

Explanations for the origins of the changes and clarification of the meanings are necessary premises to restoring exact semantic reconstructions for each comparable language, including the Kartvelian languages. The above-stated facts define the importance of the topic.

The reason for the breakdown of regular correspondences between daughter languages is generally considered to be unexplained lexical exceptions. This implies neither a deficiency in the examples nor a breach of regularity. On the contrary, the reason for the breakdown of regular correspondences lies at the intersection of linguistic and extra-linguistic factors. In such cases the existence of duplicate forms can be suggested that does not break the solidity of the protolanguage.

Reasons for the appearance of duplicate forms can be: stylistic variation, social stratification, the influence of colloquial forms on the literary language, the compatibility of the data of protolanguages with the local language subgroups, and so on. Comparative reconstructions also reveal examples when some roots with similar meanings are reconstructed.

In certain linguistic groups there usually exist stereotypes according to which one part of a word's meaning is considered to be positive, while the other, negative. Differences in the development of meanings can be regarded as the origins of taboos and euphemisms in natural languages.

At first sight it seems that an investigation of the corpus of plant names does not yield such interesting reconstructed systems as in the case of kinship or colour-terms (Berlin and Kay 1969, Soselia 2009), though it helps us to identify some biological units corresponding to the names of plants. But it is precisely this kind of research that fills gaps in our knowledge about the processes of human cognitive means to clarify the nature of the human world through categorization.

Tree names are paradoxical. On the one hand they are basic, semantic primitives, but on the other hand tree names, because of the peculiarities of their referents, are sensitive to ecological changes and the migration processes of a speech community. P. Friedrich's opinion about the Proto-Indo-European arboreal system may be extended to the whole corpus of plant names. Thus, plant names, their meanings and the botanical realities to which they correspond, are assumed to constitute a set of interdependent systems. The nature of such systems can only be discovered and interpreted on the basis of conjoined approaches, or analytical systems (Friedrich 1970). The first approach is linguistic-phonological: morphological parameters constitute a linguistic system. The second is a semantic approach: semantic features which define morphemes, words and sets of word-families constitute a semantic system. And the third approach is lexical: the reconstructed lexicon may relate to data and systems that are neither linguistic nor semantic (e.g. archaeological, palaeo-botanical data). Such information constitutes an external system (Friedrich 1970: 1–4).

The integrated approach seeks all relevant evidence to get complete information about the historical existence of the speakers in question, including the ecological environment (fauna, flora, geographical setting, climate) and human habitation and migration in the environment, as well as culture in the broadest sense (including both material and spiritual culture) (Gamkrelidze 1999).

Exact semantic reconstructions of the proto-forms calls for the scrupulous etymological analysis of the reconstructed stems oriented towards the proper lexical-semantic groups, allowing us to restore the initial meanings of the stems in the systems, to explain the words' transitions from one lexical subsystem to another, etc.

Such an approach will permit us not only to account for the semantic changes, but tentatively to define the direction and manner of the changes. To establish criteria for the verification of semantic changes is as necessary as those for the verification of phonetic changes. Phonetic reconstructions are based on ranges of phonemes corresponding to the comparable languages. Semantic reconstructions are difficult because there are diverse semantic nuances; the set of semantic positions is complex and their frequency is less than phonetic ones. Practically each phonetic usage of words is a separate semantic position, and usually sufficient data is not available to build the semantic ranges.

The simplest way in such investigations is to register the movements and deviations of similar meanings in different languages, which would help us to restore the exact proto-meanings.

G. Klimov, who gives high praise to the 'Etymological Dictionary of the Kartvelian Languages' (Fähnrich and Sardschweladze 1995), asserts: like all important research, this monograph clearly shows the range of problems of comparative study of Kartvelian languages and etymological investigations, the solution of which becomes more and more urgent.

First of all, we must mention the task of the adequate semantic reconstruction of the archetypes. This task is complicated in the case of genetically isolated language groups. It seems that inadequate attention to this aspect of reconstruction in Kartvelian studies prompted the above-mentioned authors to give up reconstruction of meaning. There is still a lot to be done in this sphere (Klimov 1998).

The foregoing theoretical discussion prompts the author to bring to light new roots of Proto-Kartvelian plant names, make a more precise analysis of old ones, to show the existence of borrowed forms on the proto-level, to compare the Proto-Kartvelian arboreal system with the Proto-Indo-European and Caucasian plant names data, showing their similarities and differences. All this makes the classification of languages possible. They can (or cannot) be considered as entities of the same structural-typological (or genetic) classes.

Friedrich (1970: 139–40) wrote:

> Both the wide diffusion and the emotional intensity of these ancient patterns of culture – not paralleled by those for any other tree – suggests that the oak was one of the underlying themes in PIE culture, as a basic life symbol and a root of myth and of sacrament. The oak was a nexus of symbolic articulation between the semantic system of the tree names and the cultural system of religious beliefs and ritual conserving the supernatural.

The 'oak' and its inhabiting pure soul is known in the West and also in the East (Frazer 1993). The cult of oak is widespread in the Caucasus, too, especially in the Kartvelian traditions (Javakhishvili 1986).

Th. V. Gamkrelidze and V.V. Ivanov reconstructed two stems in Proto-Indo-European: I.*$t'e/oru_c$-/*$t're/ou_c$- with the meaning 'tree, oak' and II. *$p[^h]erk[^h]^ou$-/*$p[^h]eru$- with the meaning 'oak' (Gamkrelidze and Ivanov 1995). They analysed these meanings on the basis of wide complexes of mythological phenomena. Examples of taboo are given, which were realized either as a substitution of the roots with other new words or as phonetically modified forms of the same roots.

We have a typologically similar picture for the meaning 'oak' in the Kartvelian languages. The following are reconstructed: *c_1qan 'oak': Georg. çqn-, çqn-et-i (toponym): Megr. čqon-, čqon-i 'oak' : Laz. čkon-||mčkon-||mčon-, čkon-i||mčkon-i||mčon-i 'oak' and another root: *z_1el- 'tree' : Georg. ʒel- ʒel-i 'tree' (old Georg.) : Megr. ʒa-, ʒa- 'tree' ʒal-ep-i 'trees' o-ʒal-e-š -i (type of vine) če-ʒa- 'poplar' 'white tree' : Laz. ʒa||nʒa||mʒa 'tree' ʒal-ep-e 'trees' – for the Georgian-Zanian unity period (Klimov 1998, Fähnrich and Sardschweladze 1995).

The root *z_1el- would have had another meaning – 'oak', besides the meaning 'tree', which is presented as a separate Svanian form: ʒihra||ʒīra||ʒira. What is the reason for the difference of forms? Are they lexical exceptions? Let us analyse these roots starting from the end of the stem:

1) -*ra* is the derivational suffix of plant names in Svan, i.e. Georg. çip-el-i : Megr. çip-ur-i : Laz. çip-/nçip- çip-ur-i : Svan. çip- çip-ra 'beech'; Georg. rc_1xila : Megr. c_1xim-ur-i/ c_1xem-ur-i : Svan. $c_1xəm$-ra||c_1xwim-ra||c_1xum- 'hornbeam' etc.

2) The last non-syllabic [*l] (i.e. after vowels or syllabic sonant) in Svan, as a rule, gives the spirant |š| (Gamkrelidze and Machavariani 1965). Compare Georg. çul-i : Svan. $c_1uš$ etc. In some cases [*l] > š>h, which may be lost (or substitute Ø): Georg. gul-i : Svan. (lšx.) gu<guh<*guš ('heart').

3) Georg. *e* : Megr., Laz. *a* : Svan. *e* is the regular phonemic correspondence for the Kartvelian vowel system. However, sometimes other vowel correspondences can be found as well, for example: Georg. *e* : Megr., Laz. *i* : Svan. *i*. *nen- Georg. en-a 'language, tongue, word' : Megr. nin- nin-a 'language, tongue, word' : Laz. nen- nin-a 'language, tongue, word' : Svan. nin-/nᴣn- nin- 'language'; *c_1el- Georg.

çel- çel-i : Megr. či-/čə- : Laz. ču-/mču- : Svan. čil-, čin- 'intestine,
gut' etc.

4) Georg. ʒ: Megr. ʒ : Laz. ʒ : Svan. ʒ is the regular phonemic correspondence in the Kartvelian languages as well.

Thus, for the Proto-Kartvelian level the root *$ʒ_1$el- is restored with
the meaning 'tree, oak' on the basis of such correspondences: Georg. ʒel-i :
Megr. ʒa : Laz. ʒa||nʒa||mʒa : Svan. ʒihra||ʒīra||ʒira. I think that the coexist-
ence of different roots, *$c_1$qan- and *$ʒ_1$el- 'tree, oak', is connected with an
ancient human tradition of beliefs regarding trees (cf. from the typological
point of view a similar picture for the PIE languages).

It is very rare for plants and their fruits to have different names. This
kind of exception occurs in Georgian muxa- 'oak' and rḳo- 'acorn'. In old
Georgian texts and modern dialects rḳo-ḳrḳo- 'acorn' means not only the
fruit but also the tree. G. Klimov has reconstructed the archetype *ḳrḳo- for
the Georgian-Zan unity period (Klimov 1998). A. Shanidze has connected
this root with the Indo-European (Latin) quercus 'oak' (Shanidze 1947).

The roots muxa and rḳo are widespread in many Kartvelian toponyms:
muxiani, muxrani, didmuxa, rḳoni, čqondidi, ʒihra etc. (Tschumburidze
1985). The root is borrowed from Kartvelian into the Caucasian languages:
Avar. mik' 'oak', 'acorn'; Darg. mijˉ (Urakh.)|| mig (Akush.) : Lak. murxˉ
'tree' (←*murxˉ') : Lezg. mjw : Tab. máqw : Rut. máxw : Tsakh. mòq : Ud.
máq (Gigineishvili 1972).

One important question arises: What is the etymology of muxa? In the
oldest Georgian lexicon of Sulkhan-Saba Orbeliani (17th c.) we can find
some interesting verbal forms: muxva, momuxva, damuxva 'cut, separate'.
According to Saba's explanation, everything which has bark-like dismemberable small parts is called muxa (Orbeliani 1991). I think that this is the
reason that the names of fruits with dismemberable barks are: muxanesvi
'type of melon', muxamsxali 'type of pear', muxamßvane 'type of apple', etc.

Typologically many plants are named according to their whole appearance, external features of leaves, and colours of fruit So the unexpected
lexical form muxa, which has no phonemically corresponding roots in
other Kartvelian languages, is replaced by a duplicate form, maybe recalled
on the basis of taboo related to tree-beliefs, which through the centuries

preserved the original aspects to the present day in Kartvelian folklore, legends, fairytales, architectural ornaments, songs, etc.

Bibliography

Berlin, Brent, and Paul Kay. 1969. *Basic Color terms: Their universality and evolution.* Berkley: University of California Press.

Fähnrich, Heinz, and Surab Sardschweladze. 1995. *Etymologisches Wörterbuch der Kartwel-Sprachen.* Leiden: E.J. Brill.

Frazer, James George. 1993. *The Golden Bough.* London. (Russian translation: Золотая ветвь, 1980, Moscow).

Friedrich, Paul. 1970. *Proto-Indo-European Trees.* Chicago: University of Chicago Press.

Gamkrelidze, Thomas V. 1999. On Linguistic Paleontology of Culture. *Time Depth in Historical Linguistics*, ed. by Colin Renfrew, April McMahon and Larry Trask, 456–61. Cambridge: The McDonald Institute for Archeological Research.

Gamkrelidze, Thomas V., and Vyacheslav V. Ivanov. 1995. *Indo-European and the Indo-Europeans: A Reconstruction and Historical Typological Analysis of a Proto-Language and Proto-Culture*, 2 vols, with a Preface by Roman Jakobson. Berlin: Mouton de Gruyter. English version by Johanna Nichols.

Gamkrelidze, Thomas V., and Givi Machavariani. 1965. The System of Sonants and Ablaut in Katvelian Languages. Tbilisi, TSU, 81–2.

Gigineishvili, Bakar K. 1972. Comparative Reconstruction and Modification in Proto-Language (Voprosy Yazykoznanja, 4, 1977), Comparative Phonetics of Daghestan's Languages, Tbilisi, TSU, 98.

Javakhishvili, Ivane. 1986. *A History of the Georgian People*, vol. 5. Tbilisi: Metsniereba.

Klimov, Georgi A. 1998. *Etymological Dictionary of the Kartvelian Languages.* Berlin: Mouton.

Orbeliani, Sulkhan-Saba. 1991. *Leksik'oni kartuli.* Tbilisi: Merani.

Rayfield, Donald. 1988. *Dendronims and the Relation of Caucasian Languages.* Tbilisi: Mnatobi, 9.

Shanidze, Akaki. 1947. Etymological Research: *rk̇o* and *muxa.* Proc. Scient. Session, Tbilisi: TSU.

Soselia, Ether. 2009. *Semantic Universals and the Kartvelian Languages: Patterns of Colour Categorization.* Tbilisi: Nekeri.

Tschumburidze, Surab. 1985. Die Namen der Eiche in Georgischen Toponymen. *Georgica*, Jena – Tbilissi, Heft 8, 8–9.

Wierzbicka, Anna. 1996. *Semantics: Primes and Universals*. Oxford: Oxford University Press.

Discussion (Extract)

BEEDHAM: May I ask a question regarding Saussure's notion of the linguistic sign. You said that form cannot be studied in isolation from content. You also said that every language builds its own world picture. You are concerned with languages which go back so far in time that there is no direct written evidence of their existence and their structure, we can only assume that they existed and try to reconstruct how they looked, what their structure was; in other words, you are concerned with proto-languages. You have also said that by looking at a reconstructed formal structure of a proto-language we can deduce both material objects and abstract ideas in the culture and the minds of the people who spoke that language. One of the great controversies in linguistics is does form determine meaning or does meaning determine form. Which is it in your approach: is your synchronic analysis of a proto-language based on the view that form determines meaning, or is it based on the view that meaning determines form?

IVANISHVILI: As is known, every natural language has a meaning plan and an expression plan, they do not exist without each other. The language sign is the synthesis of them. Your question is more philosophical than linguistic.

MARINA JIKIA

10 The Non-Suffixal Derivation of Intensive Forms in Turkish

ABSTRACT

The structure of word-forms in Turkish seems unproblematic, with Turkish being an agglutinative language: suffixes – it is well known that the only derivational morphemes in Turkish are suffixes – are joined to the stem or word base in a fairly clear manner. However, intensive forms of adjectives, adverbs and nouns may be created in Turkish by means of partial reduplication in which prefix-like morphemes are used. This is the use of 'interfixes' in Turkish – I propose calling the items in question 'interfix' – they bind part of root with root.

More than 150 units in Turkish intensify by doubling the first syllable and adding or replacing its final consonant with -p-, -s-, -m-, -r-, -pA-, -rIl-, -rma-, -pis-, -ram-, -re-, -se-, -ş-, -t- (the last 9 of these affixes are discussed first).

High productivity of this kind of word-formation is illustrated by the following. Both simple and derived units are reduplicated: boş 'empty', bo-m-boş 'totally empty'; ıssız 'uninhabited', ı-p-ıssız 'absolutely deserted'. Alongside native Turkic words Arabic or Persian loanwords are partially doubled, as well as new borrowings: direkt (<Fr. directe) 'direct', di-m-direkt 'straight'.

This word formation type is confirmed in language contacts, too: in the Ingilo dialect of Georgian (which is widespread in Azerbaijan) and in Udian some intensive forms are produced according to the Azerbaijani model using Georgian adjectives: c'itel 'red', c'i-m-c'itel 'deep red'; cariel 'empty', ca-m-cariel 'completely empty', etc. The reduplicated syllable (i.e. the first) is accented, whereas Turkic words usually have an accent on the last syllable.

Rightside agglutination, i.e. suffixation, is one of the main traits of Turkic languages. But we can now affirm the presence of prefix-type morphemes, joined from the left side to the word-bases or stems. This is non-suffixal derivation. In Turkish issues of accentuation and affixation type are interconnected. Their detailed specification lays the ground for a more adequate interpretation of the main typological traits of Turkic languages.

Turkic languages form a closely related group with genetically similar traits: synharmonism, obvious phonetic concordance, and extreme closeness of grammatical structure and vocabulary. In the word formation of this language family suffixation prevails, though there are forms of analytical word formation: twin words, compound verbs, differently realized reduplication, etc.

In the present paper I will consider words which form an intensive by means of partial reduplication. Reduplication is partial or full, exact or approximate repetition of the first syllable, root or stem of a word. It is one of the morphophonemic means of word formation, and whilst performing various functions is very wide-spread in languages of different kinds of structure. In some African languages the plural of a noun is formed by reduplication; in Proto-Indo-European Perfect was expressed by repeating the ablauted stem and special person indices. Reduplication is often used for noun and verb compound formation (Мельчук 2000: 48–61). In Georgian, reduplication can denote plurality, recurrence, intensity; it is often employed to derive compound nouns and verbs (Butskhrikidze 2005: 35–8).

Reduplication is also variously realized in Turkish. In the present paper partial reduplication is examined as one of the means of forming the superlative of adjectives and an intensive not manifested with a suffix. Hitherto there has been no Turkic philological research dedicated to this word formation means, yet it is a device common to all Turkic languages. It is formed in the following way: the first open syllable of a word (often that of an adjective or an adverb, more rarely that of a noun) is taken and after that a morpheme-intensifier is manifested, followed by a duplicated word. E.g. Azerbaijani *yaşıl* 'green', *yamyaşıl* 'very green'; Altaian кызыл 'red', кы-п-кызыл 'deep red'; Bashkir кызыл 'red', кы-п-кызыл 'deep red'; Gagauz бийаз 'white', би-м-бийаз 'very white'; Kazakh жаксы 'good', жа-п-жаксы 'best'; Karaim толу 'full', то-п-толу 'over-full'; Karakalpak кызыл 'red', кы-п-кызыл 'deep red'; Karachai-Balkar сары 'yellow', са-п-сары 'intense yellow'; Kirghiz *oop* 'heavy', *o-n-oop* 'very heavy'; Crimean-Tatar айдын 'light', а-п-айдын 'very light'; Kumik янгыз 'alone', я-п-янгыз 'totally alone'; Nogai кызыл 'red', кы-п-кызыл 'deep red'; Tatar *zur* 'big', *zu-p-zur* 'very big'; Tuvinian кызыл 'red', кы-п-кызыл 'too red'; Turkish *temiz* 'clean', *te-r-temiz* 'quite clean'; Turkmen гони 'straight', го-с-гони 'absolutely straight'; Uigur каттик 'firm', ка-п-каттик 'too firm'; Khakass арыг 'clean', а-п-арыг 'too clean'; Shor кара 'black', ка-п-кара 'jet black'; Yakut урун 'clear, light', у-п-урун 'too light', etc.

More often than not, in descriptive grammars, manuals, and reference books the forms obtained through partial reduplication are interpreted either as the superlative degree of adjectives, showing the kind or quality of a person or thing, or as adverbs, characterizing the quality of an action or state. However, languages have a separate set of comparative and superlative forms, used in the comparison of things or persons. A partially reduplicated form expresses the high degree of a quality, not comparison.

According to Sapir in this connection it is reasonable to conclude that nouns, as well as verbs, by their nature can be graded (Sapir 1944: 94–5); therefore, adjectives and adverbs of quality are not the only parts of speech showing a grading. Hence, potentially it is possible to grade different types of substantives; a grading marker in one or another degree of its manifestation may be expressed also by a substantive (Кононов 1956). This is confirmed by some reduplicated substantival word-formations, though in Turkish substantives do not feature degrees of comparison: *buz* 'ice', *bumbuz* 'very cold'; *çarşı* 'market', *çamçarşı* 'from everywhere, from every side'; *çevre* 'circle', *çepçevre* 'around, all around'; *gündüz* 'day', *güpegündüz* 'in daytime'; *halat* 'rope', *hamhalat* 'rough, uncouth; dullard, bumpkin'; *hayal* 'dream', *hamhayal* 'fantasy, illusion'; *ışık* 'light', *ıpışık* 'very bright'; *parça* 'piece', *paramparça* 'cut into pieces'; *tekerlek* 'wheel', *testekerlek* 'completely round'; *yaz* 'summer', *yamyaz* 'midsummer', etc.

Such reduplicated word-forms do not express comparative or superlative degree, as there is no object they are compared with. They are best classified as a means of intensification of the basic meaning of a given element.

Words of Turkish origin as well as borrowed stems are reduplicated by this kind of shortened repetition: from Arab. *mavi* 'blue', *ma-s-mavi* 'deep blue', *beyaz* 'white', *be-m-beyaz* 'snow-white'; Pers. *aşikar* 'clear', *a-p-aşikar* 'completely clear', *bedava* 'free, gratuitous', *be-s-bedava* 'very cheap'; Fr. *direkt* 'direct', *di-m-direkt* 'straight', etc.

In order to express an intensified feature root stems as well as derived stems are reduplicated: *bulanık* 'turbid', *bu-s-bulanık* 'very turbid', *ıssız* 'uninhabited', *ı-p-ıssız* 'completely deserted', etc.

Qualitative traits are given to things: *tarla yemyeşiliyor* 'the cornfield turns green'; motivated adjectives become abstract: *apaklık* 'very whiteness', *bambaşkalık* 'too differentness', *ipincelik* '(the) most thinness', etc.

In Turkic languages partial reduplication is a morphophonemic device which consists of doubling the first open syllable. In this connection in the Russian, French, English and Turkish specialist literature there is a brief mention of the following type: The first vowel sound or two sounds (consonant and vowel of this same word) are added to the beginning of a word. After it a morpheme-intensifier is placed, followed by the reduplicating words. If the first syllable is closed the final consonants are dropped: *kırmızı* 'red', *kıpkırmızı* 'quite red', *dinç* 'robust', *dipdinç* 'very robust', *çevre* 'surroundings', *çepeçevre* 'all around'.

In contrast to other Turkic languages, in 150 examples of Turkish an intensifying morpheme is revealed by thirteen morphologically conditioned allomorphs, though in the literature only four allomorphs are usually distinguished: -p-, -m-, -s-, -r- (Banguoğlu 1990: 348–9, Lewis 1967: 159–60). Although allomorphs -pA-, -rma-, -rIl-, -re- are mentioned, they are not considered to be allomorphs of this type (Zulfikar 1980: 64). The rest – -ram-, -se-, -s-, -t-, -pis- – are introduced as intensifying morphemes for the first time in the present paper. The capital letters indicate synharmonism, though because of the absence of phonologically conditioned allomorphs the assimilation of voiced and voiceless is not applicable.

Concerning the choice of allomorphs: if the anlaut is a vowel the allomorph -p- is used, if the anlaut is a consonant the following is observed:

a) In this word-formation the coincidence of initial consonant and affix-intensifier is inadmissible: *mavi* – *ma-m-mavi, *pis* – *pi-p-pis, *sivri* – *si-s-sivri

b) If the initial consonant is b-, allomorphs -p- and -r- are excluded;

c) If the initial consonant is g-, the allomorph -s is excluded;

d) If the initial consonants are p- or t-, the allomorph -m- is excluded;

e) If the initial consonants are b-, g-, h-, y-, the allomorph -r- is excluded.

The formulation of rules of allomorph choice is complicated because of free variation in some of the allomorphs (Deny 1945: 231). For example, the word *çevre* 'circle' has four of them: *çe-p-çevre, çe-pe-çevre, çe-re-çevre, çe-s-çevre* 'from every side'.

Turkic languages have a fixed accent at the end of a word. During partial reduplication the word is lengthened by adding one or two syllables. One syllable words become two: *dik – dimdik, gök – gömgök* or three syllables: *genç – gepegenç*. Two syllable words become three: *baya – basbaya, koca – koskoca* or four syllables: *sıklam – sırılsıklam, gündüz – güpegündüz*, and three syllable words becomes four: *yuvarlak – yusyuvarlak, çıplaklık – çırçıplaklık* and five syllables: *karışık – karmakarışık, dağınık – darmadağınık*, etc.

Instead of the expected accent a much stronger accent appears on the first syllable: *yuvarlak – yu'syuvarlak*, and in the case of the presence of an intensifier echo syllable in the affix the second syllable becomes accentuated: *karma'karışık, sırı'lsıklam* (Zimmer 1970: 161).

It appears that the accentuation of a Turkish word is changed (Ergin 1967: 355–6), and in consequence the paradigm of word accent is destroyed.

Rightside agglutination, i.e. suffixation, is one of the main traits of Turkic languages (Gencan 1997: 11). It has now become possible to state the presence of prefix-type morphemes, joined from the left side to word-bases or stems. While the following kinds of morpheme exist – prefix, infix, interfix, transfix, confix, circumfix, ambifix – interfix is preferred. Intensifier morphemes are dissociated and determined as interfixes, which serve for binding (part of) root or stem with root or stem.

In this small fragment of Turkish grammar issues of accentuation and affixation type are interconnected. The new data lay the ground for a more adequate interpretation of the main typological traits of Turkic languages.

Turkic languages are considered to be only suffixal (Ediskun 1996: 155). But in a word-formation process having dominant suffixation, for the expression of intensity intensifier morphemes function with thirteen allomorphs, a state of affairs which differs partially from Greenberg's 27th universal ('If a language is exclusively suffixing, it is postpositional; if it is exclusively prefixing, it is prepositional' (Greenberg 1966: 101)), because one has to do with a non-suffixal derivation process in Turkish.

Here we see expressions of extreme degree in Georgian and Udian influenced by Azerbaijani. In these latter a totally new form of intensive appears, following the Azerbaijani model, by means of reduplication of the first syllable and the interfix -*m*-: Georg. *koxe* 'unripe' *ko-m-koxe* 'very unripe'; *c'iteli* 'red', *c'i-m-c'iteli* 'deep red'; *yia* 'open', *yi-m-yia* 'wide open'; *umarilo* 'unsalty, unsalted', *u-m-umarilo* 'completely unsalted'; *pexşola* 'barefoot', *pe-m-pexşola* 'totally barefoot'; *cariel* 'empty', *ca-m-cariel* 'completely empty'. Exactly the same occurs in Udian with a unified -p- allomorph: *neşum* 'yellow', *ne-p-neşum* 'very yellow', *keže* 'sour', *ke-p-keže* 'very sour'; *çoça* 'red', *ço-p-çoça* 'deep red', etc.

This small fragment of Turkish grammar is important for the specifications of the main properties of Turkic languages, because two typological characteristics of native lexical items – only suffixation, and accent on the last syllable – are changed.

In order to illustrate the increasing dynamics of the forms examined above further examples are given in the Appendix.

Bibliography

Banguoğlu, T. 1990. *Türkçenin grameri* [Turkish Grammar]. Ankara: Türk Tarih Kurumu Basım Evi.
Butskhrikidz, M. 2005. Reduplicative Patterns in Georgian. *Tipologiuri Dziebani* [Typological Researches] V. Tbilisi: universali.
Deny, J. 1945. *Türk Dili Grameri*. Translated into Turkish from the French by A.U. Elove. Ankara: Osmanlı Lehçesi. (French original: *Grammaire de la Langue Turque (dialecte osmanlı)*, Paris 1921).
Ediskun, H. 1996. *Türk Dilbilgisi, Sesbilgisi – Biçimbilgisi – Cümlebilgisi* [Turkish Grammar, Phonetics – Morphology – Syntax]. İstanbul: Remzi Kitab Evi A.Ş.
Ergin, M. 1967. *Türk Dil Bilgisi* [Turkish Grammar]. Sofya: Narodna prosveta.
Gencan, T.N. 1997. *Dilbilgisi* [Grammar]. İstanbul: Kanaat Yayınları Golden Print.
Greenberg, J.H. 1966. Some universals of grammar with particular reference to the order of meaningful elements. *Universals of language*, ed. by J.H. Greenberg, second edition, 48–61. Cambridge, Mass.: MIT Press.

Кононов, А.Н. 1956. *Грамматика современного турецкого литературного языка* [Grammar of the Modern Turkish Literary Language]. Москва-Ленинград: Издательство Академии Наук СССР.

Lewis, G.L. 1967. *Turkish Grammar*. Oxford: Clarendon Press.

Мельчук, И.А. 2000. *Курс общей морфологии* [A Course in General Morphology], Т. III. Москва: Языки русской культуры.

Sapir, E. 1944. Grading: a study in semantics. *Philosophy of Science* 11/2: 93–116.

Zimmer, K.E. 1970. Some Observations on Non-Final Stress in Turkish. *Journal of the American Oriental Society* 90/1: 160–2.

Zulfikar, H. 1980. *Yabancılar için Türkçe Dil Bilgisi* [Turkish Grammar for Foreigners]. Ankara: Ankara Üniversitesi Basımevi.

Appendix

Table 10.1. Prefix-like morphemes (interfixes) in Turkish

acı	bitter	p	a-p-acı	very bitter
açık	open	p	a-p-açık	wide open
açıklık	clearness	p	a-p-açıklık	openness
ak	white	p	a-p-ak	very, all white
ansız, ansızın	suddenly suddenly	p p	a-p-ansız a-p-ansızın	all of a sudden
aşikar	clear	p	a-p-aşikar	completely clear
aydın	light	p	a-p-aydın	absolutely light
aydınlık	daylight	p	a-p-aydınlık	very light
ayrı	apart	p	a-p-ayrı	quite separate
az	little	p	a-p-az	too little
başka	other	m	ba-m-başk	totally different
başkalık	diversity	m	ba-m-başkalık	differentness

baya	simple	s	ba-s-baya	very common
bayağı	simple	m	ba-m-bayağı	ba-m-bayağı
		s	ba-s-bayağı	ba-s-bayağı
bedava	free, gratis	s	be-s-bedava	very cheap
belli	evident	s	be-s-belli	obvious
		se	be-se-belli	
beter	worse	s	be-s-beter	the worst
beyaz	white	m	be-m-beyaz	snow-white
bok	ordure	m	bo-m-bok	utterly useless
boş	empty	m	bo-m- boş	absolutely empty
boz	grey	m	bo-m-boz	quite grey
böyük	big	s	bö-s-böyük	very big
bulanık	turbid	s	bu-s-bulanı	very turbid
buruşuk	crumpled	m	bu-m-buruşu	very crumpled
buz ice	ice	m	bu-m-buz	cold, very cold
bütün	whole	s	büs-bütün	altogether, entirely
car	market	r	ca-r-car	ca-r-car
cavlak	naked, bald		ca-s-cavlak	completely naked
çevre	circumference	p	çe-p-çevre	all around
çabuk	quick	r	ça-r-çabuk	very quickly
çıplak	naked	r	çı-r-çıplak	stark naked
		rll	çı-rıl-çıplak	
*dağan	scattered	r	da-r-dağan	in a clutter
*dağanlık	scattered	r	da-r-dağanlık	
dağın	untidy	r	da-r-dağın	
dağın	untidy	rma	da-rma-dağın	very untidy
dağınık	untidy	p	da-p-dağınık	
		rma	da-rma-dağınık	
dar, daracık	narrow	p	da-p-dar	very narrow
		p	da-p-daracık	
		s	da-s-daracık	
derin	deep	p	de-p-derin	too deep

dızlak	naked, bald	m	dı-m-dızlak	quite bald
dik	upright	m	di-m-dik	very steep
dinç	strong	p	di-p-dinç	too strong
direct	direct	m	di-m-direkt	absolutely direct
diri	alive	p	di-p-diri	very alive
doğru	straight	p s	do-p- doğru do-s-doğru	perfectly correct
dolu	full	p s	do-p- dolu do-s-dolu	over-filled
duru	clear	p	du-p-duru	very clear
düz	flat	m p pA be	dü-m-düz dü-p-düz dü-pe-düz dü-be-düz	absolutely flat
eski	old	p	e-p-eski	quite old
eyü, *eyi, *eyice	good	p	e-p-ey e-p-eyce	rather a lot (of) (the) best
genç	young	p pA	ge-p- genç ge-pe-genç	very young
geniş	wide	m	ge-m-geniş	quite wide
gök	sky	m	gö-m-gök	quite blue
gündüz	(in) daylight	pA	gü-pe-gündüz	(in) broad daylight
güzel	beautiful	p	gü-p-güzel	very beautiful
halat	rope	m	ha-m-halat	rough, uncouth
hayal	dream	m	ha-m-hayal	fantasy, illusion
hayalli	unreal	m	ha-m-hayalli	dreamy
hayranlık	admiration	t	ha-t-hayranlık	adoration
hazır	ready	p	ha-p- hazır	completely ready
ırak	far	p	ı-p-ırak	too far
ıslak	wet	p	ı-p-ıslak	very wet

ıssız	uninhabited	p	ı-p-ıssız	absolutely desert
ışık	light	p	ı-p-ışık	very bright
ihtiyar	old	p	i-p-ihtiyar	too old
ince, incecik	thin	p	i-p-ince i-p-incecik	too thin
incelik	thinness	p	i-p-incelik	(the) most thinness
iri	ivast	p	i-p-iri	very vast
*kacak	dishes	p	ka-p-kacak	pots and pans
kara	black	p	ka-p-kara	pitch black
karanlık	darkness	p ş	ka-p-karanlık ka-ş-karanlık	complete darkness
karış	untidy	rma	ka-rma-karış	very untidy
karışık	mixed	m rma	ka-m-karışık ka-rma-karışık	in a mess in utter disorder
katı	hard	p s	ka-p-katı ka-s-katı	very hard, rigid
kavlak	peeled	s	ka-s-kavlak	very peeled
kırmızı	red	p	kı-p-kırmızı	quite red
kısa	short	p	kı-p-kısa	too short
kıvrak	lithe	s	kı-s-kıvrak	tightly bound
kızıl	red	p	kı-p-kızıl	fully red
koca	big	s	ko-s-koca	huge
kocaman	huge	s	ko-s-kocaman	colossal
kolay	easy	p	ko-p-kolay	very easy
koyu	dark	p	ko-p-koyu	fully dark
kör	blind	p	kö-p-kör	absolutely blind
kötü	bad	p	kö-p-kötü	very bad
kuru	dry	p	ku-p-kuru	bone-dry
kütük	drunk	s	kü-s-kütük	very drunk

mavi	blue	s	ma-s-mavi	blue-blue
mavilik	blue colour	s	ma-s-mavilik	blueness
mor	violet	s	mo-s-mor	violet
olgun	ripe	p	o-p-olgun	fully ripe
ölgün	withered	p	ö-p-ölgün	very withered
parça	piece	ram	pa-ram-parça	broken to bits
pembe	pink	s	pe-s-pembe	very pink
perişan	scattered	r s	pe-r-perişan pe-s-perişan	in confusion
*pirik	old	m	pi-m-pirik	very old
pis	dirty	m	pi-m-pis	too dirty
sağ	alined	pA	sa-pa-sağ	in good health
sağlam	healthy	p pA	sa-p-sağlam sa-pa-sağlam	sound and well
sakin	quiet	p	sa-p-sakin	totally quiet
sarı	yellow	p	sa-p-sarı	bright yellow
sefil	miserable	r rIl	se-r-sefil se-ril-sefil	very miserable
serpe	freely	re	se-re-serpe	quite freely
sert	hard	m	se-m-sert	too hard
sıcak	hot	m p	sı-m-sıcak sı-p-sıcak	very hot
sıkı	tight	m	sı-m-sıkı	very tight
sıklam	wet	r rIl	sı-r-sıklam sı-rıl-sıklam	sopping wet
siyah	black	m p	si-m-siyah si-p-siyah	pitch black
sivri	sharp	p	si-p-sivri	sharp
şirin	pretty	m p	şi-m-şirin şi-p-şirin	very pretty
takır	empty	m	ta-m-takır	quite empty

tamam	complete	s	ta-s-tamam	quite complete
tatlı	sweet	p	ta-p-tatlı	fully sweet
taze	fresh	p pA	ta-p-taze ta-pa-taze	very fresh
tekerlek	wheel	s	te-s-tekerlek	very round
temiz	clean	r	te-r-temiz	absolutely clean
top	ball	r	to-r-top	quite round
topaç	fat	s	to-s-topaç	quite fat
toparlak	round	s	to-s-toparlak	quite round
ucuz	cheap	p	u-p-ucuz	very cheap
ufak	small	p	u-p-ufak	too small
uslu	quiet	p	u-p-uslu	fairly quiet
uygun	suitable	p	u-p-uygun	very adequate
uzun	long	p	u-p-uzun	extremely long
yakın	near	p	ya-p-yakın	very near
yalnız	alone	p pA	ya-p-yalnız ya-pa-yalnız	totally alone
yarık	split	p	ya-p-yarık	very split
yassı	flat	m	ya-m-yassı	very flat
yaş	tear	m	ya-m-yaş	very much tears
yaz	summer	m	ya-m-yaz	very summery
yeni	new	p pis s	ye-p-yeni ye-pis-yeni ye-s-yeni	brand-new
yeşil	green	m p	ye-m-yeşil ye-p-yeşil	fully green
yumru	bump	s	yu-s-yumru	very bumpy
yuvarlak	round	s	yu-s-yuvarlak	quite round
zayıf	weak	p	za-p-zayıf	very weak

Discussion (Extract)

BEEDHAM: Would you clarify your use of the term 'suffix'. Usually the affix at the end of a word is called a suffix; any morpheme preceding the suffix which isn't the root is called 'infix', 'interfix', etc., but not suffix.

JIKIA: In grammars of Turkish the term 'suffix' is used to mean any morpheme to the right of the stem, not necessarily the last one. So by 'suffixation' is meant the addition of affixes to the right of the stem, i.e. the addition of suffixes. So what is odd and irregular about the reduplication I have described is that it involves the addition of an affix to the left of the stem, i.e. a prefix-type morpheme, intensifiers. They are different to prefixes, in fact they are interfixes, because they serve to bind roots to roots.

BASSAC: I want to express my pleasure at seeing the difficult problem known in Turkish grammar as that of 'üsteleme sıfatları' tackled in this conference, and have many questions to ask. My first question is: is this reduplication as productive with derived adjectives such as *açımsı* (cross-like) from *aç* (cross)?

JIKIA: This reduplication is productive on only derived words with the following suffixes: -lIk, -sIz, -AcIk, -Ik, -lam, -ArlAk.

BASSAC: Is there any difference between the reduplicated form in *p* and *p* + vowel such as *yapyalnız* and *yapayalnız*, and do you think that there is a motivation for the presence of the vowel and that these forms have the same meaning?

JIKIA: There does not seem to be any variation in meaning and the presence of the vowel is largely unmotivated as far as I know.

BASSAC: Is there a difference between intensive forms built by reduplication and those built with *çok* ('very')?

JIKIA: No, definitely not, these two forms are unambiguously equivalent.

CHRISTOPHER GLEDHILL

11   On the Discourse Functions and Contrastive Phraseology of Equivalent Light Verb Constructions Involving 'make' and 'take'

ABSTRACT

The verbs *make* and *take* are used in a wide range of light verb constructions (LVC) such as *make / take + bath, call, joke*, etc. The alternation of *make / take* in these constructions can usually be explained by the meaning of the light verb (*make* as creation, *take* as reaction). However, a small set of expressions do not appear to follow this pattern: *make / take + decision, note, effort, time*. In this paper, I examine the phraseology of these expressions in the British National Corpus. Using the framework of Systemic Functional Grammar (SFG), I show that this particular group of LVCs are (mostly) used in verbal group complexes of the form: *make / take + N + to* V. In SFG terms, this is a 'grammatical metaphor' in which the LVCs express an evaluation of the following predicator. I argue that it is only when we analyse the extended phraseology of these 'exceptions' that we can see how these expressions still broadly follow the regular patterns of English.

Introduction

Light verb constructions (LVCs) (such as *bring to mind, give a talk, make a decision*, etc.) differ from other verb phrases (such as *bring to market, give a gift, make a cake*, etc.), in that they are composed of a 'predicative' noun, which refers to a specific process (*mind, talk, decision*), and a 'light' verb, which re-frames this process in terms of a general metaphor (*bring, give, make*, etc.).[1] In this paper, I focus on the particular phenomenon of 'equivalent' LVCs in English. Equivalent LVCs are constructions in which two or more alternative light verbs can be used, such as *give / have + talk, make / take + decision*, etc. Generally speaking, it is possible to explain the choice between light Vs such as *make* and *take* in equivalent LVCs by looking at the meaning of the noun (N) in the expression. For example, the Ns which are used exclusively with *make* (+ *amends, contact, deal, fun, gesture, love, sense …*) appear to refer to psychological or social behaviours: these processes are necessarily complex and involve various stages. On the other hand, the Ns which only occur with *take* (+ *action, bite, care, chance, charge, heart, issue, umbrage …*) tend to express psychological or physical reactions: these can be seen as actions or states of mind which are the result of a single, particular decision to act. This general difference may explain the distribution of *make* or *take* among a large number of LVCs. A similar distinction can be proposed to explain equivalent expressions which allow for both light Vs, but this time the onus is on the meaning of the light V. Generally, the subjects of many LVCs with *make* tend to have the underlying semantic role of 'initiator, creator' or in grammatical terms Agent (*make + bath, call, exception, joke, point*, etc.), in contrast to Subjects of many LVCs with *take* which tend to function as 'possessor, receiver' or Medium[2] (*take + bath, call, exception, joke, point*, etc.).

However, not all equivalent LVCs can be explained in these terms. In this paper I focus on a small set of constructions which appear to be exceptions to the general pattern, at least when observed out of context: *make / take + (a) decision, (a) note, (a, the) effort* and *(the or zero) time*. The hypothesis I wish to test here is that far from being interchangeable, each of these LVCs in fact has a consistent and contrastive pattern of use. This is in keeping with the structuralist principle, set out again recently

1 This article is based on a paper read at the *Summer School and Conference on the Method of Lexical Exceptions*, St Andrews 2–8 Sept. 2007. I am very grateful to Tom Bloor for comments on a previous draft. I am solely responsibile for any errors remaining.
2 In Systemic Functional Grammar initial capitals are conventionally used to refer to terms which are particular to the model.

by Beedham 2005, that apparent 'exceptions' point to an alternative regular system within a given language. However, in this paper, I attempt to show that this kind of observation can only be carried out by analysing the phraseology of a particular sign in a representative sample of texts (such as the British National Corpus, BNC³). By 'phraseology', I am not only referring here to idiomatic expressions, but to the more general tendency for signs (either lexical or grammatical items) to habitually co-occur with other signs in a particular communicative context (Firth 1957, Sinclair 1991). A related hypothesis I wish to explore here is that the phraseology of any given light V construction usually involves a much more regular extended lexico-grammatical environment than we would normally expect. Thus, my survey of the BNC below suggests that the expressions *make / take +
decision, note, effort* and *time* differ from many other LVCs in that they are typically used in 'verbal group complexes', structures which express an abstract form of evaluation in relation to the following non-finite clause. I would suggest that this is a significant feature of this particular group of expressions.

The linguistic literature on LVCs has been primarily concerned with issues of categorization. This debate is clearly of interest to syntacticians and lexicologists, whose aim is to study the particular place of linguistic signs in relation to each other within the abstract language system. But it is less relevant to discourse-oriented linguists, who are interested in how the language system creates meaning in different communicative contexts, and how signs are used in naturally-occurring texts. For this reason, in the section titled 'LVCs in mainstream grammar' I only give a very brief discussion of the defining features of LVCs. Although LVCs have attracted much attention in formal grammar and lexicology, there has been less research on them in functional or discourse-oriented linguistics. This is surprising, given that the difference between a V such as *to decide* and its equivalent LVCs, such as *to + come to / make / take / reach*, etc.+ *decision* is just as

---

3   The British National Corpus (BNC) is a representative corpus of 100 million words of spoken and (mostly) written texts in British English dating from the 1980s and 1990s (as reported in Aston and Burnard 1998).

likely to be found in the communicative functions of these phrases as in the semantics and structure of their constituent parts. In order to address this issue, in the following section titled 'LVCs in Systemic Functional Grammar' I set out the analysis of LVCs from the point of view of the discourse-oriented model of language, Systemic Functional Grammar (SFG, Halliday 1985, Bloor and Bloor 2004, Halliday and Matthiessen 2004). According to this approach, LVCs can be seen as part of a broader class of 'extended predicates', whose function is to express a particularly abstract (but also very productive) form of 'grammatical metaphor' (this point has been made previously in Gledhill 2008, 2009). In support of this analysis, in the penultimate section titled 'LVCs in the British National Corpus' I present a corpus-based analysis of the LVCs *make / take + decision / note* (with their equivalent Vs *to decide* and *to note*) and the LVCs *make / take + effort, time* (which do not have equivalent Vs).

LVCs in mainstream grammar

LVCs can be seen as both partially grammaticalized and partially lexicalized phrases (Brinton and Akimoto 1999, Brinton and Traugott 2005). On the one hand, all LVCs share a relatively predictable, productive structure (light V + predicative N) and semantics (including lexical aspect). On the other hand, when we look at LVCs not as a class, but as individual expressions, their structure and semantics are relatively specialized (this is especially true of LVCs with a 'non-referential' N). In the following discussion, I discuss these issues in terms of compositional and lexical aspect (2.1), and the syntactic constraints on the predicative N (2.2).

LVCs and aspect

Jespersen (1942) observed that LVCs express a process as an 'isolated instance':

> The most usual meaning of substantives derived from and identical in form with a verb is the action or an isolated instance of the action. This is particularly frequent in such everyday combinations [...] after *have* and similar 'light' verbs. They are in accordance with the general tendency of Mod E to place an insignificant verb, to which marks of person and tense are attached, before the really important idea [...] Such constructions also offer an easy means of adding some descriptive trait in the form of an adjunct: *we had a delightful bathe, a quiet smoke*, etc. They thus in some way form a parallel to those with a 'cognate object': *fight the good fight*, etc. (Jespersen 1942 VI: 117).

Subsequent linguists agree that LVCs make an important contribution to the expression of 'aspect', whether in contrast to other equivalent LVCs or equivalent simple Vs (Vendler 1967, Smith 1991, Cotte 1998, Ballier 2003, inter alia). One of the problems commonly addressed in the literature is the extent to which the aspect of any given LVC is compositional, i.e. determined by modifiers of the LVC, or lexical, i.e. motivated by the underlying meaning of the predicative N. It has also been noted (for example in Celle 2004) that the modification of an LVC by an article such as *a/an* signals that a process is countable (and thus compatible with 'accomplishments' or bounded time-frames, as in as in *have a meal, take a break*), while the absence of an article signals that the process is uncountable (compatible with states and atelic processes, such as *make sense, take shelter*). In addition, as Hiroe (2007) has argued, the semantics of the N, at least for certain categories of LVC, appears to be decisive in determining the type of (lexical) aspect expressed by the LVC. Hiroe has thus suggested two broad types of LVC. The first group (invented examples 1a–c, from Hiroe 2007: 6–7) can express either an 'activity' (compatible with phrases of duration: the '*for* test') or an 'accomplishment' (with phrases of bounded time-spans: the '*in* test'):

1a. John **did** a **dance** for/in ten minutes. = Activity or Accomplishment
1b. Prof. Smith **gave** a **lecture** on molecular biology for/in an hour.
    = Activity or Accomplishment
1c. John **took** a deep **breath** for/in three seconds. = Activity or
    Accomplishment

By contrast, a second group of LVCs (invented examples 2a–c) is incompatible with phrases of duration, and thus only express an 'activity' (i.e. a process which is dynamic, durative, atelic):

2a. John **had** a **sleep** for/*in an hour = Activity not Accomplishment[4]
2b. Mary **took** a **rest** for/*in half an hour. = Activity not
    Accomplishment
2c. John **made** a **contribution** to the charity for/*in ten years. Activity
    not Accomplishment

Hiroe suggests that the second group is 'imperfective' because it involves Ns which express no inherent endpoint. He claims that this semantic trait supersedes the usual interpretation of the indefinite article.

It would be interesting to test this hypothesis with corpus data. As can be seen in the naturally occurring examples observed below, very few examples of LVCs in *make / take* are used in the same context as time expressions, which makes it difficult to use this kind of data to carry out formal tests for aspect. However, since it is not the aim of this paper to discuss grammatical aspect at any length, it is sufficient to observe, even in the invented examples cited above (1a–c, 2a–c), that individual LVCs express much finer gradations of meaning than suggested by categories such as 'activity', 'accomplishment' and so on. In addition, as many linguists have argued, the role of the light V is also a determining factor in the overall semantics of any given LVC. For example, Wierzbicka (1982) suggests that families of related LVCs such as *have a + bite, break, walk / take a + bite, break, walk* express very specific, but regular categories of aspect, which

---

4   The judgements about grammaticality made here are those of Hiroe, not mine.

she claims can be formulated in terms of the primitive meanings of the light Vs. According to Wierzbicka, LVCs with *have* represent a process as a repeatable state that has no external goal, while LVCs with *take* represent a process as the final result of a goal-oriented, initial motion (1982: 794–5). A similar point is made by Quirk et al. 1985: 752, who distinguish between *give*, *have* and *do* in expressing different levels of conscious planning or volition, as in the following series:

3a. She shrieked.
3b. She **gave** a **shriek.** ('an involuntary shriek')
3c. She **had** a good **shriek.** ('a voluntary shriek for own enjoyment')
3d. She **did** a (good) **shriek.** ('a performance before an audience')

Many attempts have been made to provide a formal analysis of the contribution of different light Vs to the meanings of LVCs. But as Butt (2003) points out, in a discussion of LVCs expressing semelfactive 'punctual' aspect (4b), the relationship between the aspect expressed by lexical Vs and their equivalent LVC or the aspect expressed by LVCs as a family of expressions is not always symmetrical or predictable:

4a. Kim coughed for / *in five minutes. (Activity only)
4b. Kim **had** a **cough** *for / *in five minutes. (neither Activity nor Accomplishment)

The ambiguity of (4b) is instructive (is the process expressed by the N, in which case the aspect is akin to an instantaneous 'achievement', or the V, in which case the aspect is a stative relation?). Butt concludes that the semantics of light Vs cannot be explained in the same terms as grammatical aspect:

> Light verbs serve to further structure or modulate the event described by the main verb in a manner that is quite distinct from auxiliaries, modals or other main verbs. (Butt 2003: 3).

It is interesting that Butt uses the term 'modulate' in this respect, because in Systemic Functional Grammar, 'Modulation' refers to the modification of a lexical verb by a preceding 'verbal group complex'. As we see below, some LVCs (although certainly not all) play an important role in these structures. In these contexts LVCs such as *make a decision to* +V, *take time to* +V express meanings which are comparable with, but not quite the same as aspect and modality.

The syntax of LVCs

There have been many attempts to identify the formal characteristics of LVCs. Most analysts propose sub-categories rather than a general class of expression. Thus, for example, generative grammar (Björkman 1978, Grimshaw and Mester 1988, Kearns 1989, Di-Sciullo and Rosen 1991 inter alia) makes a broad distinction between 'predicate nominal' and so-called 'pure light verb' constructions. Predicate nominals allow for passivization of the LVC, pronominalization of the N, pre- or post-modification of the N, and other grammatical paraphrases (these examples are mostly from Kearns 1989):[5]

5a. The commission **made** an **inspection** of the building.
5b. An **inspection** of the building was **made** last week.
5c. The commission's **inspection** of the building was rather cursory, ...
5d. Are you referring to the **inspection** which they **made** of the building? (etc.)

Since the N in a nominal predicate is said to be 'de-verbal' and 'referential', this kind of construction has a relatively productive, unconstrained syntax. In comparison, the predicative N in a (pure) light verb construction is considered to have all the properties of a 'bare' infinitive (on the basis of which the rest of the phrase is said to be derived), and is thus considered to be 'non-referential'. As we have seen, because the aspect of 'pure' LVCs is said to be lexical, and thus determined primarily by the process expressed

---

5   For the purposes of exposition, I have re-invented some of these invented examples.

in the predicative N, the articles and other modifiers in these constructions are highly constrained in contrast with predicate nominals:

6a. John **gave** the roses a **prune**
6b. *The roses were **given** a **prune** by John
6c. *John's **prune** of the roses was successful ...
6d. *John **gave** the roses the **prune** of their life (etc.)[6]

Wierzbicka (1982) makes the same distinction between equivalent 'cognate object' expressions such as *to have a think* and de-verbal LVCs such as *have a thought*. Since the N in *have a think* is predicative, it is not as grammatically productive as a de-verbal N (*to have the thought that, to have second thoughts* appear grammatical, but not *?to have the think that, ?to have second thinks*).

Although the term LVC has been adopted by many linguists, various related concepts have been proposed, notably the 'support verb construction' (Vivès 1984, Giry-Schneider 1987, Gross 1989, 2005 and others). An SVC is a verb phrase built around a (theoretically) meaningless 'support V' and a 'predicative N' whose semantic arguments are taken on as the syntactic arguments of the phrase as a whole. As with the generative light V, the SVC is seen to be a central mechanism in the construction of phrase structure. Unlike LVCs, however, SVCs are conceived in theory as a family of structures which all share the same predicative element, regardless of the semantic contribution of the support V (a similar concept is proposed by Allerton 2002). This means that 'non-light' (full or predicative) Vs can be categorized as (different related types of) SVCs. For example, the basic predicate *Max ordered Luke to +V* and the SVC *Max gave Luke an order to +V* are related to a 'converse' construction *Luke got an order from Max to +V* and various other constructions such as *Luke has an order to +V / Luke was given an order by Max to +V*, etc. (Gross 2005: 167 [my translation]).

---

6   Kearns notes, however, that most of these will work when used with the gerund *pruning*. I should add that the acceptability judgements about these examples are those of Kearns, not mine.

Although 'SVC' is often taken to be a very inclusive category of expression, the notion excludes many examples which other analysts would consider to be legitimate LVCs (such as *bring + to book*, *make / take + effort*, *make / take + time*, *take seriously*, etc.).

Some analysts, notably Pottelberge (2000), have suggested that it is not possible to identify a general overall category of LVCs. Similarly, others (Poulsen 2005, Barrier 2006, Storrer 2006) have suggested that it is not possible to identify any reliable defining characteristics for sub-categories, such as 'pure' LVCs or SVCs. Following Brinton and Traugott (2005), I have argued (Gledhill 2008, Todiraşcu and Gledhill 2008, Gledhill 2009) that it is more realistic to analyse LVCs on a continuum of 'extended predicates' ranging from partially lexicalized constructions to highly lexicalized phrases. Of course, it is natural that functionalists and other discourse-oriented linguists have a tendency to see grammatical phenomena in terms of variation and 'lexical diffusion'. They are therefore more comfortable with the gradual notion of a continuum and less preoccupied by the need to make a clear distinction between LVCs and other sequences (as they are with the distinction between grammar and lexis). On the other hand, formal linguists argue that it is absolutely necessary to establish watertight formal categories. For these analysts, a light verb construction (or support verb, stretched verb etc.) is by necessity a much more limited category of expression than the kinds of extended predicate that functional linguists are prepared to work with.

LVCs in Systemic Functional Grammar

In this section I set out the analysis of LVCs according to Systemic Functional Grammar (SFG, Halliday 1985, Halliday and Matthiessen 2004). The following text is split into two sections, which correspond to the two 'systems' of meaning at which it is relevant to analyse LVCs in this model: 'Transitivity' and 'Mood'. There is also a third major system in SFG, 'Theme', that is to say the organization of language in the form of messages and texts. It can be shown that LVCs also have an important role to play in theme and information structure. In addition, the presence or absence of an article (*make a decision, make all the decisions that matter*) can often be explained in terms of cohesive or textual reference.[7] However, space precludes me from addressing these issues in this paper.

LVCs and Transitivity

In SFG, the Transitivity system is concerned with how language represents ideas and experience in the form of lexical processes. As in other models, SFG makes a broad distinction between semantic roles which are non-essential or extrinsic to a process (such as Circumstantials), and 'participants' which are intrinsic to a process (material processes have Actors and Goals, mental processes have Sensers and Phenomena, relational processes have Carriers and Attributes, and so on). However, Halliday suggests that there exists an intermediate category, which is treated syntactically as though it were a participant, but from the point of view of meaning is part and parcel of the process:

> There may be in each type of clause one element which is not so much an entity participating in the process as a refinement of the process itself. (Halliday and Matthiessen 2004: 295)

Halliday uses the term 'Range' for the participant role of any element which determines the type or extent of the process expressed by the predicate as a whole (Halliday 1985: 149, Banks 2000, Bloor and Bloor 2004: 114–16). This distinction can be seen in (7a–d),[8] in which the N *note* has a variety of meanings, depending on its participant role in the clause. The following

---

7   Since determiner usage is not the focus of this paper, in the following sections I use a '+' sign to avoid, in most cases, having to specify each time that an article (*a, the* or zero) may or may not be used with a particular LVC.

8   Unless otherwise stated, all the numbered examples from this point on are taken from the BNC.

tables set out the usual way these examples are visualized in SFG notation (the middle line corresponds to clause function, the bottom line corresponds to participant role):

7a. Ace	took	the note	and	read	it
Subject	Finite/Predicator	Complement	//	Finite/Predicator	Complement
Actor	Material Process	Goal		Mental Process	Phenomenon

7b. On 15 December,	Fhimah	made	a note	in his diary ...
Adjunct	Subject	Finite/Predicator	Complement	Adjunct
Time	Actor	Material Process	Range	Location

7c. The women	took	note	of where the body was laid to rest
Subject	Finite/Predicator	Complement	Complement [[Embedded clause]]
Senser	Mental Process	Range	Phenomenon

7d. I	made	a mental note	that	I mustn't say anything ...
Subject	Finite/Predicator	Complement	//	Projected clause
Senser	Mental Process	Range		Phenomenon

In example (7a), *note* is an 'object' (a letter or some other message) which is moved or transferred, and thus has the participant role of Goal (of a material process). However, in examples (7b–d), *note* refers to different kinds of process, and thus has the participant role of Range. Thus, in (7b) *note* refers to a more abstract kind of material object: it can be understood either an abstract 'piece of writing' (a message scratched on paper), or perhaps more realistically as a material process: the 'act of writing' or 'making notes'. In (7c), we can observe that *note* refers much more clearly to a process, and there has been a change in process type; here *take note* expresses a psychological mental process equivalent to 'to notice, to remark'. Finally, in (7d) *made a mental note* explicitly refers to a mental process, but this time with the meaning 'to think, to remark to oneself'. This analysis can be verified by the presence of a 'projected' subordinate clause (this being a potential formal test for mental and verbal processes). In fact, *make a mental note to* + V is a prime example of a lexicalized phrase (which we encounter again in the corpus analysis).

It is important to state at this point that Halliday's concept of Range is not the same as 'predicative' in traditional grammar. In SFG, Range is a participant role which is determined in relation to the clause as a whole, and cannot be seen as an intrinsic property of one particular element in the clause or a lexical class (such as the 'predicative' status of a verb, adjective or noun). In this respect, Halliday uses the term to refer to variety of functions in the clause, which are not necessarily predicative:

> [...] the scope, type, extent, quality or quantity of the process or simply a restatement of the process itself in a nominal form (Halliday 1985: 149)

Furthermore, Halliday makes a distinction between two types of Range. First, 'Process Range' defines or names the lexical process expressed in the clause. We have seen this in examples (7a–d) above, but Process Range can be expressed by elements other than complements, in particular 'obligatory' adverbials and prepositional phrases (*bear in mind, bring into play, take into account, take lightly*). I have suggested previously (Gledhill 2005) that these elements have the clause function of 'extended predicator', as can be visualized in the following analysis (7e):

7e. I	take	seriously	any allegations of misbehaviour ...
Subject	Finite/Predicator	Extended Predicator	Complement
Senser	Mental Process	Process Range	Phenomenon

A second category, 'Entity Range', delimits the extent of the process expressed by a predicator. This type of Range expresses a variety of functions, such as the specification of a process type (*Dante wrote +his epic poem*), the specification of extent (*Matthew Webb first swam +the English Channel*, which is not the same as the Circumstantial: *+across the English*

Channel), the product of resultative constructions (*Van Gogh had painted the canvas +one shade of blue*), and so on. Entity Range can also be seen in 'caused movement' constructions (7f–g), some of which (7g) resemble LVCs in that they have a relatively light V, an obligatory 'extended predicator' and an equivalent lexical V 'to shelve':

   7f. He knelt on the car park gravel to **stow in his daypack** the grated cheese sandwiches.[9]
   7g. Nathalie **put on the shelf** every piece of fiddle music she had collected in Nova Scotia.[10]

It can be seen in these and previous examples that expressions of Entity Range often serve to express the outcome or 'endpoint' of a process, and therefore contribute to the expression of compositional aspect, as mentioned above.

I mentioned above that SFG does not consider LVCs to be a separate sub-category of expression, but rather as part of a gradual continuum which extends from simple transitive constructions to more metaphorical forms of speech. However, it is precisely this notion of metaphor which makes LVCs stand out from other predicates. From the point of view of SFG, all LVCs can essentially be considered to be examples of 'grammatical metaphor'. According to Halliday and Matthiessen, grammatical metaphor refers to a transfer of meaning from a 'congruent' (non-metaphorical) mode of expression to a more metaphorical mode (2004: 592–3). Halliday and Martin (1993) claim that this form of expression has had a particularly important role to play in technical and scientific English (as can be seen in such abstractions as *give effect to, have an impact on, have an important role to play, take possession of*, etc.). It is perhaps no accident that many examples of LVCs examined in the corpus analysis in this paper belong to the same type of discourse. In addition, I would suggest that LVCs present a rather complex form of metaphorical expression, in that they involve increasingly abstract cyclical layers of meaning:

9   From: McEwan, Ian. 1998. *Amsterdam*. London: Anchor Books, p76.
10   Cited in Ernst 2002: 208–9.

Grammatical Metaphor (1) the re-expression (nominalization) of a congruent event (*to note*) as a metaphorical entity (*a note.*)

Grammatical Metaphor (2) the reformulation of this process (GM1) as a participant in a more abstract process (*have* = 'possess', *give* = 'transmit', *make* = 'create', *take* = 'appropriate'...)

Grammatical Metaphor (3) the re-interpretation of the whole expression (GM2) as a new composite process (which is not evident until equivalent LVCs are compared: *have a word* 'talk' vs. *have words* 'dispute', *make notes* 'write notes' vs. *take note* 'to notice', etc.).

In the next section, we see that this cycle is taken one step further, since some LVCs are used in verbal group complexes to express (an abstract) evaluation of the process expressed by the following verb.

LVCs and Mood

The Mood system in SFG is concerned with how language expresses interpersonal relationships in the form of speech functions. The primary speech functions of English include Mood type (indicative, imperative, etc.), Modality, Polarity, and so on. Just as LVCs have a significant role to play in Transitivity (the representation of the world in terms of lexical processes), LVCs are also involved in the expression of interpersonal meanings. Most LVCs probably express some form of evaluation of the lexical process expressed in the predicate as a whole, but in this section I focus on a small group of LVCs which fulfil this role in the particular context of 'verbal group (VG) complexes' (Halliday and Matthiessen 2004: 497–508, Bloor and Bloor 2004: 149–51). A VG complex is a serial verb structure in which the first verb (V1) introduces a second, non-finite verb (V2). In SFG terms, the V1 does not express a process of its own, but rather serves to pick out a particular facet of the lexical process expressed by V2. As is evident in examples such as *have the opportunity to do it, make the effort to do it, make a mess of doing it,* the N signals an explicit evaluation of the following V2 by labelling it as an *opportunity, an effort, a mess,* etc. In structures such as these, the VG complex can be analysed as a form of grammatical metaphor (as discussed in the previous section).

Halliday and Matthiessen (2004: 497–508) suggest that the V1 in a VG complex can express various types of meaning in relation to the V2: 'Phase' expresses the aspect or potential time-frame of a process (*to keep meowing*), 'Conation' evaluates the actual or attempted realization of a process (*to try to measure the speed of light*) and 'Modulation' signals the circumstances or potential means by which a process is realized (*to help to lead the resistance*). A fourth term, 'Projection', is used for VG complexes in which the V1 is a Mental process (*to expect to win the ballot*). Since in cases of Projection, the V1 is an independent process in relation to the V2, this structure is not strictly speaking a VG complex but rather a (non-finite) clause complex. In Table 11.1, I have drawn up a summary of these different categories. Halliday and Matthiessen (2004) provide several examples of Vs (listed below, under the examples 8a–8d) but they do not give examples of LVCs. For comparison, I have suggested some examples (9a–d) which reflect the patterns observed in the data analysis.

Table 11.1 Light Verb Constructions and verbal group complexes

Type of VG relation	Meaning of V1	Single V examples	LVC examples
Phase	V1 = aspect (when V2 is realized)	8a. He just **kept** meow**ing** the whole time	9a. Titch **took time to** consider the question
		Other Vs: *begin to, get + ing, seem to, start +ing*	Other LVCs: *take ages to, take long to, take a moment to, take a while to,*
Conation	V1 = polarity (whether V2 is realized)	8b. Galileo **tried to** measure the speed of light	9b. Please **make** every **effort to** attend
		Other Vs: *avoid +ing, fail to, learn to, manage to*	Other LVCs: *be able to, have a go at +ing, make a bid to, take care to, make a point of +ing*

Modulation	V1 = modality (by what means V2 is realized)	8c. Barbara Castle **helped to** lead the resistance	9c. Everyone **has the right to** say no.
		Other Vs: *happen to, hasten to, insist on +ing, remember to, tend to*	Other LVCs: *get the chance to, have the authority to, have a duty to, have the potential to*
Projection	V1 = mental process	8d. She **expected to** win the ballot	9d. I had to **make a decision to** stay in this line of work
		Other Vs: *decide to, enjoy +ing, intend to, promise to, remember +ing*	Other LVCs: *have the option to, make a choice to, make a promise to, take a decision to*

The clause relations Phase, Conation and Modulation have not been explored as thoroughly as other features of SFG. Perhaps this is because, when considering VG complexes, the categories are difficult to identify in naturally-occurring examples. However, in theory, it is not difficult to identify cases of Phase, since this often corresponds to a lexicalized expression of aspect that can be fairly straightforwardly compared with evaluative adjuncts of time such as *finally, initially, little by little*, etc. Typical examples of Phase include periphrastic constructions such as *to + be about to do, go on doing, stop doing*, etc. In these structures, the subject is a participant of the process expressed by V2, and the process expressed by V1 cannot be specified without reference to V2. As far as LVCs are concerned, in the corpus analysis in the following section, I found only one (possibly marginal) example of Phase: *take + ages, long, a moment, time, a while +V2*. Most of these are impersonal, postposed clauses (*It takes + time + to do this = To do this + takes + time* in contrast to *make time* which does not share the same pattern or meaning).

'Conation' is an evaluation of the extent to which a process is actualized or enabled, a meaning that is analogous to 'polarity' (as in the sequence: *X did it, X nearly did not do it, X nearly did it, X did not do it*). Among the examples given by Halliday and Matthiessen (2004: 511), Conation can be most clearly seen in causatives which express how participant X enables participant Y to do something (the examples given include: *X encouraged, instructed, taught, trained Y to* V). In these structures, it can be inferred that the process in V2 is actualized, or an attempt has been made to do so. In addition, and unlike Phase, the subject in a Conation structure has two different participant roles: one for V1 (often the 'Behaver' of a behavioural process, such as *help, learn, manage,* etc.) and V2 (some other participant role). In LVCs, the light V *take* often expresses this meaning (such as *take + action, care, effort, measures, pains, steps, time, trouble* +V2). These expressions all refer to the cognitive or physical 'effort' (and also 'time') that has been, or was nearly, expended in realizing a process.

Finally, 'Modulation' expresses an evaluation of the means by which a process is actualized. Modulation can be thought of as a lexicalized form of 'modality', in that the V1 expresses meanings to do with deontic permission or potential (*X can / may do Y*) or epistemic inference and possibility (*X could have / might have done Y*). The light V *have* is often used in LVCs which express these kinds of meaning (*have + the capacity, the opportunity, the potential, the responsibility, the right* +V2). Examples such as these can be distinguished from Conation by considering whether the process in V2 is effectively realized or only potentially realized: in *X has a go at doing Y* the process is (nearly) realized, and the V1 expresses an evaluation of this attempt, while in *X has a chance to do Y* the process is only potentially realized, and the V1 focuses on this eventuality. This seems to be a criterial distinction between Conation and Modulation. In addition, as with Phase, Halliday and Matthiessen (2004: 508) suggest that because the role of the V1 is simply to modify the process expressed in the following V2, in cases of Modulation, the V1 does not express a separate process, and thus resists probes such as the passive construction. In the data analysis below, I suggest the light V *make* (in contrast with *take*) tends to be used with VGs expressing Modulation. It might be objected that, since the V *decide* and its equivalent LVCs *make / take + decision* are mental processes, they should primarily express 'Projection' (as noted above in 8d, 9d). However, it seems to me that in the case of *decide* and *note* there may be a correlation between the meanings of the clauses projected by Vs and LVCs on the one hand and clause relations on the other. This can be summarized as: *decide / note* + clause = Phase, *take + decision / note* + clause = Conation, *make + decision / note* + clause = Modulation.

LVCs in the British National Corpus

The aim in this section is to explore the contrastive use of the light verbs *make* and *take*, principally in relation to the equivalent LVCs *make / take + decision* and equivalent full V (*to decide*). These observations are then compared briefly with a small set of similar LVCs, namely *make / take + note, effort time*. I would contend that this small group of expressions has a somewhat different set of lexical patterns to that of other equivalent LVCs in *make + take*. This initial observation is based on a survey of 50 LVCs involving *make* and / or *take*, summarized in Table 11.2.

Table 11.2.The distribution of *make* and *take* in fifty different Light Verb Constructions

Exclusive LVCs (not interchangeable, when the Complement expresses Process Range)	10a. Different light verb: **make +** (an) appointment, (an) arrangement, (an) attempt, (a) change, (a) complaint, (a) concession, (o) contact, (o) conversation, (a) deal, (a) demand, (a) discovery, (an) enquiry, (an) excuse, (a) fortune, (some / o) friends, (o) fun, (an) investment, (a) list (of), (o) love, (o) mention, (a) mistake, (o) sense, (a) wish ... **take +** action, (a) bite, (o) care, (a) chance, (o) charge, (a) class, (o) exercise, (o) heart, (a, the) lead, (a) look, (a) nap, (a) test, (a) walk ...

Contrastive LVCs (interchangeable, but with a clear contrast in meaning)	10b. Different process, different participant: **make** (a) bath 'prepare bath' / **take** (a) bath 'bathe' **make** (a) bow 'bend down' / **take** (a) bow 'react to audience' **make** (a) break 'escape' / **take** (a) break 'pause' **make** (an) exception 'recognise unique case' / **take** (o) exception 'react badly' **make** (a) hint 'suggest' / **take** (a) hint 'understand' **make** (a) meal 'prepare' / **take** (a) meal 'eat' **make** (a) point 'communicate idea' / **take** (a) point 'understand' **make** (o) trouble 'cause problems' / **take** (the) trouble 'care'
	10c. Similar process, different participant [Transitive / Ergative]: **make** (a) bid [Actor / Agent] / **take** (a) bid [Actor / Beneficiary] **make** (a) call [Actor / Agent] / **take** (a) call [Actor / Medium] **make** (an) opportunity [Actor / Agent] / **take** (the) opportunity [Actor / Beneficiary] **make** (a) picture [Actor / Agent] / **take** (a) picture [Actor / Medium]
Interchangeable LVCs (interchangeable, with a slight contrast in meaning)	10d. Similar process type, similar participant: **make** (a) decision / **take** (a) decision **make** (an) effort / **take** (an) effort **make** (a, zero) note / **take** (a, zero) note **make** (the, zero) time / **take** (the, zero) time

Note. The articles (*a, the*, zero) mentioned here are only indicative. As mentioned earlier, I do not focus on determiner usage here, and thus use a '+' sign for the citation forms of LVCs.

As shown in Table 11.2, I propose a basic distinction between 'Exclusive LVCs' (10a), 'Contrastive LVCs' (10b–c), and 'Interchangeable LVCs' (10d). Space precludes me from examining the Exclusive LVCs (10a) in any detail. As mentioned in the Introduction, both groups of LVCs present some very general differences of meaning: *make* as a light V seems to have a preference for mental or verbal processes, *take* as a light V tends to be used with material or behavioural processes. This general trend can also be observed in the lexicogrammatical patterns of the Contrastive and Interchangeable LVCs.

Contrastive LVCs (10b) involve a change in meaning either of the lexical process, or if there is no change in process type, a change of participant role. For example, *make / take + bath* express two different types of material process (roughly glossed as 'run a bath, prepare a bath' vs. 'bathe, enjoy a bath'). In some cases, as noted in (10c), both LVCs refer to the same process, but their participants play subtly different roles. In SFG, this difference can be captured by analysing the lexical process in terms of two simultaneous perspectives: 'transitive' and 'ergative' (Halliday and Matthiessen 2004: 280–302). From a transitive perspective, an external 'source' or 'initiator' is seen as the primary participant of the process. Thus the (invented) examples:

10e. *Pat makes nice photographs*
10f. *Pat takes nice photographs*

would both be analysed transitively as *Pat* = Actor (i.e. a photographer), the only difference of meaning being in the interpretation of *photograph*: in (10e) this appears to be unambiguously a physical object or a result in which case it is a 'Goal'. In (10f) however, *photograph* can be taken to represent either a Goal (the physical object, which can be 'appropriated' or otherwise created, transferred, etc.) or a process Range (the act of taking photographs with a camera). An ergative perspective on the other hand sees the primary participant as 'inherent' to the process, and in SFG this participant is labelled 'Medium'. An ergative analysis of (10e–f) would not be very different to that of a transitive analysis, except for a change of labels (*Pat* = Agent, *photographs* = Medium or Range). However, an ergative analysis would allow us to represent a third potential reading for (10f) 'Pat is photogenic / is nice to photograph'. All of these readings can thus be represented as follows (using transitive / ergative labels simultaneously):

10e. *Pat* (Actor / Agent) *makes* (Material process: 'creates') *nice photographs* (Goal / Medium)
10f. (ii) *Pat* (Actor / Agent) *takes* (Material process: 'appropriates, receives') *nice photographs* (Goal / Medium)

10f. (i) *Pat* (Actor / Agent) *takes* (Material process: 'photographs')
nice photographs (Range / Range)

10f. (iii) *Pat* (Actor / Medium) *takes* (Material process: 'is the photogenic subject of') *nice photographs* (Range / Range)

Although it is possible to represent these differences from a purely transitive perspective (by seeing *Pat* as some kind of 'Beneficiary' in sense iii),
an ergative or 'middle' analysis appears to present a much more systematic
way of analysing such examples. It is for this reason that in Table 11.2 I have
proposed a dual analysis for various other LVCs (examples 10c) which
appear to have little difference in meaning in terms of lexical process, but
which have different participant roles. Thus for example, *make + bid, call,
opportunity, picture* all appear to have the roles of Actor / Agent (depending
on the specific process), as opposed to *take + bid, call, opportunity, picture*
which can be analysed as Actor / Medium.

Of course, it is entirely unsurprising to find that the light Vs *make*
and *take* are associated with different semantic roles. As I mentioned in
the introduction, the alternation between *take* and *make* in LVCs can
usually be explained by appealing to the general semantics of the light V:
LVCs with *make* prototypically express 'agency, creation' (expressed as a
complex, multi-stage process), while LVCs with *take* usually refer to some
kind of 'appropriation, reception' (which takes place as a single, punctual
event). However, it is surprising to see that a small number of examples
(*make / take + decision, effort, note, time*) cannot be explained in this way.
This small group of 'Interchangeable LVCs' (10d) can be expressed with
both *make* and *take* as light Vs, yet, out of context, these LVCs cannot be
as easily distinguished in terms of participant or process type as the examples listed in (10a–c). It might be argued that *make + note* and *take + note*
express different process types ('write a note' or 'think'): but I would contend that, without the aid of corpus-based evidence, it would be difficult
for us to say that one or the other is associated with these interpretations
(in fact, as we see below, there is a clear distinction, but it is not realized
in terms of process type). In addition, the four expressions I have identified here are probably not the only examples of this type (some possible
variants are discussed below).

The final point in relation to interchangeable LVCs, is that when we come to look at the corpus data, these LVCs can in fact be distinguished in term of subtly different process and participant types. Thus in the data analysis below, we see that *make / take* are not in fact interchangeable; rather they have different but regular lexicogrammatical patterns. I discuss the implications of this in the conclusion.

The contrastive phraseology of to decide, make + decision and take + decision

The V *to decide* occurs over 25000 times in the BNC. The frequency of the equivalent LVC *make + decision* (counting active and passive forms) is approximately 1521 and *take + decision* approximately 922. The frequency of alternative expressions such as *reach + decision* is much lower (approximately 128).[11] If we compare the typical lexicogrammar of each form, *decide* has a preference for finite, rankshifted and non-finite clauses, whereas its equivalent LVCs tend to prefer non-finite clauses or are used alone (as we see below, this preference is reversed for the V *to note* and its equivalent LVCs).

When *decide* introduces finite (projected) clauses, it expresses a cognitive or mental process equivalent to 'to realize, to understand'. The projected clause is either a proposition or a state of affairs (11a–d) or in some examples (11e), a personal resolution about some future action (as we see below, the pattern in 11e is shared by *make + decision*, but not *take + decision*):

11a. the French people **decided that** France's honour was at stake.[12]
11b. Hari **decided that** her mother must be told the truth.

---

11 A similar proportion has been observed (Gledhill 2008, Todiraşcu and Gledhill 2008) in English, French and Romanian. However, these examples were observed in 'technocratic' texts (legal documents of the European Union). There is some correlation between LVCs and text types, but I have no space to discuss this here.

12 Unless otherwise stated, from this example onwards I use the convention of only citing five examples taken from the BNC for each pattern.

    11c. Shortly after the film began, Liz Taylor **decided** enough was
        enough.
    11d. I **decided** I would postpone hostilities for a while.
    11e. if you **decide** you want to go sort of four, fourish or threeish ...

I can find only 7 examples of finite clauses projected by *make / take + deci-*
sion in the BNC. These do, however, present a regular pattern, in that the
modal *should* is always used in the subordinate clause. Here the meaning
of the LVC is something like 'recommend':

    12a. Alternatively, we can **make** the **decision that** decent wages <u>should</u>
        be paid to all workers.
    12b. it was not until September 18 that a **decision** was **made that** a
        section 105 investigation <u>should</u> be carried out.
    12c. indeed, in 1945, a conscious **decision** was **made that** it <u>should</u>
        remain so.
    12d. A **decision** was **made that** the delivery <u>should</u> be by Caesarean.
    12e. and the **decision** was **taken that** SERPS <u>should</u> be replaced.

As mentioned above, *decide* also introduces various types of rankshifted
clause (headed by the interrogatives *how*, *if*, *what*, *when*, *which*). In these
contexts, the process expressed by the V1 is closer to 'choose', and is usually accompanied by some modal expression expressing duty. Rankshifted
clauses headed by *whether* also belong to this pattern, and in many cases
the V2 (here underlined) refers to a choice about whether to commence,
continue or conclude a certain activity:

    13a. But the IWC has yet to **decide whether** to <u>continue</u> or <u>end</u> the
        moratorium, ...
    13b. then it's for the client to **decide whether** to <u>proceed</u>.
    13c. the Disciplinary Committee then has to **decide whether** to <u>go</u>
        <u>ahead</u> with the inquiry in his absence.
    13d. George Bush must **decide whether** to <u>renew</u> China's trading
        privileges.

13e. the latter have to **decide whether** to <u>stop</u> trying or to resort to more unconventional means.

The LVCs *make / take* + *decision* introduce very few rankshifted clauses. I only find 12 in the BNC, and these most often involve non-finite clauses introduced by prepositions (*make* + *decision as to whether / decision on which* etc.). These examples are similar to *make* + *decision that* (13a–e), and the LVC can similarly be paraphrased by 'to recommend (that)':

14a. When the parents are equally decent and competent, or the reverse, it is very difficult to **make** a **decision as to where** <u>the children should reside</u> on breakdown of the parents' marriage.

14b. It is the human being who will be faced with the opportunity and perhaps the temptation to be violent, and who will **make** the **decision as to which** <u>path to follow.</u>

14c. Those who have to **make** the **decision whether** to <u>keep or discard</u> are often people who have spent their lives among books.

14d. See if you can get a similar report significantly quicker elsewhere and then **make** a **decision as to whether** <u>a less powerful but quicker report will do.</u>

14e. the test which I need to adopt when I go to the site again, is to look at it and er simply **make** a **decision as to whether** or not in my opinion <u>the land is more properly a part of this built-up area.</u>

I now turn to patterns in which the V *decide* and LVCs *make / take* + *decision* introduce non-finite clauses. As with the rankshifted clauses mentioned above (13a–e), non-finites introduced by *decide* often involve idiomatic expressions of delay and postponement, such as: *call it a day*, *stall for time*, *wait and see*. This is such a regular phraseology that I have given a longer sample than usual to illustrate the variety of 'time-span' phrases used in the non-finite clause (here underlined):

15a. That evening I **decided** to <u>begin</u> my search around the shower area.

15b. There was nothing. They had **decided to** <u>call it a day,</u> that was all.

15c. He **decided** <u>to carry on</u> and returned to training four weeks ago.

15d. Upon getting airborne, Crocker **decided to** <u>continue</u> the trip which meant flying with two ...

15e. I **decided to** <u>delay</u> informing him of my visit to the Orne.

15f. he was trying to chat me up, I **decided to** <u>end</u> the conversation and get off the train.

15g. At the end of last season I had all but **decided to** <u>finish my career</u> playing junior rugby.

15h. At the same time it was **decided to** <u>go ahead</u> with a new 14,000 square foot facility.

15i. Nigel **decided to** <u>leave things a few weeks</u> then issue an invitation.

15j. the committee **decided to** <u>postpone</u> the proposed trip to Llangollen.

15k. we were a few days behind schedule by this time I **decided to** <u>press on</u> while the weather held .

15l. That's the usual procedure. Adam **decided to** <u>stall for time</u>.

15m. After my mother died he **decided to** <u>stay on</u> and **make** a living hunting.

15n. It was **decided to** <u>take no further action</u> with regard to the matter.

15o. He'd come across that before now. He **decided to** <u>wait and see</u> what happened.

Negative contexts follow the same pattern:

15p. If you **decide not to** <u>go ahead</u>, just return the policy within 15 days.

15q. So, and the person who's speaking **decides not to** <u>go on</u>, so perhaps the conversation has stopped.

15r. Preston **decided not to** <u>pursue the subject</u>.

15s. The committee **decided not to** <u>take any further action</u> against four ...

15t. At half-past eleven the house was so quiet they **decided not to** <u>wait</u> until midnight.

I estimate that at least half of the non-finite clauses introduced by *decide* involve this kind of time expression in the BNC. Of the examples which do not follow the pattern, the projected non-finite clause still appears to involve some change in a course of action or a new psychological position (in aspectual terms this is 'inceptive'). This is not signalled explicitly, but can be gathered from elements in the immediate context (here underlined):

16a. <u>So</u> I've **decided to** ask Mrs Dean to come upstairs.
16b. He had <u>obviously</u> **decided to** be pleasant to her.
16c. <u>Back on the ground</u> again he **decided to** break the news.
16d. My <u>just married</u> son **decided to** build a wall in his back garden.
16e. <u>if we hear for example</u> that Saudi Arabia has **decided to** buy a series of British tanks ...

In sum, the series of examples (11, 13, 15) suggest that *decide* typically introduces non-finite projected clauses which express the commencement, continuation or conclusion of a process. This is a similar meaning to that of Phase, discussed above (although structurally it is not the same: here lexical aspect is expressed in the V2, or gathered from the surrounding context). If the V *decide* is associated with the projection of clauses expressing some form of Phase, I would suggest that the non-finite clauses introduced by the LVCs *make / take + decision* tend to express meanings related to Conation or Modulation. Thus, the LVC *make + decision* + non-finite clause tends to project non-finites in which the emphasis is less on the time-frame or ongoing process than on engaging in a potentially new process:

17a. So some farmers **make** the **decision to** <u>change</u> the crops in each field from one year to the next.
17b. **Making** the **decision to** <u>come in</u> is difficult for an investor.
17c. the subsequent investigation of Ventura led Tony Gamble to **make** the **decision to** <u>give it a try.</u>
17d. You can really only **make** your **decision to** <u>go netting</u> in a particular area that same day.
17e. I had to **make** a **decision to** <u>put my heart into it</u> or not to bother at all; ...

The passive construction *decision + (is / was) + made + to* (which, with 410 examples, makes up over one third of all uses of *make + decision*) involves a similar pattern. Its projected non-finite clauses often refer to a physical or metaphorical movement *ahead, forward, on*, etc.:

18a. The concept of effectiveness means that a **decision is made to** <u>do something</u> and to do it effectively.
18b. If the **decision is made to** <u>go ahead</u> ...
18c. It is for that reason that, if and when the **decision is made to** <u>move forward</u> ...
18d. The police have heard nothing. Finally, the **decision is made to** <u>move in</u>.
18e. ... so the **decision was made to** <u>venture abroad</u> to play matches in Belgium.

It is interesting to note that in these series (12a–e, 13a–e, 14a–e, 17a–e) and (18a–e), the LVC *make + decision* is typically followed by modals (in 12, *should*) or preceded by modals (in 13, 14, 17 *has, have to, must*), or conditional clauses with *if* (14, 17, 18) : this leads me to suggest below that the *decision* in question may have been *made*, but the contents of the *decision*, the process in V2 has not yet been enacted or actualized.

Whereas *make + decision* + non-finite clause tends to express 'personal' *decisions* which open up the possibilities of new processes, *take + decision* + non-finite clause generally expresses 'public' *decisions* which close off or narrow down the possibilities of further action. In examples (19a–e), it is clear from the process expressed by the V2 that the *decision taken* is momentous (here underlined). This correlates with the tendency for the *decision-taker* to be in some position of authority (here in italics):

19a. They hoped to arrange a meeting with Mr Mugabe, who in his capacity as *Chancellor of the university* was believed to have **taken** the **decision to** <u>close the campus.</u>
19b. The Prime Minister: There have been twin forms of law since *this House* **took** the **decision to** <u>enter the Community</u> 20 years ago.

19c. Responsibility for **taking** the **decision to** <u>imprison a person</u> before trial is shared between *the police, Crown Prosecution Service and the courts.*

19d. Moreover, as *Eisenhower* later publicly admitted, on 17 March Washington **took** the **decision to** <u>prepare an invasion</u> of Cuba.

19e. *Tommy Gilmour, Clinton's manager,* said last night: 'Pat had tried to go through the pain barrier and keep his injury from me but *I* have **taken** the **decision to** <u>withdraw him</u> after consultation with an orthopaedic surgeon.';

As we can see from these examples *take* + *decision* + non-finite clause tends to be used when the *decision* has dramatic or irrevocable consequences. Since these consequences usually affect participants other than the *decision-taker*, it is not surprising to find many passives, a structure in which the agentive role is optional, as in the following examples:

20a. Then, with dramatic abruptness, a **decision is taken** <u>to close the institution or move on.</u>

20b. At a recent SAG board meeting a **decision was taken** <u>to cut all development projects.</u>

20c. the armed response vehicle arrived and the **decision was taken** <u>to shoot the dogs.</u>

20d. in the wake of the Chernobyl disaster, the **decision was taken** <u>to start the shut-down in 1995.</u>

20e. the **decision was taken** <u>to terminate the programme.</u>

I can now summarize the data regarding non-finite projected clauses: LVCs with *take* introduce processes that are actualized (or 'de-actualized', since they often refer to the cessation of a process). Since the passive can be used to express the resultant state of an action (Beedham 2005), it is not surprising to find so many examples of LVCs with *take* in the passive. The LVC *take* + *decision* + V2 therefore generally involves Projection + Conation. On the other hand, *make* + *decision* + V2 appears to express a more diffuse set of meanings. In most cases, it is clear that although the *decision made* in V1 is an actualized event, the process expressed in V2 is not, since (as is the case of *to decide* + V2), *make* + *decision* is typically used to introduce a new process or course of action. I would therefore suggest that *make* + *decision* + non-finite clause correlates with Projection + Modulation (an expression which focusses on how the process in the V2 is realized, or has come about.) This meaning is not always easy to detect, especially in examples where it is almost certain that the process will be realized (e.g. 18d.). Nevertheless I would suggest that even in these examples, we can only be certain that a *decision* has been *made* to engage in a new process, and the emphasis is therefore less on the details or the effects of the *decision*, but rather on the means employed (whether the *decision* is *quick*, whether the *decision* enacts a communicative act, and so on.)

Let us now turn our attention to the differences between *decide* and its equivalent LVCs in terms of modification of the predicator or the complement. The V *decide* is typically modified by manner adjuncts which have a variety of meanings: source (*by experts*), means (*by democratic vote*), content (*differently*), and evaluation (*immediately*, *impulsively*):

21a. The treatment was to be **decided** <u>by experts</u>, and the people had simply to accept it.
21b. Supposing Yorkshire or Cornwall **decided** <u>by a majority vote</u> to secede from Britain ...
21c. The irony for England was that had he **decided** <u>differently</u> he would have been
21d. playing for them.
21e. Each of them has the power to **decide** <u>immediately</u> to stop purchasing.
21d. Folly had **decided** <u>impulsively</u> that they weren't friends at all.

In contrast, the LVC *make* + *decision* is typically modified by circumstantial adjuncts of time (the most frequent being *quickly*):

22a. a place on the United board that he would **make** his **decision** <u>at the end of this season.</u>
22b. I think the **decision** was **made** <u>long ago</u>. I cannot go back now.

22c. Thus, for example, in a police operational matter it may well be that one individual must make a decision and **make** that **decision** quickly.

22d. the bloke says we're going to sit down and **make a decision** tonight.

22e. FIDE was scheduled to **make a decision** yesterday.

The LVC *take + decision* tends to be modified by prepositional phrases in passive constructions. These are manner adjuncts which express the cognitive effort involved, or the reasons which motivated the *decision-taker*:

23a. the **decision** was **taken** after careful consideration.

23b. The spokesman stressed: 'This **decision** was **taken** after a great deal of thought and heartache'.

23c. The parliamentary candidate, yesterday revealed the **decision** was **taken** for financial reasons.

23d. Could it be that the **decision** was **taken** in a temporary depression from drugs?

23e. The **decision** was **taken** reluctantly by the company ...

The modification of Vs by adjuncts can be compared to the pre-modification of Ns in LVCs. The typical adjectives used in LVCs tend to correlate with the patterns observed above for adjuncts, namely: (22a–e) *make + decision* + time expression, (23a–e) *take + decision* + manner. There are four main patterns of pre-modification for *make + decision*. The first typically expresses an evaluation of the speed of the *decision*, and is preceded by various modals of necessity:

24a. GORDON Hamilton remains hopeful of a return to competitive rugby – but he won't **make** any hasty **decisions**.

24b. I had to **make** an instant **decision**, so I steered Foinavon to the right – the outside – to get away from the main part of the melee.

24c. The stewards inquiry had to **make** a quick **decision**; any defect in natural justice at that stage would be cured by the hearing before the full committee of the Jockey Club.

24d. This can happen at a time when you are under pressure and need to **make** a rapid **decision.**

24e. The most common cause of serious accidents on wire launches is **making** a snap **decision** to turn off for a 360° turn without ensuring that there is enough speed.

The second pattern is essentially a variation of (24a–e) involving classifying adjectives: *make* + *final, initial, preliminary* + *decision.* These items set out different stages in the *decision-making* process. In a third pattern (25a–e, below) the modifier evaluates the result or quality of a *decision*:

25a. By inhibiting our initial instinctive action we have the choice to **make** entirely different **decisions.**

25b. The weathermen are your best ally in **making** a good **decision** and probably the best coastal forecasts are those provided by 'Marineline'.

25c. It is designed to help each applicant to **make** an informed **decision** before applying for a particular programme of study.

25d. But if they are to **make** the right **decisions**, they must realise that the promise will turn to ashes.

25e. As adults, however, many of us cripple ourselves with fears of making mistakes, of **making** a wrong **decision**, of failing, of feeling embarrassed, of repeating the past.

The fourth and final pattern *make* + *all* + *decisions* is used to define the overall responsibilities of someone or some organization:

26a. The council **makes all the decisions** which concern the society's policy, but on major issues, the members' opinions are sought through ballots and general meetings.

26b. The leader **makes all the decisions** and issues instructions, expecting them to be obeyed without question.

26c. The manager still **makes all the decisions**, but believes that subordinates need to be motivated to accept them before they will do what he wants them to.

26d. They depict a stereotyped norm where <u>father</u> **makes all the deci-sions**, goes out to work and waits for his meals to be prepared by the wife with occasional assistance of the daughter.

26e. [as <u>the head of the family</u>] you no longer have to **make all your decisions** in terms of money.

The LVC *take + decision* has essentially one pre-modification and one post-modification pattern. The pre-modifiers evaluate the effort (*bold, difficult, hard, risky*) involved in the *decision* rather than evaluating timing or result:

27a. Countless numbers of people are looking to their leaders and representatives to **take <u>bold</u> decisions** now – and not to put off these critical decisions that will ultimately cause our grandchildren to curse us.

27b. And he made clear that despite the government's small majority, they would be prepared to **take <u>difficult</u> decisions** about how to reduce the enormous government deficit.

27c. From time to time national committees will have to **take <u>hard</u> decisions** about the strategy for that particular sector, that's what they're there for.

27d. Investors were reluctant anyway to **take <u>major</u> decisions** until the Budget details are known and the Chancellor has shown whether growth or control of the borrowing requirement is his top priority.

27e. To develop ideas at this stage means **taking <u>risky</u> decisions**, so the BTG must have the cash to throw after promising ideas.

The second pattern involves post-modification of the N by prepositional phrases headed by *against, on* or *upon*. In these examples, the post-modifier specifies the topic or 'matter' of the *decision*. It is notable that this degree of qualification is usually absent in *make + decision*:

28a. 'We would want to find out more about the circumstances of what happened before we **take a decision** <u>on future screenings</u>,' said company spokesman Richard Frost.

28b. He gave warning that the longer the Council of Ministers waited before **taking** a **decision** <u>on the former</u>, the more time trading partners had to change their minds on the latter.

28c. The fundamental considerations in **taking** a **decision** <u>on loans</u> are laid out in another Midland Bank booklet called 'How to Borrow Money' by Margaret Dibben.

28d. The House itself will **take** a **decision** <u>on the matter</u> later this evening when the Question will be put whether the Bill should or should not be considered in Committee of the whole House.

28e. they've **taken** a **decision** <u>on the preferred route.</u>

It is now possible to summarize some of the general differences between the the simple V *decide* and its equivalent LVCs *make / take + decision*. It is a general principle of phraseology (following Firth 1957, Sinclair 1991) that the meanings of expressions change in subtle ways according to their lexicogrammatical contexts. Thus I would propose the following simple glosses for the different patterns observed in this section: *decide* + finite clause = 'realise, understand', *decide* + rankshifted clause = 'choose which', *decide* + non-finite clause 'to choose to, to be determined to', *make + decision* + finite clause = 'recommend', *make + decision* + non-finite clause = 'deliberate', *take + decision* + non-finite clause = 'decree', *take + decision* + N modifier 'decide a specific case'. Generally speaking, the meanings of the LVCs move the process of *deciding* away from the private domain of the mind to the more public domains of social interaction (*decision-making*) or social regulation (*decision-taking*).

It is also possible to make some generalizations about the contrastive role of the light verbs in these expressions, especially in relation to their use in VG complexes. Generally, the simple V *decide* regularly introduces finite, rankshifted and non-finite clauses which express a similar meaning to Phase (an evaluation about the timing of an ongoing or new process). By contrast, *make + decision* is generally used to introduce non-finite clauses which express a meaning akin to Modulation (an evaluation about the means or the manner by which a new process is to be realized). The LVC *make + decision* is also used on its own (an evaluation about the quality of an ongoing process). By contrast, *take + decision* typically introduces non-finites which express a similar meaning to Conation (a statement about whether an ongoing process is to be successfully actualized). This LVC is also used on its own with some form of pre- or post-modification (a specification of the process in terms of effort or matter/manner). It is important to reiterate here that the meanings of Phase, Conation and Modulation are not introduced by the V or the LVCs themselves, but by the (non-)finite clauses. In other words, the clause relations of Phase, Modulation and Conation must be seen as part of the phraseology (the extended lexicogrammatical context) of these constructions.

The contrastive phraseology of to note, make + note and take + note

In this section, I compare the simple V *to note* and its equivalent LVCs with *decide* and *make / take + decision*. In terms of semantics, *decide* and *note* both refer to cognitive processes (equivalent to *to think*), although *note* as an N or V can also be used for perceptions (*to note something*) as well as material processes (*to note something down*). Structurally speaking, the V *to note* cannot introduce non-finite clauses, and many finite examples of *to note* occur in impersonal passive or postposed ('extraposed') clauses. However, I would suggest that *to note* is analogous to *to decide* in terms of its basic process type. Thus, when *note* introduces finite clauses its meaning is typically 'to consider, notice, realise', which as we have seen is similar to the meaning of *decide* in the same contexts:

29a. **It is** important **to note that** a void charge still remains valid against the company.
29b. **It is** interesting **to note** a similar problem with attempts to put some of his ideas into practice.
29c. In Chapter Two **it was noted that** although presidents face many difficulties in imposing their will on the American political system ...
29d. Labov **notes that** questions formulated without preparation can often be lengthy and unclear.

29e. <u>observers</u> **noted that** the ideas which it promoted were gathering increasing support in Russia.

The LVCs *make* and *take* + *note* appear in two contrastively distinct lexicogrammatical patterns. As we saw above, the LVC *make* + *note* can either express a material process 'writing, take notes', or a mental process 'to remind oneself, to attempt to remember'. This ambiguity is not always resolved in context (for example, 30c–d), although the LVC is typically accompanied by prepositional phrases which suggest which type of process may be involved:

30a. On 15 December, Fhimah **made** a **note** <u>in his diary</u>, reminding himself to take some Air Malta luggage tags from the airport.
30b. Haunted by penury for the rest of her life, she habitually **made notes** <u>over other people's letters</u> and wrote her own on the back of old laundry bills.
30c. Right. Must **make** a **note** <u>of that</u>. Yes I wanted to erm outline ...
30d. But thanks for the point, and I mean, I'll **make** a **note** <u>of that</u> and take it up to the health authority.
30e. Firstly, **make** a **note** <u>of all of the bully words and phrases</u> that James Bolham uses

Make + *note* does not introduce non-finite clauses. But as mentioned above, the expression *make* + *mental note* clearly refers to a cognitive process, and thus can project a variety of finite and non-finite clauses. While the V *note* means 'to consider, notice', *make a mental note* + non-finite clause is closer to 'to decide, determine' (and once again, this is similar to *decide* + non-finite clause, which we saw earlier):

31a. I **made** a **mental note** <u>that I mustn't say anything to annoy my prim secretary</u>, ...
31b. I **made** a **mental note** <u>to ask for an application form on the way out</u>.
31c. He **made** a **mental note** <u>to find out who was the snorer and who the complainant</u>.

31d. Sarah **made** a **mental note** <u>to go and see Janine</u>.
31e. He looked at his brother's open face, and **made** a **mental note** <u>to tell his mother</u> what was going down with him.

In contrast, *take + note* is typically used to express mental processes, and more specifically reactions to messages. As can be seen in the examples below (32–3) *take + note* is essentially a lexicalized phrase (the N *note* can be seen as 'non-referential', and therefore largely fixed in place, although there is one example of *Note was taken … * in the BNC). Typically, the Subjects of *take note* (as we have seen with *take + decision*) are persons of authority or administrative bodies, and there is usually some reference to a communicative act or message in the context (here underlined):

32a. The meeting also **took note** of a <u>memo</u> from D G Mann to C Will.
32b. The administration also **took note** of the <u>fears</u> of American oil companies that their interests might suffer elsewhere in the Middle East.
32c. Julia **took note** of Ian's <u>tone</u> as well as his words.
32d. now the erm the <u>question</u> you did pose me, sir, which er I did **take** a **note** of, but I wonder if you'd be kind enough to repeat …
32e. HEREFORD player-coach Greg Downs was delighted his players **took note** of his pre-match <u>warnings</u>.

A similar meaning can be seen in a small number of finite clauses (I find 7 in the BNC):

33a. 'British Rail, the EC, car manufacturers – these and others should **take note** that we will not be letting up in our battle for consumer rights.'
33b. And further **take note** that over 100 PFF aircrew managed the ton (100 sorties).
33c. At about then I **took note** that there weren't in fact any other boats moving on the river and I remembered that often the locks closed for maintenance in winter …

33d. EFTA [...] signed a declaration on co-operation with Albania; and **took note** that both the Czech Republic and the Slovak Republic had declared ...

33e. [the House] **took note** that the Home Secretary would define the Government's attitude towards this question ...

Is it possible to explain the general differences between *to note* and *make / take + note*? In contrast to the V *decide*, which has a wide-ranging and complex lexicogrammar, the V *note* and its LVCs are evidently more restricted and specialized. In addition, *make / take + note* are not typically used in the context of VG complexes (except for the expression *make a mental note* +V2). However, I believe that the contrasts between *note* and *make / take + note* directly parallel the differences between *decide* and *make / take + decision*. In terms of lexical process type, both patterns share the same lexico-grammatical patterns and their corresponding meanings, as suggested by the following glosses: *to note* + finite clause = 'to consider, notice', *make + note* = 'write' or 'attempt to remember', *make + mental note* + non-finite clause = 'determine, decide', *take + note* = 'realise, react', and so on. More generally, I would suggest that *take + decision* and *take + note* are both used in contexts where the process of *decision* or *noting* is assumed to be actualized, and the focus of the clause is on the resultant state or consequences (expressed either in V2 or elsewhere in the context). In other words, these two LVCs tend to correlate with the clause relations Projection + Conation. In comparison, *make + note* and *make + decision* concentrate on the circumstances of *noting* or *deciding*, which are seen as leading up to the actualization of a further process (expressed either in V2 or elsewhere in the context). This correlates with the clause relations Projection + Modulation.

The contrastive phraseology of make + effort / take + effort

In the above we have seen that *make / take + decision, note* are (usually) mental processes which can be used alone as VG complexes to introduce projections. In contrast, the LVCs *make / take + effort* are (abstract) behavioural processes which can be used in VG complexes to express the clausal relation of Modulation (in the case of *make*) or Conation (the case of *take*). It is not surprising that abstract Ns such as *effort, time, trouble* are used very productively in these structures, since they have polyvalent meanings, and can be qualified in various ways. In the case of *make / take + effort*, the corpus evidence suggests that *make + effort* is used exclusively in VG complexes with a personal subject, whereas *take + effort* is used exclusively in impersonal postposed clauses. This difference in form reflects a subtle contrast in meaning. The sequence *make + effort* has two basic sub-patterns. The LVC *make + effort + V2* expresses an attempt to achieve success in some social role or 'behaviour':

34a. Please **make every effort to** <u>attend and encourage your class members to come</u> as well.

34a. No matter how tired or worried you may feel, it's important to **make the effort to** <u>be pleasant and friendly to customers.</u>

34a. the indications are that he **made an effort to** <u>behave</u> in a way appropriate to his new position.

34a. During my term, I want to **make every effort to** <u>ensure that they will be used.</u>

34a. Chatichai had nevertheless **made every effort to** <u>maintain traditional close relations with China.</u>

The second pattern, *make an effort and*, is similarly used with personal subjects, but the process expressed in V2 is a reaction to some communicative event or challenge:

35a. When he had answered my questions he **made an effort and** <u>blurted out</u> one of his own.

35b. If, on the other hand, you are not, then you need to **make the effort and** <u>change the priority you give</u> to the organisation of time.

35c. And I would be standing there with my runny nose. So he'd **make an effort and** <u>play a game</u>. And then he'd suggest hide-and-seek ...

35d. He did not want to speak to anyone, let alone Ford, but he **made an effort** *and* <u>confirmed</u> that the Colonel had indeed heard a cannon's report ...

35e. She suddenly realised how tired she was, but she **made an effort and** <u>told him</u> that she was travelling to Rome to join her aunt and uncle.

We saw above that the subjects of *take* + *decision, note* often tend to be persons in authority or organizations. A similarly regular pattern can be seen with *take* + *effort*, which is almost exclusively used with impersonal subjects and post-posed clauses. In contrast to clauses introduced by *make* + *effort* (35, 36) which tend to express communication or social behaviour, *take* + *effort* tends to introduce non-finite (postposed) clauses which express material processes or metaphorical movement:

36a. **It takes** little **effort** of the imagination **to** <u>put oneself in Theo's shoes</u>, and feel the grey, correct, judicious side of his character.

36b. no matter how talented or hardworking you are, if you're a woman **it always takes extra effort** and drive **to** <u>succeed in business</u>.

36c. **It need not take** much **effort to** <u>write to the local paper</u>, or phone a councillor, with a complaint.

36d. **It took an effort to** <u>bring her thoughts under control</u>.

36e. **It took some effort to** <u>stay upright</u> with such variations in terrain.

The contrastive phraseology of make + time and take + time

We have seen that the LVCs *make / take* + *effort* are both express (abstract) behavioural processes which are used in VG complexes to express the clause relation of Modulation (in the case of *make*) or Conation (in the case of *take*). A similar pattern can be seen for *make / take* + *time*, except that these LVCs are relational processes (analogous to the V *have* and the LVC *to have time to*). The typical context of *make* + *time* + non-finite clause involves a person who interrupts an ongoing activity to gain some benefit or fulfil a social duty or role:

37a. Friends will be in touch this afternoon and you'll need to **make time to** <u>accommodate them this evening</u>.

37b. In Acts 6 we find the apostles <u>cutting out other responsibilities</u> to **make time to** '<u>devote</u> themselves to prayer and the ministry of the word' (Acts 6: 4).

37c. The most important thing in socialising is that you **make the time** and spend the effort **to** <u>keep those friends that you do have</u>.

37d. We are thinking about those children who, whatever their socio-economic background, have parents who have the time, or somehow **make the time, to** <u>talk with them</u>, to read to them, to read for themselves, and so to offer an example.

37e. Despite his busy schedule, he **made time to** <u>visit the conference</u>.

The pattern *take* + *time* + non-finite clause appears to be related to a more general construction of the form: *take* + time expression (*ages, a moment, a while*) + V2. The LVC *take time* + non-finite clause has three distinct sub-patterns. In the first pattern (38a–e), the subject is a person who reacts to a previous event or message (in terms of participant roles, this is Sayer or Senser / Middle, a role that we have seen elsewhere for LVCs with *take*). The V2 typically involves a cognitive or communicative process:

38a. The question disturbed her and she **took time** <u>to answer</u>.

38b. Greater weight is given to propositions contained in judgments where the judges **took time** to <u>consider their judgments</u>.

38c. Curtis **took time** to <u>consider his reply.</u>

38d. Titch **took time** to <u>consider the question</u>.

38e. Martin **took time** to <u>reply</u>.

This meaning, however, is quite different from the other patterns of *take* + *time*. As can be seen in (39a–e) below, *take* + *time* is also used to refer to the relative success or completion of an event, in other words Conation. In these expressions, which all involve impersonal subjects and post-posed clauses, the LVC evaluates the time taken to achieve a material process of change or development:

39a. Besides, <u>it</u> **took time** <u>to get the formula right</u>; one dose began to work on the notes alter only 24 hours.

39b. On each occasion <u>it</u> **took time** <u>to warm a new ball</u>.

39c. Thus NEP as a monetary <u>phenomenon</u> **took time** <u>to seep slowly through the various levels of society</u>.

39d. When they quit the market and ICI became our main supplier, the <u>relationship</u> **took time** to <u>bed down</u> but ICI's performance now is excellent.

39e. *The <u>solution</u> – Polaris – **took time** <u>to be developed</u>.*

Although this meaning may be interpreted in aspectual terms as Phase, it can also be seen as Conation: an evaluation of the effort and time spent in realizing (or attempting to realize) the process in the V2. As can be seen in (37c) and in other examples, the VG appears to express two separate processes, which suggests a Conation structure (the variable use of articles in 37a–e also suggests that the expression is less lexicalized than *take + time* analysed below). This is particularly evident in expressions such as *take the time and effort / take the time and trouble*:

40a. Says Marcus Lyon: 'You are always going to get the lazy buyer who wants a barn they don't want to **take the time and trouble to** <u>do</u> it themselves.'

40b. I find it amazing that reader Mrs J. **took the time and effort to** <u>castigate</u> another community Norris Green for fighting to keep an asset in an area that is one of the most socially and economically deprived in this city.

40c. ... it might have been thought that there was a place in society for young persons who had **taken the time and the trouble** needed **to** <u>give themselves some understanding</u> of the problems we have set ourselves, so that they could help to reduce the damage done, and the worse damage yet to come.

40d. Before making such statements, the hon. Gentleman should **take the time and trouble to** <u>read</u> the Further and Higher Education Bill that is going through another place.

40e. Treat these words with care; **take the time and effort to** <u>understand</u> and explain them.

Once again, the sense of 'effort' in these examples assumes that the process in the V2 has been actualized. This point may also explain why *take the time* (with a determiner, and not *take (o) time*) is also used in the expression of 'thanks', since the process referred to is assumed to have been enacted successfully and with some care and effort:

41a. Joan asked Sunday Life to <u>thank</u> the unknown person who had **taken the time to** <u>care</u> for her son's grave.

41b. Freya <u>thanked</u> me at the end of her letter for '**taking the time to** <u>care</u> about a subject so little understood'.

41c. <u>Thank you</u> for **taking the time** to <u>complete the questionnaire</u> and we wish you luck in the prize draw.

41d. I would like to <u>thank you</u> and your colleagues for **taking the time to** <u>meet me</u> and some of my branch officials on Tuesday.

41e. To all my brothers and sisters who **took the time to** <u>visit</u> and send cards when I was ill, <u>thank you</u> for the encouraging words and scripture.

Conclusion

Things fall apart; the centre cannot hold. A cursory glance at the data presented above might suggest that the phraseology of English is nothing but a diffracted mass of idiosyncratic phrases. However, I have made every effort in this paper to show that this is not the case. On the contrary, the patterns observed in this paper confirm the structuralist idea that irregularities are not 'exceptions to the rule', but rather conceal deeper regular patterns of use and meanings, if they can be found (as argued, among others, by Beedham 2005). Having said this, it is also important to stress the fact that the regularities observed here are not absolute: in the data analysis above I have taken the decision to omit many sub-patterns which seemed contradictory, including examples which would have required individual treatment. The complexity of the data suggests to me that the alternation of *make* / *take* in light verb constructions constitutes a currently unstable part of the English language (at least as regards the LVCs I have examined here, and the kinds of English represented in the British National Corpus).

How is the empirical linguist to make any sense of this kind of data? The position taken in this paper is that of J.R. Firth and the 'contextualist' school of language (Firth 1957, Sinclair 1991). Firth insists that the meaning of a sign depends not on its place in an abstract system, but on its habitual context of use in discourse. In other words, every sign is used in the regular and recurrent lexicogrammatical environment of other signs (its 'collocations'), and at the same time, each lexicogrammatical pattern has a habitual and distinctive meaning (its 'phraseology'). The terms collocation and phraseology are often used to refer to fixed idiomatic expressions, but as I have shown in this paper, although the expressions *make* / *take* + *decision*, *note*, *effort* and *time* all have regular and recurrent patterns of use, they are also used very productively, in a variety of particular contexts which stretch beyond the immediate environment of the two or more signs of the light verb expression itself.

I have stated above that the alternation of *make* / *take* in LVCs is a particularly unstable area of phraseology in Modern English. However, some general remarks can be made. The alternation between *make* and *take* in most equivalent light verb constructions can usually be explained in terms of Transitivity or more specifically Ergativity (Halliday 1985): the subject of LVCs with *make* is typically an Agent of some kind (*make* + *call, point*) while the subject of LVCs with *take* has a more passive or 'receptive' role of Medium (*take* + *call, point*). But as we have seen, this distinction does not seem to work for *make* / *take* + *decision, note, effort* and *time*. It would appear that this small set of apparent exceptions have a particular role to play in the expression of Mood, that is to say the abstract evaluation of a lexical process. Formally speaking, and unlike other LVCs which can be used with both *make* and *take*, each of these LVCs is used in verbal group complexes of the form *make* / *take* (V1) + *decision* / *note* / *effort* / *time*

+ non-finite clause (V2). In this context, LVCs with *make* focus on the manner of *decision-making* or *note-making*, rather than on the results of the *decision* or act of *noting* (or other process expressed with *effect / time*). This clause relation is termed 'Modulation' (Halliday 1985). More generally, LVCs with *make* also tend to express an 'opening out' to a new or virtual process (expressed by the following clause or V2). This general phraseology may explain why we often find pre-modifiers of N which evaluate the different stages or cognitive effort involved in a *decision-making* process: as in *making + final, good, hasty, informed, preliminary + decision.*

In contrast, LVCs with *take* + non-finite clause imply that the event expressed in the projected clause is already actualized. Here the focus is not on the lexical process but on the effects or the details of the process expressed in V2, a clause relation that is called 'Conation' (Halliday 1985). A more general function of this pattern is to express a 'closing off' or a 'reaction' to an ongoing or already actualized process (expressed in V2). This meaning is also compatible with a stative, 'ascriptive' reading of grammatical structures such as the passive (*a decision was taken* +V2) or extraposition (*it takes time to* +V2, *it took little effort* + V2). This may explain why we often find pre-modifiers such as *bold, courageous, difficult, hard, tough*, which do not evaluate the quality of the *decision* as such, but are rather the qualities of a *decision-taker*. Since the results of these *decisions* are typically negative 'closures', it is not surprising that the subject is often left diplomatically unmentioned. I need make no comment here about the cultural values implied by this phraseology.

I would like to end this paper by pointing out one or two issues which are not problems as such, but rather opportunities for subsequent research. In the first place, the BNC (Aston and Burnard 1998) is an archive of (primarily written) British English of the 1980s–1990s. This degree of synchronicity and representativeness is in itself an advantage. But it leaves out the possibility (in fact the likelihood) that *make / take* in North American and other major varieties of English have their own phraseological patterns, in LVCs and elsewhere. This is related to a second point, which is that while I have looked at LVCs from the Systemic Functional perspective of Transitivity and Mood, I have not had space to analyse them in terms of Theme. There is clearly a textual function involved in the expression of nominalized processes, and this point requires more detailed analysis. Finally, I have discussed the general properties of LVCs and the rather unique subset of LVCs *make / take + decision, note, effort* and *time*. But it is important to bear in mind that these phraseological patterns still make up a large family of related phrases. This fact is often forgotten by prescriptive grammarians and other commentators, who generally assume that two different signs can only be contrastively defined in terms of each other. This can be seen in many on-line discussions of language, which often pick out *make / take + decision*, without relating them to structurally similar expressions. Thus for example, 'language conservatives' put the difference down to dialect (with no consensus on whether *take + decision* is a British import into American English, or the other way round), such as:

> It has always been my understanding that you should use the following; you take a decision, not, you make a decision. Can you help me here? Which is correct? Thank you ... According to Bryan Garner, 'take a decision' is a Britishism that began to 'invade' the United States in the late 20th century. 'Make a decision' prevails, still, in the US.[13]

Other 'language mavens' suggest a basic semantic difference relating to lexical aspect:

> I don't want to be a nitpicker but I can see a shade of difference between the two. Accepting that they both mean decide. Make a decision suggests make your mind up rather than as it were sit on the fence. Take a decison [sic] is make your mind up and follow through. The reason why I pick on this is that I hear the expression used as follows: A country takes the decision to go to war. And then the war starts.[14]

Finally, some comments appear to have been based on thorough analysis. The following (almost undoubtedly written by a lexicographer, with training perhaps in corpus linguistics) emphasizes both aspect and register (referring to formality), as well as hinting at lexical patterns:

---

13   From <http://grammar.ccc.commnet.edu/grammar/grammarlogs4/grammarlogs570.htm>, accessed 11 August 2011.

14   From <http://www.english-test.net/forum/ftopic12105.html>, accessed 11 August 2011.

The phrase 'making a decision' is the more common phrase. It can refer to the actual moment where a course of action is chosen (and just that moment), but also sometimes to the whole process leading up to it (where one might undertake research, have discussions, think and so on, in order to prepare oneself for the decision itself): 'The committee took several months to make a decision.' The phrase 'taking a decision', by contrast, only refers to the decisive moment itself, and not to the process leading up to it. It has more formal connotation, and an implication that the decision will have serious consequences, and that the person deciding will be responsible for them; it has a sense of finality about it. (psmears, 21 Jan 2011)[15]

As I have shown in this paper, this comment is highly accurate: the corpus data suggest that *take + decision* has a clear preference for subjects which have a role of 'authority', and the LVC is often used with 'momentous', already-actualized decisions. However, it is still necessary for the empirical linguist to corroborate these remarks, and of course to explain any tendencies observed in terms of a theory of language. In this paper, I have argued that lexical preferences of this type can be explained in terms of the general meaning of the light verb, and that this is not just a tendency for the equivalent LVCs *make / take + decision* but for all LVCs formed by *take / make*. In addition, I have attempted to show here that LVCs such as *make / take + decision / note* are not just contrastive pairs, but are also contrastive in relation to other related signs (the Vs *decide, note, notice* etc.). Finally, I have shown here that the small sub-group of LVCs (*make / take + decision, note, effort* and *time*) are all related in that they share a particular structural function: such an observation could not have been made with much confidence without the benefit of corpus-based analysis and the more general expectation that these signs might all have their own particular 'phraseology'.

---

15   From <http://english.stackexchange.com/questions/6431/what-is-the-difference-between-make-decision-and-take-decision>, accessed 6 August 2011.

Bibliography

Allerton, David. 2002. *Stretched verb constructions in English*. London: Routledge.

Aston, Guy, and Lou Burnard. 1998. *The BNC handbook: Exploring the British National Corpus with SARA*. Edinburgh: Edinburgh University Press.

Ballier, Nicolas. 2003. Les collocations en DO et le statut de verbe léger. Presented at the *ALAES – UPPA Seminar on do*, 1 Feb. 2003.

Banks, David. 2000. The range of range: a transitivity problem for systemic linguistics. *Anglophonia* 8.195–206.

Barrier, Sébastien. 2006. *Une métagrammaire pour les noms prédicatifs du français: développement et expérimentations pour les grammaires TAG*. Thèse doctorale. Université Paris VII : Denis Diderot.

Beedham, Christopher. 2005. *Language and meaning: The structural creation of reality*. Amsterdam: John Benjamins.

Björkman, Sven. 1978. *Le type avoir besoin: étude sur la coalescence verbo-nominale en français*. Uppsala: Acta Universitatis Upsaliensis.

Bloor, Thomas, and Meriel Bloor. 2004. *The Functional analysis of English: A Hallidayan approach*. 2nd edn. London: Arnold.

Brinton, Laurel, and Minoji Akimoto (eds). 1999. *Collocational and idiomatic aspects of composite predicates in the history of English*. Amsterdam: John Benjamins.

Brinton, Laurel, and Elizabeth Traugott. 2005. *Lexicalization and language change*. Cambridge: Cambridge University Press.

Butt, Miriam. 2003. The Light Verb Jungle. Workshop on Multi-Verb Constructions. Trondheim, June 26–27, 2003. From <http://www.ling.hf.ntnu.no/tross/Butt. pdf>, accessed 30 Oct. 2011.

Celle, Agnès. 2004. Constructions verbo-nominales atéliques et types de procès. *Contrastes*, ed. by Lucie Gourney and J.-M. Merle, 87–100. Paris: Ophrys.

Cotte, Pierre. 1998. *Have* n'est pas un verbe d'action: l'hypothèse de la réélaboration. *La Transitivité*, ed. by André Rousseau, 415–39. Lille: Presses Universitaires du Septentrion.

Di-Sciullo, Andrew, and Steven Rosen. 1991. Constructions à prédicats légers et quasi-légers. *Revue québécoise de linguistique* 20(1).13–37.

Ernst, Thomas. 2002. *The Syntax of Adjuncts*. Cambridge: Cambridge University Press.

Firth, John R. 1957. *Papers in linguistics 1934–1951*. Oxford: Oxford University Press.

Giry-Schneider, Jacqueline. 1987. Interprétation aspectuelle des constructions verbales à double analyse. *Linguisticae Investigationes* 2(1).24–53.

Gledhill, Christopher. 2005. Problems of adverbial placement in learner English and the British National Corpus. *Linguistics, language learning and language teaching*, ed. by David Allerton, Cornelia Tschirhold and Judith Wieser (ICSELL 10), 85–104. Basel: Schwabe.

Gledhill, Christopher. 2008. Les constructions verbo-nominales en français et en espéranto: un cas spécifique de 'glissement phraséologique'. *Zeitschrift für Französische Sprache und Literatur* 36.71–84.

Gledhill, Christopher. 2009. Vers une analyse systémique fonctionnelle des expressions verbo-nominales. *La Linguistique systémique fonctionnelle et la langue française*, ed. by David Banks, Simon Easton and Janet Ormrod, 89–126. Paris: L'Harmattan.

Grimshaw, Jane, and Armin Mester. 1988. Light verbs and θ-marking. *Linguistic Inquiry* 19.205–32.

Gross, Gaston. 1989. *Les constructions converses du français*. Genève-Paris: Droz.

Gross, Gaston. 2005. Verbes supports : Nouvel état des lieux. *Lingvisticae Investigationes* 27(2), ed. by Gaston Gross and Sylvie Pontonx, 167–9.

Halliday, Michael A.K. 1985. *An Introduction to Functional Grammar*. 1st edn. London: Arnold.

Halliday, Michael A.K., and Christian M.I.M. Matthiessen. 2004. *An Introduction to functional grammar*. 3rd Edn. London: Arnold.

Halliday, Michael A.K., and Jim R. Martin. (eds). 1993. *Writing science: literacy and discursive power*. Pittsburgh: University of Pittsburgh Press.

Hiroe, Nobuyuku. 2007. *Light verb constructions in Japanese and English*. University of Essex Press.

Hunston, Susan, and Gill Francis. 2000. *Pattern grammar – A Corpus-driven approach to the lexical grammar of English*. Amsterdam: John Benjamins.

Jespersen, Otto. 1942. *A Modern English Grammar. On historical principles. Part VI. Morphology*. London: George Allen & Unwin.

Kearns, Kate. 1989. Predicate nominals in complex predicates. *MIT Working Papers in Linguistics* 10.123–34.

Pinker, Steven. 1994. *The Language instinct*. New York: Harper Collins.

Pottelberge, Jeroen van. 2000. Light verb constructions: What they are and what they are not. *Logos and Language* 1(2).17–33.

Pottelberge, Jeroen van. 2001. *Verbonominale Konstruktionen: vom Sinn und Unsinn eines Untersuchungsgegenstandes*. Heidelberg: Winter.

Poulsen, Sonja. 2005. *Collocations as a language resource. A Functional and cognitive study in English phraseology*. PhD thesis, Institute of Language and Communication, University of Southern Denmark.

Quirk, Randolph, and Sydney Greenbaum. 1973, 1980. *A University grammar of English*. London: Longman.

Quirk, Randolph, Sydney Greenbaum, Geoffrey Leech and Jan Svartvik. 1985. *A Comprehensive grammar of the English language*. London: Longman.

Sinclair, John McH. 1991. *Corpus, concordance, collocation*. Oxford: Oxford University Press.

Smith, Carlota S. 1991. *The Parameter of Aspect*. Dordrecht: Kluwer Academic Publishers.

Storrer, Angeliker. 2006. Corpus-based investigations on German support verb constructions. *Collocations and Idioms: Linguistic, lexicographic, and computational aspects*, ed. by Christiane Fellbaum, 164–87. London: Continuum Press.

Todiraşcu, Amalia, and Christopher Gledhill. 2008. Extracting collocations in context: the case of verb-noun constructions in English and Romanian. *Recherches anglaises et nord-américaines* 41.107–22.

Vendler, Zeno. 1967. *Linguistics in Philosophy*. Ithaca: Cornell University Press.

Vivès, Robert. 1984. L'aspect dans les constructions nominales prédicatives: *avoir, prendre*, verbe support et extension aspectuelle. *Lingvisticae Investigationes* 8(1).161–85.

Wierzbicka, Anna. 1982. Why can you have a drink when you can't have an eat? *Language* 58.753–99.

Discussion (Extract)

BEEDHAM: You have combined Corpus Linguistics and Systemic Grammar to arrive at a new account of the meaning/use differences between *make* and *take* in Light Verb Constructions (LVCs) such as *to make/take a decision*. In doing so you used unusual or exceptional uses/meanings of *make* and *take* in LVCs as your starting point, on the basis of which you arrived at deeper generalizations.

I have two related questions. Firstly, corpus linguistics is obviously *parole*, but the new aspectual analysis of the passive which I have proposed was and still is conceived within *langue*. How do you square those two things in terms of the role of exceptions?

Secondly, Halliday has said that for him grammar is always lexico-grammar, and I agree with that entirely. How do you square the lexis-oriented nature of your work on LVCs with that statement by Halliday? Is lexis for you always grammatical lexis?

GLEDHILL: Can I account for the exceptional behaviour of LVCs in terms of *langue*? Maybe, but only if we refine what we mean by *langue*. The language system is usually defined in terms of purely abstract, grammatical oppositions. Oppositions such as *active / passive* and *regular / irregular* involve contrastive, closed grammatical choices, whereas LVCs (as I have shown in this paper) represent a class of phrases in which each particular expression has an asymmetrical, unpredictable relation with the others (a full V may have one or more equivalent LVCs, while many LVCs do not have a full V equivalent, etc.). Since LVCs are essentially 'lexical', should we see LVCs as a (large) set of unexplained lexical exceptions? Maybe we should. But perhaps the answer lies in the way in which we conceive of *langue* and *parole*.

In Beedham 2005 you argue that *langue / parole* should be seen in terms of a dialectic rather than a simple dichotomy. I have a great deal of sympathy with this interpretation of Saussure. But my reply to the first question requires a slightly different approach. I would argue, following J.R. Firth (1957), that *langue* is not a system of closed-class, contrastive choices, but rather a *polysystem*: according to this view, language is a human system of behaviour designed for comprehending the world and interacting with other humans, and as such it is made up of asymmetrical, complementary but also sometimes competing subsystems, all of which have evolved to fulfil particular communicative functions. As you know, Firth also argued that there is a general principle at work which he termed 'collocation' and J. Sinclair (1991) and others later reformulated as the 'idiom principle'. Put simply, all signs (and in this case, LVCs are complex multi-word signs) have a tendency to be co-selected with other signs, and consequently to be interpreted in terms of their habitual patterns of use. In this study I have observed the typical collocations of a small subgroup of LVCs (namely *make / take + decision, effort, note, time*) and found that each expression has very a consistent and contrastive phraseology. It is possible to make some generalizations about form and function in terms of the whole subset (these LVCs are related in that they use *make* and *take* interchangeably without much difference in meaning, and they are all used to introduce non-finite clauses). However, each individual expression also has its own consistent patterns of use, and this usage is consistently different to related constructions: thus *make a mental note* does not have the same range of use or distribution as *take note*, and in a similar way *make an effort to* does not share the same contexts of use as *take the effort to*, and so on. If we see language as essentially a 'system', then these are exceptions. But if language is a 'polysystem', then we are looking here at a particular subsystem of expression, which has evolved apart from its predecessors (extended predicates are descended from complex predicates) and has taken on a particular form and function in this particular language.

Is lexis for me always grammatical lexis? Yes. In this chapter, I have been conducting a study of 'phraseology' rather than of pure grammar or syntax. The term phraseology is sometimes used to refer to the study of idiomatic expressions. However, for many Systemic Functional linguists (for example Tucker 2007), phraseology refers more generally to the co-selection of lexical patterns and grammatical structures within the same stretch of text. This approach differs from the traditional study of syntax in that it assumes that grammar and lexis are not two different levels of language, but are rather two ends of the same continuum (this is known as the 'lexicogrammar': Halliday 1985). Furthermore, the phraseological approach assumes that utterances are not the products of a combination of grammatical slots and lexical fillers. Rather, both grammar and lexis are organized in the mind (or if you prefer in the *langue*) as 'lexico-grammatical patterns' (for a discussion of lexico-grammatical patterns in a Systemic Functional perspective see Gledhill 1999, 2011a/b). Lexico-grammatical patterns are not fixed sequences of signs; they involve information about the preferences of co-selection which go beyond the items themselves (*make / take + decision* + non-finite clause, *make+ effort* + non-finite clause, but not *take + effort* + non-finite clause, etc.) and about the particular senses that speakers convey and contexts in which they are likely to use these patterns (*make note* = 'remember', *take note* 'notice' etc.) The notion of lexico-grammatical pattern allows us to explain how expressions such as '*have a sit down', 'make a face'* can be invented on the spot on the basis of more regular constructions of the type *have a* + (*base* V) or *make a* (*behavioural N*). I have not fully explored the notion of 'lexico-grammatical pattern' yet. But I think it could be a useful alternative to terms such as 'construction' or '(verb, noun) phrase', because it refers explicitly to a particular kind of linguistic unit which stands halfway on the continuum between *system* (the abstract, system-oriented oppositions and structures referred to by terms such as *active / passive, causative / resulative* etc.) and *instance* (the particular sequences of lexical items which clearly have no other name than their citation form).

References to Discussion

Beedham, Christopher. 2005. *Language and meaning: The structural creation of reality*. Amsterdam: John Benjamins.

Firth, John Rupert. 1957. *Papers in linguistics 1934–1951*. Oxford : Oxford University Press.

Gledhill, Christopher. 1999. Towards a Description of English and French Phraseology. *Langue and Parole in Synchronic and Diachronic Perspective: Selected Proceedings of the XXXIst Annual Meeting of the Societas Linguistica Europaea, St. Andrews, 1998*, ed. by Christopher Beedham, 221–37. Oxford: Elsevier/Pergamon.

Gledhill, Christopher. 2011a. The lexicogrammar approach to analysing phraseology and collocation in ESP texts. *Anglais de Spécialité* 59: 5–23.

Gledhill, Christopher. 2011b. A lexicogrammar approach to checking quality: Looking at one or two cases of comparative translation. *Perspectives on Translation Quality*, ed. by Ilse Depraetere, 71–98. Berlin: Mouton de Gruyter.

Halliday, Michael A.K. 1985. *An Introduction to functional grammar*. London: Arnold.

Sinclair, J. McH. 1991. *Corpus, Concordance, Collocation*. Oxford: Oxford University Press.

Stubbs, Michael. 1994. Grammar, Text and Ideology: Computer-Assisted Methods in the Linguistics of Representation. *Applied Linguistics* 15/2: 201–23.

Tucker, Gordon H. 2007. Between lexis and grammar: towards a systemic functional approach to phraseology. *Continuing Discourse on Language: A Functional Perspective*, Vol. 2, ed. by C. Matthiessen, R. Hasan and J. Webster, 954–77. London: Equinox.

JUHANI RUDANKO

12   On a Class of Resultatives in English, with Evidence from Electronic Corpora

ABSTRACT

The paper examines the transitive *into -ing* pattern in English, as in *he had needled me into losing my temper* (British Books, Bank of English). The pattern has received considerable attention during the past decade, but earlier work has focused on usage in current English, and the present study broadens the perspective to include diachronic data. The diachronic data come from the third part of the Corpus of Late Modern English Texts, and the synchronic data from the British Books Corpus of the Bank of English Corpus. It is shown that the frequency of the pattern has gone up considerably.

It is argued further that the transitive *into -ing* pattern represents a type of construction in the sense of Adele Goldberg's work. The construction in question, to use Goldberg's terminology, is the caused motion construction. The proposal that the pattern is a construction is used as a basis in analyzing the semantic structure of matrix verbs that select the pattern. It is observed that the verb *cause* does not select the pattern, but that verbs apparently similar in meaning to *cause* do. Using a lexical exceptions approach, such verbs are then distinguished from *cause*. It is suggested further that the term 'influenced motion construction' may be a more suitable label for the pattern.

Introduction

Consider sentence 1:

(1) ... he had needled me into losing my temper. (British Books, Bank of English)

In sentence 1 the matrix verb *needle* selects three arguments. The first is the subject argument, realized by the NP *he*. The second is the direct object argument, realized by the NP *me*. The third is the prepositional complement, introduced by the preposition *into*. The pattern illustrated by sentence 1 is here called the transitive *into -ing* pattern.[1]

It is assumed here that the prepositional complement of the transitive *into -ing* pattern is sentential and has its own understood subject. This is a somewhat controversial assumption to make, but it was made by major traditional grammarians, including Otto Jespersen, who used the term 'latent subject' ([1940] 1961: 152f.) to refer to an understood subject. Apart from an appeal to tradition, there are also other reasons for making it. One reason is that the assumption makes it easy to represent the subject argument of the lower verb in an economical and straightforward way. The assumption also makes it easy to talk about the interpretation of the understood subject. In particular, it is possible to say that sentence 1 involves object control: the reference of the understood subject is controlled by the matrix object, the NP *me* in this case. In line with current work, the symbol 'PRO' is used here to represent the understood subject of 1.

It is also assumed here that the lower sentence in 1 is a nominal clause, that is, a sentence dominated by an NP node. This makes it possible to use the normal phrase structure rule for a prepositional phrase, of the type PP rewritten as Prep + NP.

The structure of sentence 1 may then be represented as in 1':

(1') $[[\text{he}]_{NP1} [\text{had}]_{Aux} [[\text{needled}]_{Verb1} [\text{me}]_{NP0} [[\text{into}]_{Prep} [[[\text{PRO}]_{NP2} [\text{losing my temper}]_{VP}]_{S2}]_{NP}]_{PP}]_{S1}$

Sentential *into -ing* complements may also be selected by matrix verbs involving subject control in English, as in sentence 2:

---

1   The author is grateful to Ian Gurney, of the University of Tampere, Finland, for reading and commenting on a preliminary version of this article, to Kristiina Tolvanen, likewise of the University of Tampere, for checking sources, and to the participants in the Conference on Lexical Exceptions for their comments. All remaining shortcomings are solely the author's responsibility.

(2) ... I am not into sitting on the rail any more ... (British Books, Bank of English)

In sentence 2 the subject argument of the lower verb *sitting* is again PRO, but this time it is controlled by the higher subject, the NP *I*. Subject control constructions deserve attention, but they are set aside in the present investigation.

Sentence 2 is easy to set aside as a subject control construction for the higher sentence does not even have an object argument. It should be added that there is also a fairly frequent type of construction in English where there is a direct object present, but where the object designates a resource at the disposal of the referent of the matrix subject, and the structure may also be viewed as one of subject control, rather than of object control. Consider sentence 3:

(3) I put everything into looking amused ... (British Books, Bank of English)

The NP *everything* is the direct object of the matrix verb *put* in sentence 3, but the understood subject of the lower verb *looking* in 3 is still controlled by the higher subject *I*, rather than by the object *everything*. After all, the sentence means that I am looking amused, or trying to do so, not that everything looks amused, or is trying to do so. Sentences of the type of 3 are therefore also excluded from the present investigation.

On the other hand, consider 4:

(4) They had been provoked into saying bitter, if stupid, things ... (British Books, Bank of English)

Higher verbs selecting the transitive *into -ing* pattern are often in the passive, as in sentence 4, and such constructions are included in the present treatment.

The general meaning of the transitive *into -ing* pattern is a function of the nature of the construction as an object control structure. Here is how Sag and Pollard have characterized the general semantics of object control:

The semantics of all verbs in this class [of verbs involving object control, JR] thus involves a soa [state of affairs JR] whose relation is of the INFLUENCE type. With respect to such soas, we may identify three semantic roles, which we will refer to as INFLUENCE (the possibly agentive influencer), INFLUENCED (the typically animate participant influenced by the influence) and SOA-ARG (the action that the influenced participant is influenced to perform (or, in the case of verbs like *prevent* and *forbid*, NOT to perform). [footnote omitted, JR] (Sag and Pollard 1991: 66; emphases in the original)

Sag and Pollard thus propose the semantic roles Influence, Influenced, and SOA-ARG for the three arguments involved. Here the more traditional role labels of Agent, Patient or Undergoer, and Goal are used for the three roles. However, the different terminology does not detract from the value of the semantic analysis that Sag and Pollard (1991) have provided.

It may be added that the transitive *into -ing* pattern is telic in nature and that the Goal argument of the pattern typically entails accomplishment. The pattern involves movement from one state to another, and further that the new state of affairs is actually reached. Thus a sentence of the type illustrated in 5 is a contradiction. (The past perfect of sentence 1 has been changed to the simple past tense in 5, for entailment properties are generally tested with sentences in the past tense.)

(5) ?He needled me into losing my temper but I did not lose my temper.

In this connection it is of interest to compare the transitive *into -ing* pattern with the *to* infinitive pattern involving object control, for there are verbs that select both patterns. *Force* and *pressure* are such verbs. Compare 6a–b, from the British Books Corpus of the Bank of English, with 7a–b, their infinitival variants. The latter have been made up, but they are well formed.

(6) a. It was a powerfully organized Catholic lobby that forced the Socialist Government in 1984 into withdrawing its offending legislation.
    b. We pressured him into telling us everything he knew about the heist, ...

(7) a. It was a powerfully organized Catholic lobby that forced the Socialist Government in 1984 to withdraw its offending legislation.

 b. We pressured him to tell us everything he knew about the heist, ...

Consider then the entailment properties of the two patterns in 8a–b and 9a–b. (6a and 7a have been modified into non-clefted sentences.)

(8) a. ?The Catholic lobby forced the Socialist Government in 1984 into withdrawing its offending legislation, but the Government did not withdraw the legislation.

 b. ?We pressured him into telling us everything he knew about the heist, but he did not do so.

(9) a. ?The Catholic lobby forced the Socialist Government in 1984 to withdraw its offending legislation, but the Government did not withdraw the legislation.

 b. We pressured him to tell us everything he knew about the heist, but did not do so.

Of the four sentences in 8a–b and 9a–b the first three are contradictions, but 9b is not (cf. Rudanko 2003: 275).

In the light of the data it therefore appears that the Goal argument of a *to* infinitive complement in an object control structure may be telic and of the accomplishment type, as in 7a, as shown by 9a. However, this is not necessarily the case, in view of 7b and 9b, and is apparently a function of the matrix verb. By contrast, in the case of the transitive *into -ing* pattern, the Goal argument appears regularly to be telic and of the accomplishment type, as is shown by 6a–b and 8a–b.

In a similar way, the transitive *into -ing* pattern is also delimited against the non-sentential pattern of Verb NP *into* NP. The latter pattern is not necessarily telic and the Goal argument does not necessarily need to be of the accomplishment type, as is shown by the lack of contradiction in 10:

(10) He urged her into the room, but she did not go into the room.

The transitive *into -ing* pattern thus has properties both of a syntactic and semantic nature that are specific to it. Such specific properties are part of the motivation for singling out the transitive *into -ing* pattern for investigation.

What is here called the transitive *into -ing* pattern has been investigated in the literature before, as in Francis et al. 1996: 396–9, Rudanko 2000 chapter 5, Hunston and Francis 2000: 101f., Rudanko 2003, and Wulff et al. 2007. It has been observed that the pattern is fairly frequent in present-day English and that matrix verbs selecting it are of a limited number of semantic types (Francis et al. 1996: 396–9, Rudanko 2000 chapter 5). Further, it has been suggested that the pattern tends to have a negative semantic prosody (Hunston and Francis 2000: 102 and, in stronger terms, Wulff et al. 2007: 274f.).[2]

However, previous studies have generally had a focus on present-day English, and the present study serves to broaden the perspective to the recent history of English. The present study uses data from two electronic corpora. The first is the third part of the Corpus of Late Modern English Texts. When the MonoConc search program is used, the size of this corpus comes out as 6,103,660 words, and the corpus covers usage from 1850 to 1920. The corpus consists of texts of written British English, and these come from the text type of books, both fiction and non-fiction. The entire corpus is examined, with its size rounded to 6.1 million words.[3]

The other corpus is the British Books Corpus of the Bank of English Corpus. This corpus is 54,681,389 words in full,[4] that is, almost ten times larger than the diachronic corpus. With this in mind, a random sample of ten per cent is considered of the tokens of the pattern found in the synchronic corpus. The size of the corpus is rounded to 5.5 million words.

2   Two more specific lines of investigation relating to the transitive *into -ing* pattern have also been prominent recently. The first, apparently first discussed in Rudanko 2000: 84, concerns interdependencies between the nature of the matrix verb and the lower predicate; for more recent, and more formal studies, see Gries and Stefanowitsch 2004 and Stefanowitsch and Gries 2005. The second concerns the spread of the pattern to innovative or unexpected usages; for this line of investigation, see Rudanko 2005, Rudanko 2006, and Rudanko 2011 chapter 3.

3   For information about the original version of the corpus, see de Smet 2005.

4   The corpus was consulted in 2007.

Diachronic data and construction grammar

Turning to the third part of the Corpus of Late Modern English Texts, it may be noted that like other diachronic corpora, the corpus is untagged, and no tagged search is possible. Another factor bearing on the choice of a search string is that insertions between the preposition *into* and the following *-ing* form, of the type *?He needled me into, apparently, losing my cool*, appear to be rare. As a consequence, the search string adopted here is *into *ing*.

The search string identifies 183 tokens in the corpus, but the majority of these are irrelevant. Irrelevant tokens are of different types. Here are some illustrations:

(11) a. I got an ugly glimpse into something worse than self-contented incapacity, ... (1885, Linton, *The Autobiography of Christopher Kirkland*)

b. ... the lobsters were plunged into boiling water to be cooked. (1855, Baker, *Eight Years' Wandering in Ceylon*)

c. ... I would rush into stating opinions of my own. (1883, Blind, *George Eliot*)

Sentences of the type of 11a–c can of course be set aside immediately: in 11a–b there is no sentential complement, and while 11c does involve a sentential complement, the construction is one of subject control.

Another exclusion concerns the phrases of the type *bring* NP *into being*, as in 12.

(12) ... without those pale preliminary students it never could have been brought into being. (1869, Bagehot, *Physics and Politics*)

While there is some variation in the choice of the verb in the combination, with *call* for instance found instead of *bring*, the expression is rather idiomatic and fixed, and the *-ing* form is nominal in nature, with the phrase being close to 'bring NP into existence'.

The investigator is also confronted by the more subtle problem of what to do about sentences of the type given in 13:

> (13) Could he ever be happy with Patrick dead, and Esclairmonde driven and harassed into being his wife? (1870, Yonge, *The Caged Lion*)

The question is whether to count, on the basis of sentence 13, the two matrix verbs, *drive* and *harass*, as selecting the transitive *into -ing* pattern or whether to include only one of them. Here the decision is made to count only one of them, the one closest to the complement. The decision is made in order to err on the side of caution and not to overestimate the incidence of matrix verbs selecting the pattern.

When the principles explained are applied, the total of relevant tokens in the material is 62. This represents a frequency of 10.0 per million words.

When the matrix verbs encountered are examined from a syntactic point of view, it is observed that they are of different types. One type of verb is illustrated by *force* and *lead*, as in 14a–b:

> (14) a. ... silence appeared to weigh upon the spirits of this worldling, and to force him, as it were, into talking to me against his own will. (1868, Collins, *The Moonstone*)
> b. I have thought it over, and will not be led into oppressing my father's widow any more. (1870, Yonge, *The Caged Lion*)

Force and *lead* are verbs that subcategorize for three arguments independently of the transitive *into -ing* pattern. Examples of such structures with three arguments can be found in the same corpus:

> (15) a. He came to meet them in a meadow named Runnymede, on the bank of the Thames, and there they forced him to sign the charter, ... (1873, Yonge, *Young Folks' History of England*)
> b. ... he found matters much changed for the better, as East had led him to expect. (1857, Hughes, *Tom Brown's School Days*)

As is seen in 15a–b, the other pattern for *force* and *lead* is the *to* infinitive pattern. The *to* infinitive pattern, similarly to the transitive *into -ing* pattern, involves object control with these verbs.

As for the second syntactic type of matrix verb in the material, *frighten* and *irritate* may serve as illustrations:

(16) a.   Suppose a wife became a rigid teetotaller in order to frighten her husband into concealing his pub-frequenting, and then wrote him blackmailing letters in another hand ... (1914, Chesterton, *The Wisdom of Father Brown*)

   b.   ... a persistently jealous husband may not improbably end by irritating an innocent wife into affording real ground for jealousy. (1893, Gissing, *The Odd Woman*)

Outside of the transitive *into -ing* pattern, verbs of the type of *frighten* and *irritate* are often found with two arguments, as in 17a–b, which are from the same corpus as other authentic data in this section:

(17) a.   His face frightened me. (1868, Collins, *The Moonstone*)

   b.   There is nothing does irritate me more than seeing other people sitting about doing nothing when I'm working. (1889, Jerome, *Three Men in a Boat*)

A third syntactic type of verb, apparently more rare, may be illustrated with *tick*, as in 18:

(18)   This Extra Day, having been overlooked long ago, was beyond the reach of measuring clocks. No clocks had ever ticked it into passing. It could never pass. Only the present passed. The past, to which this day belonged, remained where it was, endless, ... (1915, Blackwood, *The Extra Day*)

Tick is generally a verb that selects only one argument, as in 19:

(19)   On a side cupboard between the windows ticked a gilt clock, under its glass cage. (1885, Blind, *Tarantella*)

The syntactic diversity of the matrix verbs is a reason why it is proposed here that the transitive *into -ing* pattern should be viewed as a construction in the sense of Adele Goldberg's work. Regarding the notion of a construction, she writes:

> ... basic sentences of English are instances of *constructions* – form-meaning correspondences that exist independently of particular verbs. That is, it is argued that constructions themselves carry meaning, independently of the words in the sentence. (Goldberg 1995: 1)

In a later formulation she views constructions as 'conventionalized pairings of form and function' or as 'learned pairings of form with semantic or discourse function' (Goldberg 2006, 3–5).

Using Goldberg's terminology, the type of construction in question in the present case is the caused motion construction, which is a type of resultative. The syntactic form of a caused motion construction is of type 20:

(20) [SUBJ] [V OBJ OBL]

In 20 'V is a nonstative verb and OBL is a directional phrase' (Goldberg 1995: 152).

The identification of the three syntactic types of verbs may be made use of when considering the status of the transitive *into -ing* pattern as a construction. As far as the verbs selecting three arguments independently of the transitive *into -ing* pattern are concerned, we may consider 21, a simplified version of sentence 14a.

(21) The silence forced him into talking.

To analyse sentence 21, it is helpful to introduce Goldberg's distinction between participant roles and argument roles. She writes:

> Part of a verb's frame semantics includes the delimitation of *participant roles*. Participant roles are to be distinguished from the roles associated with the construction, which will be called *argument roles*. The distinction is intended to capture the fact that verbs are associated with frame-specific roles, whereas constructions are associated with more general roles such as agent, patient, goal, which correspond

roughly to Fillmore's early case roles or Gruber's thematic roles. [Note omitted, JR] Participant roles are instances of the more general argument roles and capture specific selectional restrictions as well. (Goldberg 1995: 43; italics in the original)

The participant roles of sentence 21 are Forcer, Forced and Action, and these can be matched with the argument roles of the caused motion construction in a straightforward fashion, with the Forcer participant role matched with the Agent argument role, the Forced role matched with the Undergoer (Patient) role, and the Action role matched with the Goal role.

Verbs of the other two syntactic types enhance the attractiveness of the proposal that the transitive *into -ing* pattern represents a type of the caused motion construction. Consider sentences 22a, modified from 17b, and 22b, simplified from 16b:

(22) a. Seeing other people sitting around doing nothing irritates me.
b. A jealous husband may irritate a wife into affording real ground for jealousy.

The prototypical sense of the verb *irritate*, as in sentence 22a, is 'to excite to impatient or angry feeling' (*OED*, part of sense 2), and the participant roles are Irritator and Irritated. Assuming that the transitive *into -ing* pattern represents a type of the caused motion construction, it is possible to say that the verb has that same prototypical sense even in sentence 22b, with the Irritator participant role realized by the NP *A jealous husband* and the Irritated participant role realized by the NP *a wife*. The first of these is matched with the Agent argument role of the caused motion construction, and the second is matched with the Undergoer (Patient) argument role of the caused motion construction. Sentence 22b, of course, also has a third argument role, realized by *into affording real ground for jealousy*, but this is not matched with a participant role of the verb. Rather, it is supplied by the construction.

Recalling that a construction carries a meaning of its own, it is possible to identify both a verbal meaning and a constructional meaning in a sentence of the type of 22b. Underlying such an analysis is the idea that there are two subevents involved, the verbal subevent and the constructional subevent, and that there is a specific relation between the two. Here we may quote Goldberg and Jackendoff's comments on the two types of subevent. The comments were made on the broader class of resultatives, but they apply to the transitive *into -ing* pattern, which may be viewed as a type of the caused motion construction.

> the meaning of a resultative sentence constains two separable subevents. One of them, the VERBAL SUBEVENT, is determined by the verb of the sentence. The other subevent, the CONSTRUCTIONAL SUBEVENT, is determined by the construction. A resultative sentence means more than just the conjunction of the verbal subevent and the constructional subevent ... That is, for the bulk of cases ... the verbal subevent is the MEANS by which the constructional subevent takes place. (Goldberg and Jackendoff 2004: 538; emphases in the original)

The specific semantic characterization of the relation of the two subevents predicts that part of the meaning of a sentence such as 22b is of the type 'a jealous husband may cause a wife to move into affording real ground for jealousy by means of irritating her'.

A conceivable alternative to the analysis of a sentence such as 22b as an example of the caused motion construction would be to propose two distinct senses for the verb *irritate*. One of them would be the 'ordinary' sense of 'to excite to impatient or angry feeling', as in sentence 22a, where there are two arguments. The other would be of the type, 'move (someone) into a state or action by means of irritating (the person)'.

However, when the usage of sentence 22b is viewed as an instance of the caused motion construction, it is unnecessary to propose an additional verb sense. Instead the verb has its ordinary sense in sentence 22a and in sentence 22b, and part of the meaning of the latter sentence, the movement part, is contributed by the caused motion construction. Part of the meaning of sentence 22b is then an amalgam of the sense of the verb and of the caused motion construction. Exactly as predicted by the statement by Goldberg and Jackendoff (2004), the verbal subevent expresses the means by which the constructional subevent takes place. Instead of postulating double senses for verbs such as *irritate*, it is thus possible to appeal to the notion of the caused motion construction and to express the sense of such verbs in a more simple fashion.

An account on similar lines, in principle, is available for the usage of the verb *tick* in 18. The verb *tick* normally subcategorizes for only one argument. The verb has only one participant role, which may be labelled 'Ticker'. This is matched with the Agent argument role of the caused motion construction in 18. In this case the construction then supplies the other two argument roles, Undergoer (Patient), represented by the NP *it* in sentence 18, and Goal, represented by the sentential complement *into passing*.

Accepting that the transitive *into -ing* pattern represents a type of the caused motion construction also has a consequence for the semantic analysis of matrix verbs selecting the pattern. Given that in the construction the verbal subevent expresses the means by which the constructional subevent takes place, the task of identifying semantic classes that select the pattern can be carried out on the basis of specifying the different kinds of means that are relevant. Table 12.1 is offered to characterize the meanings in question. Table 12.1 also gives information on the frequencies of individual verbs; these are given in parentheses after each entry. (For the labels of the individual classes, the present study draws on Francis et al. 1996: 396–9 and Rudanko 2000 chapter 5).

Table 12.1 Semantic classes of verbs selecting the transitive *into –ing* pattern in the third part of the Corpus of Late Modern English Texts

by means of deception or trickery	*betray* (3), *deceive* (2), *delude* (2), *entrap* (1), *fool* (1), *trick* (2) (11 tokens)
by means of exerting force or pressure, sometimes understood figuratively	*drag* (1), *draw* (1), *drive* (2), *force* (1), *hurry* (2), *harass* (1), *rouse* (2), *sting* (1), *stir up* (1), *subdue* (1), *throw* (1), *torture* (1) (15 tokens)
by means of arousing fear, irritation, anger, annoyance, confusion, surprise	*exasperate* (2), *frighten* (6), *goad* (1), *intimidate* (2), *irritate* (2), *scare* (1), *shock* (1), *startle* (2), *surprise* (3) (19 tokens)
by means of enticing, flattering or verbal persuasion	*bribe* (1), *cajole* (1), *coax* (2), *lure* (2), *seduce* (2), *soothe* (1), *talk over* (1), *wheedle* (1) (11 tokens)
by other specific means	*charm* (1), *idealize* (1), *tick* (1) (3 tokens)
by non-specific means	*lead* (2) (2 tokens)

Note. NP_1 causes NP_O to move to perform S_2 or move into the state designated by S_2.

Not everyone would agree about every aspect of the semantic characterizations offered and there is no doubt scope for making them more adequate, but the semantic classes are offered to represent major senses of the matrix verbs selecting the transitive *into -ing* pattern when these are used with the pattern. Assuming that the semantic classes are on the right lines, it is clear that verbs selecting the pattern typically express some fairly specific means of causation. Such verbs may be termed verbs of flavoured causation. By contrast, the verb *lead* is non-specific with respect to the means by which causation takes place.

Among the verbs of flavoured causation, the present material suggests that in written British English about a hundred years ago the transitive *into -ing* construction was especially common with verbs expressing emotions such as annoyance. Both *frighten* and *irritate*, used above to illustrate verbs that are commonly used with two arguments outside of the transitive *into -ing* pattern, are from this semantic class, and other verbs of the class appear to be of the same syntactic type.

Regarding other semantic classes, verbs expressing the exertion of force, those of deception and those expressing enticing were also relatively frequent. What is also noticeable is, for instance, the absence of the simple verb *talk* from the lists.

The semantic classes are also of interest from the point of view of what has been taken to be the generally negative semantic prosody of the transitive *into -ing* pattern in the literature. The negative association of the pattern has been based on data from corpora of present-day English, and the present data afford an opportunity to bring a body of diachronic data into the picture.

On the whole, the present data are consistent with a negative semantic prosody of the transitive *into -ing* pattern. The labels of some of the semantic classes point to such negative associations, as for instance in the case of verbs expressing deception or trickery. It is also noticeable that in the largest class featuring verbs of emotion, the emotions tend to be negative, of the type of fear, irritation, and anger. Under these circumstances, it is of interest to examine the material for any counterexamples, tokens where the pattern might be associated with positive overtones. Verbs that are not negative *per se* are worth examining here. *Charm, idealize,* and *lead* suggest themselves as such verbs. They are illustrated in 23a–c:

(23) a. '... I may persuade your niece to believe my eyes are grey, or perchance charm her into hating grey eyes henceforth. Where shall I find her, Sir John?' (1910, Brebner, *The Brown Mask*)

b. ... afraid of those whom he believed to be better than himself, and prone to idealize everyone into being his superior except those who were obviously a good deal beneath him. (1903, Butler, *The Way of All Flesh*)

c. I have thought it over, and will not be led into oppressing my father's widow any more. (1870, Yonge, *The Caged Lion*)

Sentence 23a seems playful in tone, and may indicate that the pattern does not always need to carry a negative semantic prosody. However, in 23b–c the pattern appears in a more negative light. Overall, looking through the lists of verbs collected, it is hard to escape the conclusion that the transitive *into -ing* pattern generally had a negative semantic prosody in written British English about a century ago.

The Transitive *into -ing* pattern in present-day English

Turning to current English, the Books Corpus of the full Bank of English was consulted. The search string used was '*into*+VBG', with the symbol 'VBG' representing the *-ing* form of a verb. The search, carried out in 2007, yielded 1577 tokens, but recalling that the Books Corpus is almost ten times larger than the Corpus of Late Modern English Texts, a random sample of 158 was generated from the total of 1577. The generation of the random sample was performed electronically by the search engine of the Bank of English Corpus.

When the same principles as were outlined above were applied in the examination of the sample of 158 tokens, it was observed that the number of relevant tokens obtained was 94. (The tagging used ensured that the proportion of relevant tokens was much higher in the present corpus than in the diachronic corpus). This represents a normalized frequency of 17.1 per million words. It may be recalled that the corresponding frequency in the diachronic corpus was 10.2 per million words. It is thus possible to claim on the basis of the present material that the transitive *into -ing* construction has become considerably more frequent in written British English in the course of the last century.

When the verbs encountered with the pattern in current English are examined from a syntactic point of view, the same three classes can be identified as in the diachronic material, that is, verbs that are independently found with three arguments, those found with two arguments, and those found with one argument. *Force* and *lead* are among those selecting three arguments independently. An illustration of *force* is provided in 24a–b, from the British Books Corpus of the Bank of English:

(24) a. ... parents should not force kids into taking sides.
     b. ... he forced society to face both issues.

As in the diachronic material, the alternative pattern involving object control is a *to* infinitive complement.

Verbs that select two arguments independently may be illustrated with *confuse*. In sentence 25a it is found with the transitive *into -ing* pattern, and in 25b it selects two arguments:

(25) a. ... eventually I managed to confuse him into taking the escape road at Thillois Hairpin so I emerged in a clear lead.
     b. Again, Winsom's interjection seemed to confuse Blair.

Perhaps the most notable change concerns verbs that are commonly found with only one argument, independently of the transitive *into -ing* pattern. The usage of *tick* in the diachronic corpus is not repeated in the current corpus, but the verb *talk* has emerged as a verb that very frequently selects the transitive *into -ing* pattern in present-day English. An illustration is given in 26a, with 26b illustrating usage with only one argument:

(26) a. He talked the government into giving him a grant to set up a Chrono-funnel of his own, and tackled the matter all over again.

     b. ... we anchored for lunch, and just talked.

To be sure, the verb *talk* can be found with NP complements, of the type *talk business*, but in such uses the semantic role of the direct object is not that of Undergoer as in 26a, which sets them apart from the transitive *into -ing* pattern.

The analysis of the transitive *into -ing* pattern as a caused motion receives further support from present-day English data. For instance, consider the matrix verb *confuse*, as in 25a–b. An ordinary meaning of the verb, immediately relevant to sentence 25b with two arguments, is 'to distract, perplex, bewilder' (*OED*, part of the definition of sense 2). The assumption that sentence 25a involves the caused motion construction then makes it possible to say that in 25a the construction supplies the third argument, the Goal argument, that the verb retains its ordinary meaning even in 25a and that part of the meaning of 25a is an amalgam of the ordinary meaning of the verb and of the meaning of the construction, taking account of the means relation between the two meanings in the sense proposed by Goldberg and Jackendoff. In other words, the verbal subevent again expresses the means by which the constructional subevent takes place, and part of the meaning of sentence 25a is along the lines 'I moved him into taking the escape road ... by means of perplexing him'.

As far as *talk* is concerned, the construction supplies two arguments, and part of the sense of sentence 26a is along the lines 'he moved the government into giving him a grant to set up a Chrono-funnel of his own by means of talking'.

Given the status of the transitive *into -ing* pattern as a type of the caused motion construction, the focus in the semantic analysis of matrix verbs is again on the nature of the means involved in the case of each verb.

Characterizations are provided in Table 12.2, which also offers information about the frequency of each matrix verb with the pattern:

Table 12.2. Matrix verbs selecting the transitive *into -ing* pattern in the British Books Corpus of the Bank of English

by means of deception or trickery	*bamboozle* (2), *beguile* (1), *bluff* (1), *brainwash* (1), *con* (3), *dupe* (1), *enmesh* (1), *fool* (4), *inveigle* (2), *lull* (1), *manipulate* (2), *mislead* (1), *trap* (1), *trick* (7) (28 tokens)
by means of exerting force or pressure	*bludgeon* (2), *browbeat* (1), *coerce* (3), *force* (6), *harass* (1), *press-gang* (1), *pressurize* (3), *push* (2), *spur* (1), *throw* (1) (21 tokens)
by means of arousing fear, irritation, anger, annoyance, confusion, surprise	*blackmail* (1), *bully* (3), *frighten* (1), *goad* (3), *intimidate* (1), *needle* (2), *provoke* (3), *shame* (3) (17 tokens)
by means of enticing, flattering or verbal persuasion	*coax* (4), *lure* (1), *persuade* (3), *pitch* (1), *rally* (1), *sweet talk* (1), *talk* (9), *tempt* (1) (21 tokens)
by other specific means	*carry* (1), *condition* (1), *guide* (1), *woo* (1) (4 tokens)
by non-specific means	*influence* (1), *lead* (2) (3 tokens)

Note. NP_1 causes NP_0 to move into performing S_2 or to move into the state expressed by S_2.

Table 12.2 shows that the verb *talk* is the most common matrix verb selecting the pattern. Overall, though, it is now the class of verbs of deception that is the most frequent with the transitive *into -ing* pattern. Comparing the two tables, it is noticeable that the major semantic classes have in general maintained their position.

Regarding the prosody of the transitive *into -ing* pattern in current British English in the light of the present material, a negative flavour inheres in many of the verbs listed in Table 12.2. As noted, the pattern has been associated with a negative semantic prosody in the literature, with Wulff (et al. 2007: 274f.) even suggesting that verbs that 'generally have a neutral or even positive connotation' have a negative interpretation when found with the *into -ing* pattern. However, the data afford us a fresh opportunity to examine the question of prosody. Looking for potential counterexamples to the view found in the literature, we might examine verbs that appear to be neutral or even positive in isolation. *Guide, influence*, and *woo* suggest themselves here. Here are illustrations:

(27) a. In the beginning you will be so uncoordinated that you will be using your hands almost all the time to guide the muscles into performing movements that will, at first, be very unfamiliar. As you continue practising your face will eventually become supple, strong and co-ordinated enough to express a whole new vocabulary.

b. ... colour can influence us into thinking that inferior food that looks attractive also tastes good and is, no doubt, good for us.

c. Gardening in England seems like a slow process of wooing growing things into giving their best. There is no finality and there would be no satisfaction if there were.

The use of the pattern in 27b is clearly linked to a negative flavour. However, 27a is neutral or even positive in tone, and 27c similarly indicates that the pattern is not invariably and inherently linked to a negative semantic prosody in present-day English.

The verbs listed in Table 12.2, as well as those listed above in Table 12.1, are also again of interest from the point of view of the overall characterization of the transitive *into -ing* pattern. In this study the proposal has been made that the pattern should be viewed as a type of the caused motion construction, with the notion of construction understood in the sense of Adele Goldberg's work. This approach, it was argued, is needed because verbs of different syntactic types select the pattern, and the assumption that the pattern represents a type of the caused motion construction gives a coherent account of the argument structure of the pattern. Another reason for regarding the pattern as a construction is the specific semantic structure of the pattern. Here it is recalled how in the tables, the different semantic classes are phrased against the background that the pattern is indeed a construction and that the different semantic classes express different means by which the constructional subevent takes place.

In view of the above, the status of the transitive *into -ing* pattern as a construction seems well motivated. However, it is a curious fact that in neither Table 12.1 nor in Table 12.2 does the verb *cause* appear, even though it is a basic verb of causation and even though it is featured in the very name of the 'caused motion construction'. It is in fact not an accidental gap, due to the limitations of corpus size, that *cause* does not feature in the lists, for sentences of the type of 28, modelled on 27b, are ill formed.

(28) *Colour can cause us into thinking that inferior food looks attractive.

On the other hand, verbs were identified in both tables – *lead* in Table 12.1 and *lead* and *influence* in Table 12.2 – that were said to express caused motion by 'non-specific means'. This raises the question of why the caused motion construction is permitted by *lead* and *influence*, but not by *cause* itself.

A full answer will need to await further work, but a lexical exceptions approach leads us to look for a distinction between the two types of verb, *lead* and *influence* on the one hand, and *cause*, on the other. A possible line of investigation here is to suggest that verbs such as *lead* and *influence*, even though they are nonspecific as to the nature of means or manner, still have a focus on the process of influencing affecting the referent of the patient undergoing the influencing. By contrast, *cause* lacks the focus on the process, and instead reports the result.

If this suggestion is on the right lines, it may be proposed that while the transitive *into -ing* pattern is a construction in English, the label 'caused motion construction' may not be the ideal label for this type of construction. Instead, the label 'influenced motion construction' may be proposed for the present pattern. This change of terminology would not affect the status of the construction within the broader class of resultative constructions.

Summary

It has been shown in earlier work that the transitive *into -ing* pattern is flourishing in present-day English. The present study provides a diachronic perspective to its study. The evidence of the Corpus of Late Modern English Texts shows that the pattern existed in English about a century ago, but was not particularly frequent at that time.

It was noted that both in the diachronic and the present-day English material there were different syntactic classes of matrix verbs that select the transitive *into -ing* pattern, verbs found with three arguments, of the type *force*, with two arguments, of the type *irritate*, and verbs with only one argument, of the type *tick* and *talk*. It is argued in this study that in order to provide a coherent account of the argument structures of the matrix verbs in question, it is helpful to view the pattern as a type of construction in the sense of Adele Goldberg's work. The construction invoked is what she calls the caused motion construction. A construction grammar analysis, it is argued here, is especially appealing in the case of verbs that generally select two arguments, or only one argument, independently of the transitive *into -ing* pattern.

Given a construction grammar analysis of the pattern, the task of analyzing the semantic structure of matrix verbs selecting the pattern amounts to examining the nature of the means of causation or influencing expressed by the matrix verbs selecting the pattern. A number of semantic classes of verbs are identified on this basis, including verbs of deception or trickery and those expressing the exertion of force or pressure. Major classes selecting the pattern were found to have remained fairly constant over the last century, but considerable differences are observed regarding the incidence of individual matrix verbs selecting the pattern. Thus *talk* was evidently very rare with the pattern a century ago, but now it is the most frequent matrix verb with it.

One or two verbs expressing fairly non-specific causation or influencing were also found in the material, including *lead*. However, *cause* was not found in the material, and it is incompatible with the pattern in present-day

English. A lexical exceptions approach was used to attempt to find an adequate way to tease the two classes of verbs apart, and it was argued that verbs selecting the transitive *into -ing* pattern involve a focus on the process of influencing, whereas *cause* reports the result. It is therefore proposed that the term 'influenced motion construction' might be a more suitable label for the construction in question.

Bibliography

De Smet, Henrik. 2005. A Corpus of Late Modern English Texts. *International Computer Archive of Modern and Medieval English ICAME Journal* 29.69–82.

Francis, Gill, Susan Hunston and Elizabeth Manning (eds). 1996. *Collins Cobuild Grammar Patterns 1: Verbs*. London: HarperCollins.

Goldberg, Adele. 1995. *Constructions. A Construction Grammar Approach to Argument Structure*. Chicago: University of Chicago Press.

Goldberg, Adele. 2006. *Constructions at Work*. Oxford: Oxford University Press.

Goldberg, Adele, and Ray Jackendoff. 2004. The English Resultative as a Family of Constructions. *Language* 80.532–68.

Gries, Stefan Th., and Anatol Stefanowitsch. 2004. Covarying Collexemes in the *Into*-Causative. *Language, Culture and Mind*, ed. by Michel Achard and Suzanne Kemmer, 225–36. Stanford, CA: CSLI Publications.

Hunston, Susan, and Gill Francis. 2000. *Pattern Grammar: a Corpus-Driven Approach to the Lexical Grammar of English*. Amsterdam: John Benjamins.

Jespersen, Otto. [1940] 1961. *A Modern English Grammar on Historical Principles. Part 5. Syntax* (Fourth Volume). London: Allen and Unwin.

OED = The Oxford English Dictionary, second edition. Prepared by J. Simpson and E. Weiner. 1989. Oxford: Clarendon Press.

Rudanko, Juhani. 2000. *Corpora and Complementation*. Lanham, MD: University Press of America.

Rudanko, Juhani. 2003. Comparing Alternate Complements of Object Control Verbs: Evidence from the Bank of English Corpus. *Corpus Analysis*, ed. by Pepi Leistyna and Charles F. Meyer, 273–84. Amsterdam: Rodopi.

Rudanko, Juhani. 2005. Lexico-Grammatical Innovation in Current British and American English: a Case Study on the Transitive *into -ing* Pattern with Evidence from the Bank of English Corpus. *Studia Neophilologica* 77.171–87.

Rudanko, Juhani. 2006. Emergent Alternation in Complement Selection: the Spread of the Transitive *into -ing* Construction in British and American English. *Journal of English Linguistics* 34.312–31.

Rudanko, Juhani. 2011. *Changes in Complementation in British and American English.* Houndsmill: Palgrave Macmillan.

Sag, Ivan, and Carl Pollard. 1991. An Integrated Theory of Complement Control. *Language* 67.63–113.

Stefanowitsch, Anatol, and Stefan Th. Gries. 2005. Covarying Collexemes. *Corpus Linguistics and Linguistic Theory* 1.1–43.

Wulff, Stefanie, Anatol Stefanowitsch and Stefan Th. Gries. 2007. Brutal Brits and Persuasive Americans. *Aspects of Meaning Construction*, ed. by G. Radden et al., 265–81. Amsterdam: John Benjamins.

Discussion (Extract)

BASSAC: Most examples in the corpus and more specifically members of the sub-class identified as *NP₁ causes NP₀ to perform S₂* seem to be good examples of compositionality of aspect, as the PP *into+ V-ing* transforms the lexical aspect of the verb from atelic to telic aspect as shown by example (1) in the corpus, *I pestered my father into letting me create a small conifer and heather garden*. Had you thought about this phenomenon and could it be used as a criterion to build a sub-class of its own?

RUDANKO: I said nothing about this but had noticed the phenomenon which actually is frequent in the examples provided but until further work is carried out on the subject, nothing can be said about a possible new sub-class of verbs built on this criterion.

PIERRE RUCART

13 Prefix Verbs in Cushitic are not Exceptions

ABSTRACT

Some Cushitic languages have a small class of verbs that are exceptions in the verbal inflectional system: whereas most verbs have only suffixes, these exceptions also use prefixes. For
example, one can find 5 verbs in Somali or 14 in Rendille. This class of prefix verbs exists
in Afar (cf. Hayward 1978), but the number of verbs in this class is much more relevant:
there are more than 300 verbs (cf. Hayward and Parker 1985). These verbs are treated as
exceptions and require either a specific marking in the lexicon or specific rule adjustments
(cf. Bliese 1981).

I will argue that prefix verbs are not exceptions to the inflectional verbal system of Afar
and that the roots of the verbs provide enough information to understand the possibility
of having prefixes for those verbs and not for others.

In Afar, I claim that verbs with prefixes and verbs with suffixes can be represented
within a single template that allows one to derive every surface structure. This template
unifies the verbal category within a specific prosodic domain.

Following this hypothesis, I argue that the difference between prefix inflection and
suffix inflection depends on the association of the root with the verbal template: prefix
verbs never exhibit a vowel between the two first root consonants whereas suffix verbs
always do. Within the Government Phonology framework (cf. Kaye, Lowenstamm and
Vergnaud 1990, Lowenstamm 1999), the initial CV position (cf. Lowenstamm 1999) of
verbal templates must be properly governed at the phonological level to remain empty.

In suffix verbs the initial CV is always properly governed and remains empty: the
inflectional markers are suffixed. On the other hand, prefix verbs never exhibit a vowel
that could properly govern the initial CV: this last cannot remain empty. However, it has
to be identified: inflectional markers are the best candidates to do that. Then one can
derive the expected verbal forms.

Thus I argue that the prefix verbs are not lexical exceptions and that they do not need
specific rules. The identification of a verbal template allows one to unify the prefix verbal
class and the suffix verbal class and to predict the expected inflected forms that seemed
to be exceptions at first. It is possible to extend this analysis to other Cushitic languages
such as Bedja, which has a large class of prefix verbs, too. This class seems to be the core of
the verbal system in Cushitic and the few exceptions in other Cushitic languages might
be explained as well.

Introduction

Some Cushitic languages have a small class of verbs that are exceptions in the verbal inflectional system: whereas the main class of verbs have only suffixes, these exceptions also use prefixes. In some languages it is only a few verbs: for example, 5 verbs in Somali[1] and 14 verbs in Rendille.[2] But in other languages this class of prefix verbs is more relevant: there are more than 300 verbs in Afar[3] or in Bedja.[4] These verbs are called *strong verbs.*[5]

In this paper I will argue that strong verbs are not exceptions to the inflectional verbal system in Afar and Bedja. The verbal roots provide enough information to understand the possibility of having prefixes for those verbs and not for the others.[6] Thus there is no need to label strong verbs in the lexicon or to write specific rules to predict their inflectional forms.

In the first part I will expose the difference between weak verbs and strong verbs. Then I will examine the vocalization of verbs in Afar then in Bedja. Finally, within the Government Phonology – CVCV option framework,[7] I will show that the Government of the initial CV position can predict the possibility of having prefixes in the case of strong verbs and not in the case of weak verbs.

---

1   Cf. Abdullahi 1996.
2   Cf. Pillinger and Galboran 1999.
3   Cf. Parker and Hayward 1985.
4   Cf. Reinisch 1893.
5   Diachronic and comparative studies in Cushitic have shown that strong verbs are the core of the Cushitic verbal system and the oldest one (cf. Zaborski 1975).
6   Verbs with only suffixes are called *weak verbs.*
7   Cf. Guerssel and Lowenstamm 1996, Lowenstamm 1999.

The weak and the strong inflections

In Afar, the three finite verbal forms are *Perfect, Imperfect* and *Purposive*. In the weak verb conjugation, the suffixes /e/, /a/ and /o/ are the markers of these forms:

(1) *dunqe*   *dunqa*   *dunqo*
    'I pushed'   'I push'   'that I push'

But in the prefix verb conjugation the realizations of these markers are different, as shown below:

(2) *uktube*   *aktube*   *aktubo*
    'I wrote'   'I write'   'that I write'

As we can see, /e/ and /o/ are still suffixes and oppose imperfect and purposive; but in both forms, /a/ is prefixed to the verbal root and seems to alternate with the initial /u/ in the perfect. In fact, this initial /u/ is a copy of the root vowel insofar as this initial vowel is always the same as the stem vowel in the perfect, and is always /a/ in the imperfect and purposive, as shown in the examples in 3:

(3) *egeere*   *ageere*   *ageero*
    'I bailed'   'I bail'   'that I bail'

    ogoose   *agoose*   *agooso*
    'I swam'   'I swim'   'that I swim'

    icfide   *acfide*   *acfido*
    'I learnt'   'I learn'   'that I learn'

Thus, I propose that there exists an aspect marker /a/ in the imperfect that alternates with a Ø marker in the perfect. These markers are prefixes in strong verbs and suffixes in weak verbs. Moreover, there are two markers of mood, /e/ and /o/, that are suffixes in both conjugations. As hiatus are not allowed in Afar, only one of the two markers can appear in weak verbs.[8]

Person markers are also prefixed to the verbal stem of strong verbs. One can observe the difference with weak verbs in the examples in 4:

(4) Weak verb: *dunuqte*   *dunqe*
                       'you pushed'   'he pushed'[9]

     Strong verb: *tuktube*   *yuktube*
                       'you wrote'   'he wrote'

Otherwise, the plural marker is always a suffix:

(5) Weak verb: *dunqen*
                       'they pushed'

     Strong verb: *yuktuben*
                       'they wrote'

We can now give the following representation of affixes ordering in Afar:[10]

(6) *Weak verb*: $\boxed{V}$ + P + A/M + N

     Strong verb: P + A + $\boxed{V}$ + M   + N

In Bedja, the three main verbal forms are *perfect, pluperfect* and *present*. Likewise, weak verbs have only suffixes, as exemplified in 7, and strong verbs have both prefixes and suffixes.

---

8   For an extensive study of the realizations of the aspect and mood marker, see Rucart 2006.
9   /y/ is always deleted in post-consonantal position (cf. Bliese 1984).
10 V = verbal root, P = person, A = aspect, M = mood, N = plural.

(7) *tamya*   *tami*   *tamiini*
    'he ate'   'he has eaten'   'he eats'

    tamta   *tamti*   *tamtiini*
    'she ate'   'she has eaten'   'she eats'

    tamtaana   *tamtiina*   *tamteena*
    'you ate'   'you have eaten'   'you eat'

The conjugation of strong verbs seems to be more complex: strong verbs have different inflections whether they are monosyllabic or disyllabic.[11] But in both cases prefixes are involved in their inflection.[12] As in Afar, there is an initial consonant for person followed by a vowel that indicates the tense, and the plural marker /na/ is a suffix, as we can see below:

(8) Monosyllabic   Disyllabic
    dif 'translate'   *ktib* 'write'

	Perfect	Pluperfect	Present	Perfect	Pluperfect	Present
3ms	*idif*	*iidif*	*endiif*	*iktib*	*iiktib*	*kantiib*
3fs	*tidif*	*tiidif*	*tendiif*	*tiktib*	*tiiktib*	*kantiib*
2pl	*tidifna*	*tiidifna*	*teedifna*	*tiktibna*	*tiiktibna*	*tekatibna*

We can represent affix ordering in Bedja as follows:[13]

---

11 I.e. their root contains two or three consonants respectively. I leave aside roots with more than three consonants, but the following analysis can be extended to them.

12 The main difference occurs in the present tense: monosyllabic verbs have a prefix /an/ and person marker in the singular, while disyllabic verbs have the same marker /an/ as an infix and no person marker in the singular (cf. Roper 1929 and Rucart 2006 for a detailed analysis of the verbal inflection).

13 V = verbal root, P = person, T = tense, N = plural.

(9) *Weak verb*: $\boxed{V}$ + P + T + N

   Strong verb: P + T + $\boxed{V}$ + N

Lexical vowels of verbs in Afar

The phonological system of Afar contains 5 vowels that can be either short or long:[14] /i/, /e/, /a/, /o/ and /u/. All of these can occur in weak verbs:

(10) *kibe*   'fill'
   burte   'despise'
   gexe   'go'
   sooke   'spin'
   fake   'open'

Weak verbs have a lexical vowel that is always located between the two first consonants. It is obviously the case when the root is monosyllabic but it is also the case when the root is disyllabic (e.g. *burte* 'despise'). Then, the representation of weak verbs will be as follows:

(11) $R_1\ V_{lex}\ R_2\ \emptyset\ R_3$ e.g.   *b u r ø t e*
      | | | | | | | | |
      C V C V C V   C V C V C V

Now, if we examine the vocalism of strong verbs, it appears that the vowel of the stem is never /a/ and that middle vowels are always long vowels:

(11) *icfide*   'learn'
   uktube   'write'

---

14   On the vocalic system of Afar, cf. Parker and Hayward 1985, Rucart 2002.

> *eteeqe* 'obey'
> *ogoose* 'swim'

The initial vowel in the perfect is a copy of the stem vowel: it is always the same and it alternates with the imperfective marker /a/ in the imperfect, as shown below:

(12) *eteeqeh* 'I obeyed' – *ateeqeh* 'I obey'
  icfideh 'I learnt' – *acfideh* 'I learn'
  ogooseh 'I swam' – *agooseh* 'I swim'
  uktubeh 'I wrote' – *aktubeh* 'I write'

It has been demonstrated that middle vowels are derived from high vowels when the root contains an underlying consonant: it explains both their timbre and their length.[15] Thus we will consider only roots with three consonants[16] that have a vocalism in /i/ or /u/. Unlike in Bedja,[17] we could not suppose that there is no lexical vowel in Afar strong verbs. Though there is a difference between weak verbs and strong verbs, which is the position of the lexical vowel. We have just seen that the lexical vowel of weak verbs is between the first two consonants of the root. In contrast, the lexical vowel (/i/ or /u/) of strong verbs is always between the second and third consonants, as in the following examples:

(13) *icfide* 'learn' *uktube* 'write'
  ifdige 'release' *ubruke* 'roll'
  ikcine 'love' *udruse* 'teach'

Thus we can give the following representation to strong verbs:

15 cf. Rucart 2002.
16 There exists a small number of strong verbs with only two root consonants, but these verbs have no lexical vowel. Their vocalism is entirely morphological, depending on the verbal form in the inflection (e.g. *e-rd-e* 'I ran', *a-rd-e* 'I run'). Cf. Rucart 2006.
17 Cf. next paragraph.

(14) $R_1 \, \varnothing \, R_2 \, V_{lex} \, R_3$ e.g.: $u \quad k \; \varnothing \; t \; u \; b \; e$

       | | | |

      C V C   V   C V

                   C V - C V C V C V

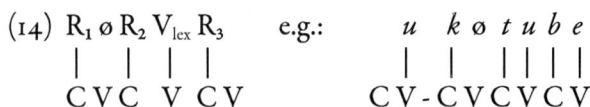

Lexical vowels of verbs in Bedja

If we first look at the vocalism of weak verbs, we can see that the five vocalic sounds of Bedja – /i/, /e/, /a/, /o/ and /u/ – are represented, as shown in examples in 15. Moreover, the vowel of the stem never changes in the conjugation. On this basis we can argue that the vowel of the stem is lexical.

(15) *taman* 'I ate'   *tami* 'I have eaten'   *tamani* 'I eat'

      duuran 'I visited'   *duuri* 'I have visited'   *duurani* 'I visit'

      kirifan 'I avoided'   *kirifi* 'I have avoided'   *kirifani* 'I avoid'

      deeran 'I dismissed' *deeri* 'I have dismissed' *deerani* 'I dismiss'

      digoogan 'I sent'   *digoogi* 'I have sent'   *digoogani* 'I send'

Now, if we look at strong verbs, we can expect the same distribution of the vocalism; but it is not the case. Strong verbs with a CVC or a CVCVC stem[18] have only /i/, /a/ and /u/ as stem vowel in the perfect tense. This stem vowel that appears in the present alternates in the present with a long /i/, no matter what the stem vowel in the perfect is. Examples in 16 present some CVC strong verbs in the perfect:

(16) *abis* 'I buried'   *anbiis* 'I bury'

      adif 'I translated'   *andiif* 'I translate'

      aʔad 'I cursed'   *anʔiid* 'I curse'

      adaʔ 'I plaited'   *andiiʔ* 'I plait'

      akul 'I compressed'   *ankiil* 'I compress'

      agur 'I cooked'   *angiir* 'I cook'

---

18   It represents 65 per cent of the strong verbs in Reinisch 1895.

Thus, the vowel doesn't seem to contribute to the lexical meaning of the verb since it can disappear in the present. And it doesn't seem to be a morphological marker of perfect since three different sounds are allowed, /i/, /a/ and /u/. Moreover, this stem vowel can also alternate with other vowels in derived stems such as the intensive form. In this case the stem vowel is always a long /a/, as show in the following examples:

(17) *dir* 'kill'   →   *daar* 'kill-INTENSIVE'
     ʔar 'grow'   →   *ʔaar* 'grow- INTENSIVE'
     nuw 'be inferior'   →   *naaw* 'be inferior- INTENSIVE'

On the one hand, two verbs do not exist that differ only on the basis of their vocalism. On the other hand, the alternation in the present and intensive shows that a stem vowel can contribute to the meaning of a verbal form. So it seems that the vowel in the perfect is not a lexical vowel.

If we observe the distribution of the vocalism comparing to the root consonants, we can see that verbs with an /a/ always have a guttural (/ʔ/ or /h/) in their root and verbs with an /u/ always have a velar (/ k/, /g/ or /w/). When the vowel is /i/, the root can contain any other consonant. The table in 18 below summarizes this distribution:

(18) Vowel \ Consonant	+ guttural	+ velar	– guttural / – velar
A	+	–	–
U	–	+	–
I	–	–	+

Thus the presence of an /a/ in the stem depends on the presence of a guttural in the verbal root and a velar root consonant is the condition for the presence of an /u/ in the stem.[19] When there is no specific consonant in the root the /i/ vowel appears in the stem. It seems to be the default vowel. Within

---

19   This influence of consonants has been noticed by Reinisch 1893, and McCarthy 1991 has shown the influence of guttural on vocalism in Semitic languages.

the Theory of Elements[20] vowels and consonants can be decomposed into Elements. Guttural consonants contain the Element A that is also the constituent of the vowel [a], and velar consonants contain the Element U that corresponds to the vowel [u]. We can assume that a consonant can provide a vocalic Element (like A or U) to an empty vocalic position of the stem. In the absence of any guttural or velar, an epenthetic Element I is inserted (corresponding to the vowel [i]) as exemplified below:[21]

(19) d I f   ʔ → A d   g → U r
      | | | | | | | | |
      C V C   C   V C   C   V C
      [dif]   [ʔad]   [gur]

Thus verbal roots do not have lexical vowels: the vocalism of the stem depends on the consonants of the root.[22]

If we examine disyllabic strong verbs,[23] the same vocalic distribution in terms of the root consonants occurs, as it shows up for the two vowels of the stem as in the following examples:

(20) *bidil*   'change'   *timuk*   'compress'
      ʔadil   'make peace'   *tukuk*   'prepare'
      biʔar   'watch over'   *hagun*   'scratch'
      kubil   'warp'   *guhar*   'cheat'

The hypothesis we made on the basis of the distribution of the vocalism of monosyllabic verbs can be extended to the vocalism of disyllabic verbs. The vocalism strictly depends on the consonant of the verbal root. This root does not need to contain any lexical vowel.

---

20   Cf. Kaye et al. 1985.
21   The arrow indicates the consonantal origin of the vocalic element.
22   Except for morphological vowel as in present or intensive forms.
23   For a detailed analysis of the vocalism of strong verbs, see Rucart 2006.

(21)   b I d I l   ? → A d I l   d I g → U y

      | | | | | | | | | | | | | | |

      C V C V C   C V C V C   C V C V C

      [bidil]   [ʔadil]   [diguy]

Thus the main difference between weak verbs and strong verbs lies in their vocalization: weak verbs have a lexical vowel in their root, whereas strong verbs have strictly consonantal roots without any vowel specifications. The representations of verbs are then as follows:

(22) Weak Verbs   Strong Verbs

     $R_1 V_{lex} R_2$ e.g. t a m $R_1 ø R_2$ e.g. d (i) f

     | | | | |

     C V C V   C V C V

     $R_1 V_{lex} R_2 V_{lex} R_3$ e.g. k i t i f $R_1 ø R_2 ø R_3$ e.g. b (i) d (i) l

     | | | | | | | |

     C V C V C V   C V C V C V

Initial CV, proper government and affix ordering

Within Government Phonology – CVCV option, Lowenstamm (1999) has proposed that templates of every major syntactic category (noun, verbs ...) have an initial CV position. This position, as any, must be identified or properly governed. That means that the nucleus, V, must be linked to a segment or must be properly governed by the next nucleus. The succession of two empty nuclei is not allowed. In the following representations, the 'initial CV' is underlined, 'GP' means *Properly Governed* and '*GP' means *not Properly Governed*, 'X' stands for any consonantal segments and 'Y' for any vocalic segments:

(23)

```
    Y X Y           Y X             X Y             X
    | | |           | |             | |             |
    C V C V         C V C V         C V C V         C V C V
     ↑___| GP        ↑⤫_| *GP        ↑___| GP        ↑⤫_| *GP
```

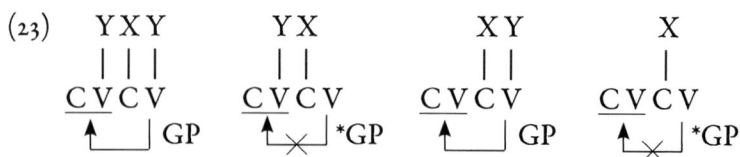

Now, if we examine the status of the initial CV of Afar verbs, we can see that the lexical vowel of weak verbs, that is between the first two consonants, always Properly Governs the initial CV, whereas the lexical vowel of weak verbs cannot. The nucleus between the first two consonants of strong verbs is always empty: thus the initial CV nucleus is never properly governed.

(24) Weak Verb   Strong Verb

```
   R₁ Vₗₑₓ R₂ ø R₃              R₁ ø R₂ Vₗₑₓ R₃
   |   |  |  |  |              |  |  |  |   |
   C V C  V   C V C V          C V C V C V  C V
    ↑___| GP                    ↑⤫_| *GP
```

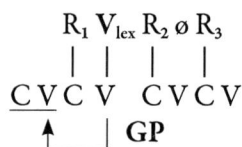

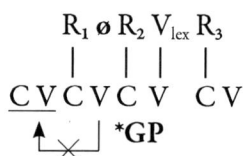

burte 'despise'   *ktub* 'write'

```
   b u  r ø t e                 k ø t u b e
   | | |   | |                  |  | | | |
   C V C V C V C V              C V C V C V C V
    ↑___| GP                     ↑⤫_| *GP
```

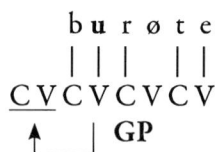

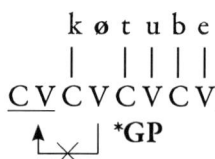

In the case of weak verbs, the initial CV can remain empty and every inflectional marker is realized as a suffix on the right edge of the verbal template, as shown in 25:

(25)

```
   b u  r ø t                   b u  r ø t a
   | | | |                      | | | |   |↗
   C V C V C V C V              C V C V C V C V     [burta] 'I despise'
    ↑___| GP
```

But in the case of strong verbs the initial CV cannot remain empty: as far as it is not Properly Governed, the initial CV has to be identified by a segment. The necessary segments can be found in the inflectional morphology like the marker of imperfect /a/. Then the consonantal marker of person can occupy the first C position. Then other inflectional markers can be suffixed to the form as the conflict on the initial CV is solved (this is the case of the mood marker /e/). This can be exemplified as in 26 for the verbal form *taktube* 'you write':

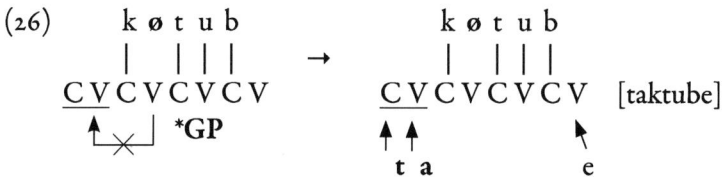

```
(26)    k ø t u b              k ø t u b
        |   | | |      →       |   | | |
        C V C V C V C V        C V C V C V C V   [taktube]
        ↑__×_|  *GP            ↑ ↑             ↖
                               t a              e
```

When there is no inflectional marker to identify the initial CV, there is a copy of the lexical vowel of the root, as in *tuktube* 'you wrote':

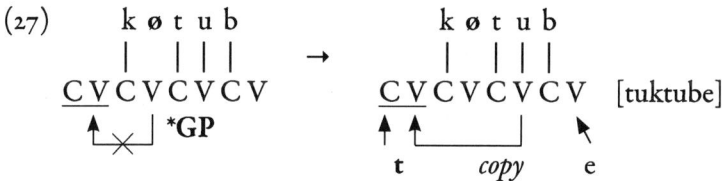

```
(27)    k ø t u b              k ø t u b
        |   | | |      →       |   | | |
        C V C V C V C V        C V C V C V C V   [tuktube]
        ↑__×_|  *GP            ↑ ↑_____|    ↖
                               t    copy         e
```

The presence of a prefix only depends on the presence or absence of a vowel between the first two consonants of the root to Properly Govern the initial CV. This corresponds to the difference between the roots of weak and strong verbs, that is, the position of the lexical vowel.

If we now examine the verbal forms in Bedja, we can give a strictly parallel explanation to the difference between the weak and the strong inflection. Weak verbs always have lexical vowels that can Properly Govern the initial CV position. Thus weak verbs have only suffixes, as far as the initial CV does not need to be identified:

(28)   t a m   t a m   t a
            | | | | | | ↙ ↙
        C V C V C   →   C V C V C V + C V   [tamta] 'she ate'
        ↑___| GP

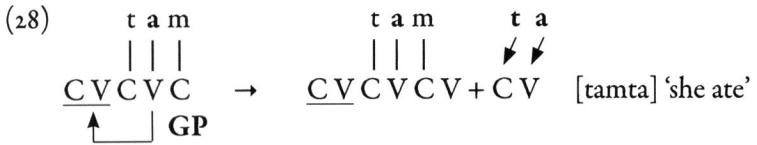

As we have seen in the previous paragraph, strong verbs have no lexical vowel. So, the initial CV is never Properly Governed: it has to be identified. Like in Afar, inflectional markers are the best candidates to do that.[24] For example, in 29, *tidif* 'she translated', the prefix markers /t/ and /i/ are linked to the initial CV because no lexical vowel can Properly Govern its nucleus. Then an /i/ is inserted in the root, in the absence of any velar or guttural consonants:

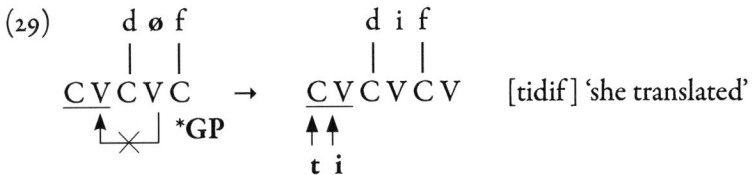

(29)   d ø f   d i f
            | | | | |
        C V C V C   →   C V C V C V   [tidif] 'she translated'
        ↑__×_| *GP   ↑↑
                          t i

Conclusion

In Afar and in Bedja, the initial CV of weak verbs is always properly governed and remains empty: the inflectional markers are suffixed. In contrast, prefix verbs never exhibit a vowel that could properly govern the initial CV: in Afar the lexical vowel is never between the first two consonants and in Bedja there is not any lexical vowel. Then the initial CV cannot remain empty. However, it has to be identified: inflectional markers are

---

24   The only difference with Afar is that strong verbs in Bedja have no lexical vowel at all. The identification of the root vocalic position only depends on the nature of the root consonants.

the best candidates to do that. Then one can derive the expected verbal forms with prefixes.

Thus prefix verbs are not lexical exceptions and they do not need any specific rules. The identification of a verbal template allows one to unify the prefix verbal class and the suffix verbal class and to predict the expected inflected forms that seemed to be exceptions. The only difference between the two verbal classes is either the existence of a lexical vowel or the position of the lexical vowel in the root.

Bibliography

Abdullahi, Mohamed Diriye. 1996. *Parlons Somali*. Paris: L'Harmattan.
Bliese, Loren F. 1981. *A Generative Grammar of Afar*. PhD dissertation, Austin, University of Texas.
Galboran, Letiwa, and Steve Philinger. 1999. *A Rendille Dictionary*. Kuschitische Sprachstudien. Köln: Rüdiger Köppe Verlag.
Guerssel, Mohamed, and Jean Lowenstamm. 1996. Ablaut in Classical Arabic Measure I Active Verbal Forms. *Studies in Afroasiatic Grammar*.122–33.
Hayward, Robert J. 1978. The Prefix Conjugation in 'Afar'. *Atti del Secondo Congresso Internazionale di Linguistica Camito-Semitica*, Firenze 16–19 aprile 1974, ed. by P. Fonzaroli, 355–68. Firenze, Istituto di Lingue Orientali, Università di Firenze – Quaderni di Semitistica, vol. 5.
Hayward, Robert J., and Enid M. Parker. 1985. An Afar – English – French Dictionary (with Grammatical Notes in English). London: SOAS.
Kaye, Jonathan; Jean Lowenstamm; and J.-R. Vergnaud. 1985. The Internal Structure of Phonological Elements; a Theory of Charm and Government. *Phonology Yearbook* 2.305–29.
Kaye, Jonathan; Jean Lowenstamm; and Jean-Roger Vergnaud. 1990. Constituent structure and Government in Phonology. *Phonology Yearbook* 7.193–231.
Lowenstamm, Jean. 1999. The beginning of the word. *Phonologica 1996, Proceedings of the 8th International Phonology Meeting*, Vienna 1996, ed. by J. Rennison and K. Kühnhammer. The Hague: Holland Academic Graphics.

McCarthy, John J. 1991. The phonetics and phonology of Semitic pharyngals. *Papers in Laboratory Phonology III*, ed. by P. Keating. Cambridge: Cambridge University Press.

Reinisch, Leo. 1893. *Die Bedauye Sprache in Nordost-Afrika*. Hölder: Wien.

Reinisch, Leo. 1895. *Worterbuch der Bedauye Sprache*. Hölder: Wien.

Roper, E.M. 1929. *Tu Bedawie – An elementary handbook for the use of Sudan government officials*. Hertford: Stephen Austin and sons.

Rucart, Pierre. 2002. The vocalism of Strong Verbs in Afar. *Berkeley Linguistics Society 27S, Afroasiatic Linguistics*. Berkeley, USA.

Rucart, Pierre. 2006. *Morphologie gabaritique et interface phonosyntaxique*. Thèse de doctorat, Paris 7.

Zaborski, Andrej. 1975. *The verb in Cushitic*. Zeszyty naukowe, Uniwersytetu Jagiellonskiego.

Notes on Contributors

RUSUDAN ASATIANI is Professor of Linguistics at Tbilisi State University, Georgia, and coordinator of the Centre for Language, Logic and Speech there. Her research interests cover the typology of syntactic structures, especially in the Kartvelian languages: Georgian, Megrelian, Laz and Svan; relations between grammatical categories and the human mind; cognitive semantics; information structure and text linguistics. Her publications include 'Word order and intonation in Georgian', *Lingua 2008* (with S. Skopeteas and C. Féry); and 'The Information Structure and Typological Peculiarities of the Georgian Passive Constructions', in *9th International Tbilisi Symposium on Logic, Language, and Computation*, Guram Bezhanishvili et al. (eds), Springer, 2013.

CHRISTIAN BASSAC is Professor of Linguistics in the language faculty at the University of Lyon 2 (France). He is a member of the research group CRTT (*Centre de Recherche en Terminologie et Traduction*) and of the INRIA (*Institut National de Recherche en Informatique et Automatique*) in the *Signes* project. His main research interests are morphology, lexical and computational semantics, and type logical grammars. Two recent publications are 'Toward a type theoretical account of lexical semantics', in *Journal of Logic, Language and Information*, 2010 (with B. Méry and C. Rétoré); and 'Philosophy, linguistics and semantic interpretation' in *Philosophy of Language and Linguistics: The Formal Turn*, Piotr Stalmaszczyk (ed.), Ontos, 2010.

CHRISTOPHER BEEDHAM has studied and taught languages and linguistics at the Universities of Salford (England), Leipzig (GDR), Aston (England), and Moscow (Soviet Union), and is now Lecturer in German at the University of St Andrews (Scotland). He has published various books and articles since 1976 on the passive and irregular verbs in German,

Russian, and English, and on the 'method of exceptions and their correlations'. He is the author of *Language and Meaning: The Structural Creation of Reality* (Benjamins, 2005).

WARWICK DANKS originally trained and worked as an analytical chemist, and his first publication in 1984 was in the field of industrial archaeology. He is now University Examinations Officer at the University of St Andrews, where he studied Arabic with Linguistics and was awarded a PhD for his thesis on the Arabic verb, in which he used the method of exceptions and their correlations. His PhD thesis was published by Benjamins in 2011 and reviewed in *Language* in 2012.

CHRISTOPHER GLEDHILL is Professor of English Linguistics at the University of Paris Diderot, having worked previously at Lille 3 and Strasbourg (France) and having been lecturer in French at St Andrews (Scotland) and Aston (England). His research interests include artificial and invented languages, genre analysis (English for Specific Purposes, Simplified Technical English), grammar (Systemic Functional Grammar), and lexicology and phraseology (Verb Noun constructions). One of his first publications, 'The Discourse Function of Collocation in Research Article Introductions', has been reprinted in Douglas Biber & Randi Reppen (eds), *Corpus Linguistics*, Sage 2012.

MARINE IVANISHVILI is Professor of Linguistics in the Department of Language Typology at Tbilisi State University, Georgia, where she was awarded a PhD in 2005 for a thesis on Proto Kartvelian plant names, under the supervision of Prof. Thomas V. Gamkrelidze. Her research interests are typological and comparative linguistics, Kartvelian languages, and logic language computation. She is co-Managing Editor of the *Journal of Language, Logic, and Computation*, and on the organising committee of the International Tbilisi Symposium on Language, Logic and Computation.

MARIKA JIKIA studied musicology as an undergraduate – she is an accomplished pianist – and theoretical linguistics as a postgraduate at Tbilisi State University, Georgia. Her Candidate of Sciences thesis was published in Russian as Структура словоформ турецкого языка, Тбилиси, Мецниереба, 1984, and her Doctor of Sciences thesis on Turkisms in Kartvelian Anthroponymics was published in Georgian (with English and Turkish summaries), Tbilisi, Sitkva, 2008. Marika is Professor and Head of the Department of Turkish Studies at Tbilisi State University. Her research areas are Turkish Studies and Kartvelian Studies: morphology, word formation, syntax (Megrelian, Laz), onomastics, poetics, typology.

MANANA KARKASHADZE studied linguistics at Tbilisi State University, Georgia. Her main research interest is the typology of the verb. She has published various articles on Kartvelian passive and antipassive verbs. Her doctoral thesis, *The typology of structural-semantic characteristics of Georgian medio-active verbs*, examines typological data from about 20 languages. She has also conducted research into the activities of Catholic missionaries in XVII century Georgia. She teaches Georgian language and classical literature at the School of Tomorrow (Momavlis Skola), Tbilisi.

PIERRE RUCART obtained his doctoral degree in Linguistics from the University of Paris 7 in 2006. His research interests cover verbal morphology and the connections between phonology and syntax. His work originally concerned the Afro-Asiatic languages and later Romance languages. Since 2010 he has been a researcher in genomics and bioinformatics at the *Conservatoire National des Arts et Métiers* in Paris, and he also teaches biotechnology.

JUHANI RUDANKO obtained his doctoral degree from the University of Tampere (Finland) in 1977 and has been Professor of English at the same university since 1998. His recent research interests include the system of English predicate complementation and political discourses in the early American Republic. His publications include *Pragmatic Approaches to Shakespeare* (University Press of America, 1993), *Prepositions and Complement Clauses* (State University of New York Press, 1996), and *Discourses of Freedom of Speech* (Palgrave Macmillan, 2012). His articles have appeared in the *Journal of Pragmatics*, *English Studies*, *Studia Neophilologica*, and the *Journal of English Linguistics*.

ETHER SOSELIA is Professor of Linguistics at Tbilisi State University, Georgia, and head of the Language Typology Department at the George Tsereteli Institute of Oriental Studies. Her research interests cover semantic typology and the typology of morpho-syntactic structures, especially in the Kartvelian languages (Georgian, Megrelian, Laz and Svan), and cognitive semantics. She has published books on the kinship terms and colour term systems in the Kartvelian languages, analysing them both synchronically and diachronically.

Index

CONTEMPORARY STUDIES IN DESCRIPTIVE LINGUISTICS

Edited by

DR GRAEME DAVIS, Research Fellow in the Department of English, University of Buckingham, UK, and Associate Lecturer, the Open University, UK, and

KARL A. BERNHARDT, Research Fellow in the Department of English, University of Buckingham, UK, and English Language Consultant with both Trinity College, London and the London Chamber of Commerce and Industry International Qualifications.

This series provides an outlet for academic monographs which offer a recent and original contribution to linguistics and which are within the descriptive tradition.

While the monographs demonstrate their debt to contemporary linguistic thought, the series does not impose limitations in terms of methodology or genre, and does not support a particular linguistic school. Rather the series welcomes new and innovative research that contributes to furthering the understanding of the description of language.

The topics of the monographs are scholarly and represent the cutting edge for their particular fields, but are also accessible to researchers outside the specific disciplines.

Contemporary Studies in Descriptive Linguistics is based at the Department of English, University of Buckingham.